ST ANTONY'S SERIES
General Editors: Archie Brown (1978–85
Pravda (1992–), all Fellows of St Antony

Recent titles include:

Daniel A. Bell, David Brown, Kanishka Jayasuriya and David Martin Jones
TOWARDS ILLIBERAL DEMOCRACY IN PACIFIC ASIA

Mats Berdal
THE UNITED STATES, NORWAY AND THE COLD WAR, 1954–60

Craig Brandist
CARNIVAL CULTURE AND THE SOVIET MODERNIST NOVEL

Sir Alec Cairncross
MANAGING THE BRITISH ECONOMY IN THE 1960s: A Treasury
Perspective

Stephanie P. Y. Chung
CHINESE BUSINESS GROUPS IN HONG KONG AND POLITICAL
CHANGES IN SOUTH CHINA, 1900–20s

Alex Danchev and Thomas Halverson (*editors*)
INTERNATIONAL PERSPECTIVES ON THE YUGOSLAV CONFLICT

Anne Deighton (*editor*)
BUILDING POSTWAR EUROPE: National Decision-Makers and European
Institutions, 1948–63

Reinhard Drifte
JAPAN'S FOREIGN POLICY IN THE 1990s: From Economic Superpower to
What Power?

Jane Ellis
THE RUSSIAN ORTHODOX CHURCH, 1985–94

Y Hakan Erdem
SLAVERY IN THE OTTOMAN EMPIRE AND ITS DEMISE, 1800–1909

João Carlos Espada
SOCIAL CITIZENSHIP RIGHTS: A Critique of F. A. Hayek and Raymond
Plant

Amitzur Ilan
THE ORIGIN OF THE ARAB–ISRAELI ARMS RACE: Arms, Embargo,
Military Power and Decision in the 1948 Palestine War

Hiroshi Ishida
SOCIAL MOBILITY IN CONTEMPORARY JAPAN

Matthew Jones
BRITAIN, THE UNITED STATES AND THE MEDITERRANEAN WAR, 1942–44

Anthony Kirk-Greene and Daniel Bach (*editors*)
STATE AND SOCIETY IN FRANCOPHONE AFRICA SINCE INDEPENDENCE

Jaroslav Krejčí and Pavel Machonin
CZECHOSLOVAKIA 1918–92: A Laboratory for Social Change

Jon Lunn
CAPITAL AND LABOUR ON THE RHODESIAN RAILWAY SYSTEM, 1888–1947

Iftikhar H. Malik
STATE AND CIVIL SOCIETY IN PAKISTAN: Politics of Authority, Ideology and Ethnicity

Rosalind Marsh
HISTORY AND LITERATURE IN CONTEMPORARY RUSSIA

Barbara Marshall
WILLY BRANDT: A Political Life

Javier Martínez Lara
BUILDING DEMOCRACY IN BRAZIL: The Politics of Constitutional Change, 1985–95

J. L. Porket
UNEMPLOYMENT IN CAPITALIST, COMMUNIST AND POST-COMMUNIST ECONOMIES

Charles Powell
JUAN CARLOS OF SPAIN: Self-Made Monarch

Neil Renwick
JAPAN'S ALLIANCE POLITICS AND DEFENCE PRODUCTION

Aron Shai
THE FATE OF BRITISH AND FRENCH FIRMS IN CHINA, 1949-54: Imperialism Imprisoned

William J. Tompson
KHRUSHCHEV: A Political Life

Christopher Tremewan
THE POLITICAL ECONOMY OF SOCIAL CONTROL IN SINGAPORE

Holly Wyatt-Walter
THE EUROPEAN COMMUNITY AND THE SECURITY DILEMMA, 1979–92

Identities in International Relations

Edited by

Jill Krause
Lecturer in International Relations
The University of Keele, England

and

Neil Renwick
Senior Lecturer in International Relations
The Nottingham Trent University, England, and
The Northern Territory University, Darwin, Australia

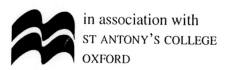

in association with
ST ANTONY'S COLLEGE
OXFORD

First published in Great Britain 1996 by
MACMILLAN PRESS LTD
Houndmills, Basingstoke, Hampshire RG21 6XS
and London
Companies and representatives
throughout the world

A catalogue record for this book is available
from the British Library.

ISBN 0–333–66077–3 hardcover
ISBN 0–333–69384–1 paperback

First published in the United States of America 1996 by
ST. MARTIN'S PRESS, INC.,
Scholarly and Reference Division,
175 Fifth Avenue,
New York, N.Y. 10010

ISBN 0–312–16435–1

Library of Congress Cataloging-in-Publication Data
Identities in international relations / edited by Jill Krause and
Neil Renwick.
p.   cm.— (St Antony's series)
Includes bibliographical references and index.
ISBN 0–312–16435–1 (cloth)
1. International relations.   2. Ethnic relations.   I. Krause,
Jill.   II. Renwick, Neil, 1957–   .   II. Series.
JX1395.I339   1996
327—dc20
96–28752
CIP

Printed and bound in Great Britain by
Antony Rowe Ltd, Chippenham, Wiltshire

Contents

Acknowledgements

There are many to whom the editors and contributors wish to express their thanks for the advice and assistance given to them during the evolution of this book. Firstly, the idea for this book originated in the tumult of second-year undergraduate classes conducted during 1994. To all the students who contributed their time and energy in the consultation and planning stages of the book and who acted as readers in the drafting stages, the editors and contributors owe an enormous debt of gratitude. Secondly, thanks are due to Jane McNeil and Peter Stokes, the long-suffering staff of the International Studies Resources Centre, and to Linda Dawes, for their patience with, and invaluable advice to, the editors. Finally, the editors would like to thank the contributors to the book for their hard work, respect for deadlines and for the quality of the contributions they have provided.

JILL KRAUSE
NEIL RENWICK

Notes on the Contributors

Richard Davies is a part-time lecturer and a research student in International Relations at the Nottingham Trent University. His doctoral research deals with the use of legislation by political elites to appeal to national identity as an instrument of legitimation. He is a graduate of the University of Kent's London Centre of International Relations and has undertaken research into Polish legislation at the Jagellonian University in Krakow. His research interests include identities in international relations, nationalism, nation-building and European integration.

Chris Farrands is Principal Lecturer in International Relations at the Nottingham Trent University, where he is Course Leader for the MA international relations programme. He has published widely in the areas of international political economy. His current research interests include: the philosophical foundations of international relations; Western European foreign and economic policy; European industrial and advanced technology.

Jill Krause is Lecturer in International Relations at Keele University and formerly Lecturer in International Relations at the Nottingham Trent University. Her research interests include gender and international theory, gender in international political economy and issues of identity in international relations. She has written and published work on all these subjects. She is also the author of *Perspectives on Gender in International Relations*.

Margaret Law is Lecturer and Research Scholar in International Relations at the Nottingham Trent University. A graduate of the Department of International Studies, she is Co-ordinator of the Idea of Europe programme. Her research interest focuses upon the international relations of the Middle East.

Lloyd Pettiford is a Lecturer and Year Tutor in International Relations at the Nottingham Trent University. A doctoral graduate of the University of Southampton, he is the author of *Changing Conceptions of Security in Central America*. His research interests are Central American politics and environmental security in international relations. His recently published work includes 'Towards a Redefinition of Security in Central America: The Case of Natural Disasters' in *Disasters: The Journal of Disaster Studies and Management*.

Nana Poku is a part-time Lecturer in International Relations and a United Nations scholar at the Nottingham Trent University. A graduate of Nottingham Trent and Coventry Universities, he is a former General Secretary of United Nations Youth and currently is an executive member of the United Nations Development Unit. A former aid worker in Sarejevo, he has also acted as the leader of a research team working in South America on behalf of the United Nations High Commission for Refugees (UNHCR). His current research deals with the institutional prospects for regional integration in post-apartheid South Africa.

Neil Renwick is Senior Lecturer in International Relations at the Nottingham Trent University and at the Northern Territory University in Darwin, Australia. A graduate of Trent Polytechnic, Durham University and the Australian National University, he has also taught at the University of Adelaide. He is Co-Director of the Nottingham Trent University Centre for Asia-Pacific Studies. He is the author of two books on international political economy and multinational corporations. His most recent publication is *Japan's Alliance Politics and Defence Production* Macmillan, 1995). His current research includes *Critical Security Issues in Northeast Asia* (Macmillan, 1995, forthcoming 1996).

Jan Aart Scholte obtained his doctorate from the University of Sussex and is now Lecturer in International Relations in the School of European Studies there. He is the author of *International Relations of Social Change, Globalisation: A Critical Introduction* and various articles that seek to bring historical-sociological perspectives into the field of international relations.

Roy Smith is Lecturer and Course Leader in International Relations at the Nottingham Trent University. He is Co-Director of the Nottingham Trent University Centre for Asia-Pacific Studies. His research interests include: pressure groups and indigenous rights; anti-nuclear movements; the United Nations; and environmental issues arising from the 1994 United Nations Global Conference on Sustainable Development in Small Island Developing States.

Roger Tooze is a former Professor of International Relations and Head of the Department of International Studies at the Nottingham Trent University and Senior Lecturer elect in the Department of International Politics, University College of Wales, Aberystwyth. He has published widely in the area of international political economy and is the author of *Globalisation, Technology and Political Economy.* Current research interests include international political economy and its theorisation; structures of power in the global political economy; international relations theory; the political economy of the Pacific Rim.

Gillian Youngs has recently been lecturing and researching in the field of international relations and has a background in journalism and communications consultancy. Previously a Senior Lecturer in International Relations the Nottingham Trent University, her research interests include critical approaches to the state and power, and the relationship between poltical, economic and cultural dimensions of globalisation. She is the author of *From International Relations to Global Relations. A Conceptual Challenge* and co-editor with Eleanore Kofman of *Globalisation: Theory and Practice.*

Introduction
Jill Krause and Neil Renwick

This collection of essays offers a radically new approach to the understanding and explanation of International Relations. The contributors are all International Relations scholars whose particular research interests in some way open up issues of identity. What all of the contributors share is a dissatisfaction with 'orthodox' approaches to the study of International Relations which have tended to reduce issues of identity to identification with the state or nation and in so doing have assumed that our identities are stable and homogeneous. There is, however, a diversity in approach. Many of the contributors locate their interest in identity in a global context within contemporary theoretical debates in International Relations and the challenges which have emerged from the intervention of postmodern and poststructuralist modes of thought and from feminist theory and cultural critiques. Others argue that identities are complex, but social and capable of explanation through argument and evidence, even if not amenable to simple explanations. The diversity of approach combined with a common desire to explore radical new approaches to understanding identities in a global perspective is one of the distinctive strengths of the text.

The text has been written primarily for International Relations undergraduates or as an introductory text for postgraduates new to the study of the subject. However, it is hoped that it will appeal to a wider readership and is written in such a way that a wider readership will find it accessible and useful. The phenomenon of 'globalisation', a central theme in many of the contributions to this text, presents radical challenges to the social sciences and humanities as a whole. The prevailing usage of 'society' has been rendered problematic by the processes of globalisation. Cultural geography, which has been largely concerned with 'mapping' processes and systems of 'inclusion' and 'exclusion', and International Relations would undoubtedly derive mutual benefits from a dialogue that aimed to expand our understanding of 'place', 'space' and identities. In the field of cultural studies where the study of identities has received most sustained attention, the founding preoccupation with national cultures is now under pressure. Recent theoretical developments within the social sciences have encouraged the breakdown of the tendency of academic disciplines to stay within their own narrow terms of reference and in so doing encouraged dialogue. It is hoped that a text of this kind which demonstrates the need for and value of a global perspective on identity, albeit in an introductory manner, will appeal to those whose main interests lie in geography, political science, sociology and cultural studies.

Students from across the Faculty of Humanities at the Nottingham Trent University were widely consulted in the planning stages of this book and their suggestions have been carefully considered and largely taken up in the initial drafting of chapters. Student involvement throughout the book's production has helped to ensure that the book has been written in a style which makes some rather abstract and difficult ideas accessible. It is hoped that the combination of the fresh research approaches of the contributors with active student involvement in its planning stages presents original and challenging alternative perspectives for students in many fields of study.

CHALLENGING THE 'ORTHODOXY'

By focusing upon the idea of identity, the aim of this book is to challenge the orthodoxy in International Relations. In their own distinctive ways, each of the contributions seeks to examine the problem of identity and meaning by 'disrupting' the conventional wisdom which privileges the nation-state as the dominant form of identity. While there has been recognition of the unsatisfactory nature of such an approach within International Relations for quite some time, it is becoming increasingly problematic in an age when identities are shaped, formed and transformed not only by factors specific to the immediate locality in which people carry out their day-to-day activities, but also by global processes. The essays in this text explore in a number of specific contexts how issues of identity are intimately connected to social processes and deeply embedded in power relations. Some of the contributions are also concerned to draw out explicitly the implications of the highly problematic nature of identity in the world for the future study of International Relations.

THE INDETERMINACY OF IDENTITY

Opening up the issue of identity to critical analysis reveals the radical indeterminacy of identity. Not only do multi-layered and diverse patterns of allegiance and identity co-exist in contemporary 'national' societies, but also globalisation has disrupted the links between identity and the territorially based nation-state. The indeterminacy of identity makes it remote to the reductionist accounts or historical generalisations characteristic of some IR scholarship. Nations are not homogeneous entities, but rather collectivities full of people with multiple identities and loyalties. A number of the contributions to this collection highlight the experiences of people who 'live between cultures' and of diasporic communities as examples of how identities are shaped by various processes associated with immigration and exile. Furthermore even the assertion of national identity can serve to set in motion a chain of events for the realisation of multi-faceted identities.

This is not to say that national identity has ceased to be important, but rather to suggest that it is only one of a number of identities which people have. Furthermore, identification with the nation can be strong or weak. At the same time, other identities, for example gender, ethnicity, social class, race or sexual preference, which are not rooted in an attachment to a particular territory can be highly significant. Religious faith may play a role in identity formation. In the post-Cold War world ethnicity is also undoubtedly a major source of collective identification. Furthermore, identities are not static, but malleable. As Lloyd Pettiford argues in this collection, in the contemporary world identity is a paradox which blurs as soon as it is asserted.

As globalisation has unsettled the construction of collective identities, territorially based conceptions of 'self' and 'other' have been challenged. In recent decades the assertion of placeless identities has challenged the 'nation' as the essential expression of collective identity. Indeed, the impact of globalisation has challenged dominant conceptions of *political space* in International Relations. Contemporary global political space is multidimensional and decentred. Global patterns of trade and capital flows, and communications from MTV and CNN to the Internet have all played a part in encouraging a radical rethinking of the relationship between the processes of identification and global political space.

IDENTITY AND THE SEARCH FOR 'AUTHENTICITY'

Identity and the activity of identification is clearly much more complex than the orthodoxy in International Relations permits. The essentialism inherent in dominant conceptions of national identity gives way under critical scrutiny to the recognition that identities are constructed and can, therefore, be deconstructed and reconstructed anew. In a condition of uncertainty and flux, where is identity centred? How is its meaning derived? It would certainly be a mistake to simply equate the processes of globalisation with the emergence of a world community at peace with itself and ready to embrace complexity, diversity and difference. Diversity, complexity and the disruption of old certainties may only serve to foster a sense of individual and collective insecurity and compel a renewed search for 'authentic' identities. The 'nation' remains a central pillar of global as well as territorial constructions of collective identities. Although, as Jan Aart Scholte's chapter argues, it may be more fruitful to concentrate our attention upon the ways in which nationalism complicates the construction of collective identities rather than continue to privilege the nation as the primary form of collective identification. Similarly ethnic revivalism and religious fundamentalisms constitute further examples of forms of essentialism characteristic of the search for security and certainty in a rapidly changing world. Rather than embracing difference and diversity, the search for authenticity inevitably involves processes of differentiation and separation from the 'other'. It may also involve the denial or suppression of other expressions of identity. Global processes of social and economic change may bring in their wake new forms of economic and social inequality and these, along with recession and the politics of fear, may serve to throw people back into a 'cult of origins'. The tragic consequences of such assertions of identity have already blighted hopes for a peaceful 'New World Order', as the old ideological divisions of the Cold War era pass into history.

THE NORMATIVE AGENDA

The worldwide upsurge in identity politics in the past three decades and the re-awakening of long-suppressed expressions of identity in the post-Cold War world have all pushed International Relations to put the question of identity onto its research agenda in recent years. This in turn has had the welcome effect of putting normative issues back into the heart of the study of International Relations. There has been a long history of thought in International Relations about problems of achieving a just international order and in thinking about the obligations which human beings owe to one another. However, in the past International Relations scholars have thought about these issues largely in terms of how human communities of nation-states relate to one another. Several authors in this collection argue that there is now an urgent need to develop new conceptions of community and work out a new basis for a just order without crushing human diversity. Does the challenge lie in finding ways to nurture a politics of identity which avoids the emphasis on opposition, exclusion, hierarchy and violence that have pervaded international relations in the past? Will a sensitivity towards identity and difference precipitate a marked decline in the level of inter-ethnic conflict and facilitate more peaceful transglobal relations? Must the problems which beset human kind – poverty, mal-development, environment degradation and resource depletion – now be viewed as global problems? Are new social movements evidence of the assertion of identities which are grounded in a concern for the future of the global community of human kind? How is it possible to encourage the development of aspects of personal identity which are compatible with evolving issues of global concern? Dare we hope for a future where identity politics does not preclude elements of self-identification towards a global citizenship?

CONCEPTUAL AND THEORETICAL CHALLENGES

Challenging the orthodoxy also gives rise to a number of theoretical challenges which are addressed in several chapters. Central to conventional approaches to the study of International Relations is the notion of state boundaries. In realist and neorealist approaches to International Relations, for example, the 'internal' domain of the reasoned peace is juxtaposed to that of an 'external' domain of unreasoned anarchy. This raises critical questions of inclusion and exclusion, of differentiation and of identification. There is a need to understand the ways in which the conceptual mapping processes of International Relations have excluded other expressions of identity. The privileging of the nation-state as the irreducible unit of identity disguises the increasingly complex ways in which identities are formed and mapped. For these reasons the state as the central unit of analysis is increasingly being challenged. It is also challenged by those who argue that International Relations needs to develop new ways of conceptualising and theorising economic and social relations in a global age. Focusing on identity encourages complex theoretical challenges to state-centric traditions in International Relations. These challenges raise important epistemological, ontological and methodological considerations which put the *political subject* and questions of political identity at the centre of the analysis. It is only in this way, as one contributor to this collection argues, that we can investigate the way identities are influenced by a complex mix of factors which span public and private realms and cross a range of social, political and economic boundaries. The challenges involved in developing new conceptual and theoretical tools of analysis, which will help us to make sense of these complexities, or involved in developing different ways of understanding the contemporary world, are revisited in the conclusion to this book, where the question is posed; *where does this take the student of International Relations?*

Prologue: States, Nationalisms and Identities – Thinking in IR Theory
Roger Tooze

There is a need for new ways of perceiving the world, for a new paradigm of social change. The nation-state is primarily a way of imagining the world, and its institutions. . . . That it was such a powerful model is proved by the difficulty of imagining what comes after it.[1]

For many inhabitants of the world the consequences of the link between the state and nationality are only all too apparent – they are caught in the (literal) crossfire of competing territorial claims which are driven and legitimated by appeals to, and the appeal of, a hyper-nationalism and enforced by the exercise of military power. For others the struggle for identity may involve other kinds of conflict, not as violent but equally important, with the territorial state within which they live being an instrument of suppression to deny the realisation of individual and collective identity (and the enabling social power that accompanies this) based on ethnicity, race, religion, class, gender or sexuality. Yet, such are the conditions of material life in the world today, that my sense is that where the actuality or the expectation of physical and violent struggle does not prevail, the majority of us are far too preoccupied with the demands of the socio-economic structure we live within to step back and think about the nature of 'our nationality' in any great depth. Although the search for and the achievement of 'identity' throughout human history has proven to be as powerful a force as the struggle for economic well-being, and often perhaps much more powerful, many of us now take our political identity as given or non-contentious. In the 'New World Order' of post-1989 world politics it is confidently claimed by political leaders and academic commentators that wars of territory, and subsequent enforced redefinitions of 'nationality' and political loyalty are in the past, at least for the 'advanced industrial economies' (AIEs) that produce much of the world's wealth.

Of course, we are continually confronted by appeals to and expectations of nationality and nationalism whatever country or territorial space we inhabit, whether it be a call from government [the state] for extreme patriotism or the cry for increased consumption of 'home-produced' goods ('Buy Japanese/French/American'!) or merely in the course of our daily existence as citizens. These are politically routine, utilised to legitimate a bewildering array of seemingly contradictory policies, often predictable (with often predictable results – either apathy or equally unthinking obeisance), and are frequently trivial. However, the appeals to nationalism are always politically important – nationalism is still regarded as a (if not 'the') prime driver of and legitimator for political, government and state policy and action, both internal and external. Moreover, in that the distribution of power within political, social and economic structures, including global structures, tends to ensure that these structures are reproduced, political legitimacy and loyalty (i.e. nationalism) has a fundamental role in this process.

But wherever we live today, we live within a political structure that is itself based on the state and the assumed identity that nation equals state, or perhaps more appropriately given the sources of power, *state equals nation*. It is *this specific political identity* (i.e. state = nation) that has dominated the development of thinking about international relations, at least for the past fifty years. It is this collective identity which is one of the principal starting points for the subject of International Relations (IR) and the corpus of theory associated with IR. Such is the strength of the assumption that the particular historical conjuncture of state and nation that has been experienced and created over the past two centuries is, in fact, *both universal over time and space* and the 'natural' and desired end condition or organisation of political community, that the whole language of politics and especially international politics is constructed on this basis. This discourse is predicated on the unproblematic assertion that the definition of what constitutes (and what *should* constitute) the proper realm or domain of individual political identity (and hence loyalty) is the nation and the ideology of nationalism. But by 'nationalism' is meant *a (or the) nation as the prime location of political identity and loyalty within the context of the state*. This means that every 'nation' needs, demands or is entitled to a 'state' as the prime form of political representation and power. What is then up for discussion and political resolution is how and to what extent 'nationalism' and/or 'state' are constructed and influenced and what effect 'nationalisms' have on the international system, rather than the initial assertion itself. This is evident in every contemporary 'nationality' dispute – in Quebec, in Bosnia and in Palestine.

Notwithstanding the embedded and established nature of political identity for most of us, a whole raft of developments has recently brought the question of 'identity' and political loyalty to the fore – both in the practice and theory of world politics. Previously unquestioned or dormant links between identity, nationality and state have been challenged by the urgent search for meaningful identity within a highly complex and changing global social structure, with major actual and potential political consequences. Different ways of understanding identity and different analyses of the political construction and consequences of 'new' identities – from political geography, sociology, history, social psychology and political science – have led to further questioning of the nature of political identity and how we understand that identity.

Given the above, what do International Relations and IR theory offer to those seeking understanding and explanation of the current questioning and political activity over identity and nationalism? Well, not as much as could be expected. And not as much as many of us in IR, including the contributors to this volume, would want and would see as necessary for IR to justify its claims to knowledge in this field. IR is clearly hampered by its implicit analytical and normative assumption that state equals (or should equal) nation and that nationalism must be the fundamental, legitimate ideology within an inter-state system. That is, all other political loyalties or ideologies should ultimately be subservient to the demands of nationalism. IR theory is equally hampered by the fact that its very language embeds a certain understanding of history and certain value structures and definitions that make it more problematic to dissect some of the important issues within the relationships of state, nationalism and identity. Moreover, IR is further limited by the fact that what are presented as its principal mainstream theories (at least by most in the United States) – neorealism and neoliberalism – seem unable to shed much explanatory light on the problems of identity. This is partly as a result of the issues and problems specified as central to the theories, partly a result of the units of analysis that each identifies as most relevant and partly that the assumptions held by practitioners of both theories concerning how we understand human behaviour make it difficult for them to identify and explain the nature and problems of identity and nationalism.

Neither of the two orthodox theories of IR sees identity as a major analytical or political problem. Although their principle foci – problems of anarchy, international co-operation, security, international political economy, institutions and state capabilities – are each constituted or at least influenced by the nature and conditions of political identity, the construction of this identity is assumed to be unproblematic, beyond the analysis, neorealism and neoliberalism both take the state as the basic unit. Neorealism is not interested in individual or sub-state levels of activity, except perhaps where these activities would have a direct and immediate impact upon the capability of a state for international interaction. It accepts as unproblematic that the prime identity of those who inhabit a state is provided by that state itself, therefore there is no need to move 'below' the level of the state. It also accepts the legitimacy of national self-determination as a constitutive principle of *international* relations, that is, every nation has a right to a 'state' and the international community is made up of such states and relations between and among states. Nationalism is accepted as a dynamic for change, often deadly, but nonetheless legitimate. Within this view, codified over many years by IR theorists, there is little room to question the core assumptions, the nature of identity and its construction as a social process and the potential disaggregation of the state. Neoliberalism similarly allows little room for such fundamental questioning of the unit of analysis, although the state is viewed more as a collective, but nonetheless remains as the necessary core unit of analysis. In sum, both the orthodox theories treat the boundaries of the state as 'preordained social facts' rather than as the temporary outcome of strategies of social struggle necessary to problematise identity.[2]

Probably the most difficult problem for those wishing to use orthodox theories of IR to understand issues of identity, state and nationalism is that they are both prefaced on a view of knowledge that separates subject and object, and that views the 'subjective' as an illegitimate basis for knowledge in IR. What this means, for me at least, is that orthodox IR theory is incapable of capturing the subjective and intersubjective nature of identity. And incapable of allowing an analysis where inter-subjective understanding(s) can become objective reality through the process of action – if individuals and groups act as if identity is problematic, it is problematic. As Robert Cox succinctly expresses the point: 'What is subjective in understanding becomes objective through action'. The state and the nation are themselves such intersubjective entities – they have no physical existence beyond everyone acting as though they are real entities.[3]

Clearly, the questions raised by our concern about identity, nationalism and state cannot be responded to from within the current mainstream of IR theory – thinking in IR theory here only seems to complete a tautological circle and cannot encompass the subjective nature of identity. Hence, we must venture outside of the orthodox to consider other ways in which IR theory can help. We are not the only group of scholars who have come to this conclusion – the continuing centrality of culture and identity is increasingly recognised by US scholars critical of the orthodoxy.[4] Yet the issues discussed here have a much wider impact: in order to make sense of them we must engage in a process of returning IR theory to normative concerns and away from the claim that IR theory simply deals with 'facts',[5] we must incorporate an analysis of intersubjective realities and the historical processes by which they become part of objective reality – imagined communities are real, and we must understand that thinking in IR theory is itself constitutive of the reality of international relations.

Notes

1. Matthew Horsman and Andrew Marshall, *After the Nation State*, (London: HarperCollins, 1995) p. 269.
2. Enrico Augelli and Craig N. Murphy 'Gramsci and international relations: a general perspective with examples from recent US policy toward the Third World' in Stephen Gill (ed.) *Gramsci, Historical Materialism and International Relations* (Cambridge University Press, 1993) p. 139.
3. Robert W. Cox, 'Towards a post-hegemonic conceptualization of world order: reflections on the relevancy of Ibn Khaldun' in James N. Rosenau and Ernst-Otto Czempiel (eds), *Governance without Government: Order and Change in World Politics* (Cambridge University Press, 1992), p. 133.
4. See *The Return of Culture and Identity in IR Theory*, ed. Yosef Lapid and Friedrich Kratochwil (Boulder, Co.: Lynne Rienner, 1995).
5. For an overview of the contemporary condition of IR theory, see Ken Booth and Steve Smith (eds), *International Relations Theory Today* (Cambridge: Polity Press, 1995).

1 Society, Modernity and Social Change: Approaches to Nationalism and Identity
Chris Farrands

INTRODUCTION

At first sight, our identity would appear to be above all a question of psychology. It is to do with who we feel we are, where we feel we belong, who we belong with, who is inside this group and who is excluded from it. But these individual inner feelings are surrounded by a social and economic context, and it very quickly becomes clear that questions of identity cannot be handled by looking only at the level of the individual person. They are social, economic, political and cultural questions. This chapter looks at ways in which accounts of identity in International Relations (IR) have been linked to ideas of social change and social cohesion in particular historical frameworks, especially in the conditions of what contemporary social science calls 'modernity'.

How does our individual psychology link to the study of international relations? We acquire our identity from our families, our work, our peer relationships, the groups we associate with (church, mosque, community, sports club, football team, who we shop with, the music we like and dislike, and the magazines we aspire to read). We also acquire our identity from the ways in which we respond to the various predicaments in which life puts us, including the threats we experience. Our identity is built from these responses. Some writers would argue that our identity is a focus for the achievement of a certain integrity of the personality.[1] Others, most influentially R.D. Laing[2] have suggested that identity and personality are a battlefield of influences which is much more likely to collapse under strain, including the strain of what is misleadingly called 'everyday life'. But this psychological context is framed socially, culturally, and economically. Both as individuals and as members of groups with a position in power hierarchies and interests, we are in touch with the sources of our identity even if we have no real influence over them or are unconscious of their impact. We also have access to identity to the extent that we have an ability to participate in rituals or processes which identify us, whether or not we can effectively manipulate the key symbols of the society that we belong to. If we are excluded or alienated from this society, that in turn is fundamental to our identity. But each individual is so locked into these frameworks of identity through groups and collectivities that any discussion of identity will very quickly lead to national and broader collective identities which are engaged in international relations at a diversity of levels. Our identity is not simply a nice question of where we feel comfortable. Our identity is about who we would kill, who we would kill for, what kind of moral community we identify with, or, to touch on the greatest taboo, whom we would eat.

Whether we approach International Relations as it has more traditionally been understood as a 'world of states' or as an arena populated first of all by citizens, questions of identity have become increasingly important. The main received idea of identity in International Relations has been nationalism and the linkages between the nation and the state.[3] This book as a whole takes as its starting point the proposition that identity is much broader in scope and much more diverse than a focus on nationalism and state ideology would suggest. This chapter also goes beyond the bounds of conventional thinking on nationalism in international relations. But because it looks at more traditional theory, and because it to some extent acts as a foil against which the other chapters in the book will lever, this chapter will spend some time looking at established views of nationalism, nationality and ethnicity.

NATIONALISM AND MODERNIST APPROACHES TO IDENTITY

Political Nationalism

One influential view of nationalism argues that nationalism (i) is the primary or only significant focus of allegiance in the modern world, including in international politics, (ii) is essentially political as opposed to economic, social, cultural or religious in origins, and that politics constitute an autonomous field of human activity and human study, (iii) has its origins in the French Revolution, or perhaps in an Atlantic Revolution which links the experience of the American and French revolutions and the emergence of new trading and economic patterns in the later eighteenth century, or at least has grown out of the birth of 'modernity', (iv) is explained mainly through the examination of the political ideas which shape it, (v) forms a corrupting, irrational or harmful ideology which weakens social order and intellectual reason alike. This view is shared by Kedourie and Minogue, and to some extent also by Gellner.[4] It is a fundamentally conservative view, rooted intellectually in Burke's[5] critique of the French revolution. It also reflects a kind of superior distaste for the populism of much democratic nationalism, as well as a fundamental rationalism. Although this contempt for the social roots of nationalism and identity is found in some orthodox or realist writing in International Relations, the reader who knows some other IR theory should be wary of identifying this narrow view (of political nationalism as a force separated from other influences and processes) with traditional realist writing in IR, since there are a number of important realist writers in the subject who take nationalism seriously, including Ivo Ducachek,[6] Cornelia Navari,[7] Robert Purnell,[8] Arnold Wolfers,[9] and Alfred Cobban.[10] Some realists may ignore or underestimate the importance of identity in their single-minded pursuit of a mechanical model of international relations based on a system of states, but others take nationalism and other identities as critical not simply as foundations of state identity but also as challenges and qualifications to the order of states.

The Social Bases of Identity

Against the narrow, conservative, often rather snobbish, and unhistorical account of nationalism offered by the 'political nationalists', there is a second broader approach to identity questions in international relations. It is exemplified in particular in the work of Antony Smith[11] and Antony Giddens.[12] Both point to the impossibility of talking about identity in social relations without looking at the complex of interactions between the social and the psychological and the political at different levels. Both recognise that, while there may well be something distinctive about *modern* nationalism, there are many kinds of nationalism rooted in different times and experiences. Smith argues that forms of identity are shaped by social change and the stresses which radical change, including invasion, structural economic transformation and the uprooting of established forms of life bring about. Giddens is not primarily a scholar of nationalism at all, but a writer who has been led to look at ideas of political identity through a set of larger theoretical concerns about social structure and social change which makes his views particularly challenging to more conventional accounts rooted in a narrow idea of what 'international politics' ought to be about. Both are important in their rejection of the idea of a uniquely 'political' basis for identity and in their attempt to explore how social, economic, cultural and political dimensions of human societies interact in shaping and transforming identities. Both also see nationalism as one form of identity, but one contested amongst many. Both look at the reshaping of identities under the influence of changes such as the globalisation of economy and culture. They provide a starting point for a re-assessment of the importance of nationalism in international relations not because they reject the idea that it *is* important but because they offer a distinctive and coherent account of *how* it is important.

The Indeterminacy of Modern Nationalism

These arguments provide a starting point, but they also leave open the questions of what we mean by nationalism. If we can establish as a starting point on the one hand that nationalism cannot simply be explained as an autonomous 'political' activity, and on the other hand that there are important social bases for all forms of identity which might count in IR, then what can we say more specifically? What is nationalism and what function does it play in international relations? There is a temptation to play an academic trick at this point and just refuse to offer a definition altogether.

There are some good reasons to do this: to say 'nationalism is x' implies that it is clearly definable and specific when it is much more uncertain than that. But students of the subject need firmer initial guidance. So it may be useful to say that many definitions of nationalism have been offered. None are completely satisfactory but some are certainly better than others. I would suggest that it is useful initially to think of nationalism in the terms used by Purnell, that 'a nation is a nation when it thinks it is a nation', but that there are varied and difficult but not unknowable or random reasons why some groups of people tend to adopt nationalities whilst others do not or cannot.[13] In due course the reader will need to treat that definition as critically as she/he would approach anything else that is said on this subject, but it provides a useful starting point.

It may be more useful to consider some examples. Jewish identity is probably the oldest established form of nationalism, and is certainly the oldest recorded in written history. It is rooted in the family and in the religious practices and law which put the family at the heart of social life. It is also rooted in specific historical experiences of exile, slavery and recovery or freedom which have been repeated several times even before the Holocaust and the pogroms of this century. The escape from Egypt and the captivity in Babylon inspires the literature and the consciousness of others, especially black Afro-Americans, but it remains something which gives unique shape to Jewish identity. Zionism was something different, part of a particularly European socialist vision, articulated in Yiddish not Hebrew, and linked to other late romantic nationalist visions in Austria-Hungary and Ireland in form. But since the foundation of the state of Israel in 1948, Zionism has fused with Jewish national identity and has been deliberately re-focused around the new state. Irish nationalism is founded in a struggle against the English which goes back centuries, but which took a particular form during the seventeenth century Wars of Religion, was redefined in the late nineteenth century by a highly refined cultural elite, and then battered into its current shape in a series of conflicts within itself as well as with the British. Indian nationalism has always been peculiar and divided, since Indian society is itself dispersed and divided. There is the middle class dominated old anti-colonial nationalism of the Congress Party, but equally there is today the nationalism of local ethnic groups which deny legitimacy to Delhi and the more fundamentalist and more working class religious based nationalism of the Hindu BJP. Scots nationalism is not, as Welsh nationalism undoubtedly is, shaped primarily by cultural forces – Scots nationalists have to represent at least three cultures (English language in the central region, Lowland Scots elsewhere, and Gaelic in the north and north west). Scotland had its own monarchy for many years, and retains its own law and education system. Hatred of the English shapes Scots nationalism but is not its defining characteristic, and economic factors have in the last generation been much more significant in the growth of Scottish nationalist sentiment than they have been in shaping Welsh nationalism. American nationalism may be the most complex and difficult to account for if we think that nationalisms may have a common essence and a common set of causes: it is difficult to find what might unite Americans, with their regional, ethnic, historical, religious and cultural variations, but American nationalism does exist amongst the competing identities of the country in some respects at least. Japanese nationalism appears to be the most straightforward to understand, in the sense that Japanese people share an identifiable language, history and culture, are almost unique in having a state which is genuinely co-terminous with the boundaries of the ethnic Japanese population, and Japan may be almost the only country we could cite where genuine 'national self-determination' is a part of the political reality.

These examples suggest that there is no single identifiable cause or set of causes of nationalism. We cannot, these examples also suggest, expect to find single-factor explanations of identity. Identities are complex webs of culture, economic necessity, political choice, experience and expectations. Each example of nationalism is different for each nation, and over time nationalisms may change more than their supporters would easily recognise, for the myth of continuity is very important in all nationalisms. Different forms of identity are invoked by different experiences: if we recognise a sexual re-orientation towards homosexuality in ourselves, suffer anti-Semitism where it had only been experienced at second hand before, or find our home team suddenly projected onto the world stage by success, our idea of what matters to us is likely to change. This is not trivial, and it is in some way purely individual. But it is not purely subjective, it is not only down to individual psychology, it is social and, most important, it is capable of explanation through reasoned argument and the use of soundly used evidence, even if it is not amenable to simple explanations. One thing central to modern identity is the sense of history. Our identity is part of our history, defined by our sense of history and validated by history. This may not be logical, for our history (that is to say our received account of our past) is equally shaped and legitimated by our identity. But it is powerful and real. But beyond noting the importance of the relationship between history and all forms of identity, identity remains radically indeterminate. This makes it interesting. It makes it remote to the kinds of scientific or historical generalisation which have sometimes characterised writing on International Relations.

Nationalism, Nationality, Traditional Society and Modernity

Almost all accounts of nationalism set it in a historical context: even though nationalism is found in many different societies and at many different times, each form of nationalism is nonetheless historically specific. Nationalism can be said to have existed in more traditional societies, as the example of Jewish nationalism recorded in the Old Testament books of the bible shows. But it is more difficult to say, for example, whether the response of the native peoples of central and southern America to the arrival of the first Europeans was really a nationalist response, or whether it should be explained in some other way, even though nationalism clearly was a part of the response to European settlement in the Great Plains of North American two or three centuries later. Hobsbawm among others identifies the emergence of nationalism with the creation of great competing industrial empires, taking a kind of Marxist view of the economic determination of political ideas, and, like the writers called 'political nationalists' earlier, sees the origins of what we call nationalism in the industrial revolution.[14] Giddens locates modern nationalism as a form of identity in a particular conception of space and time which characterises the industrial revolution. The development of railways, unified national markets, national education systems, national media all contribute to a refocussing of loyalties and allegiances in his account. However, the new nationalism which emerges is neither wholly unique nor simply determined by economic structures.[15] We have thus in effect a three way debate in the literature which has in fact characterised the academic debate on nationalism for almost all of this century: firstly, there is an argument that nationalism is located in ideas and in a distinctive political realm. Secondly, there is a view that nationalism arises as a result of changing economic forces which either determine or at least largely determine its character. Finally, there is a sociological view which has the advantage of challenging the more simple arguments of the economic or political determinists but the disadvantage of being more difficult to pin down, and is sometimes, especially in Giddens'case, very opaque.

The language of modern writing on nationalism makes some key distinctions which structure the argument. Other chapters in this book will look critically at this language and suggest that this structuring of the arguments about identity is distorting in a number of ways. But it is important here to explain how this language is used. Nationalism is generally seen as an explicit and politically mobilised expression of a certain level of shared identity. Even if nationalism cannot be reduced to the 'autonomous' sphere of the political divorced from economic, social and cultural processes, it is nonetheless distinctively political among other things. Nationality, on the other hand, is used in two quite different ways, firstly to describe a legal status of belonging to a specified nation (as in the British Nationality Act), and secondly to describe a broad cultural and social affiliation which may or may not be politically mobilised. In this second sense, nationality is always a component of nationalism, but nationalism is more than nationality.[16] Nationalism is said to be a feature of modern societies or at least to take a distinctive form in modern societies. In traditional societies, identity is articulated through local institutions and the sense of space is highly localised: people do not travel widely, at least not commonly, nor do they have access to diverse sources of information. They live within traditional roles within a time scale which is unchanging. This creates forms of identity which are distinctive in themselves and different from those in modern (or so called 'postmodern' societies).

CRITICISMS OF THE MODERNIST APPROACH

The Uses of Nationalism

Nationalism has always been used as part of a political game, and the ways in which nationalism is used help to give it a shape. In the Roman Empire, a series of historical myths about the origins of Rome and the evolution of the Roman Republic were taught by political leaders and repeated by historians to show the glory, but also the legitimacy, of the Empire. British history teachers and publicists in the school system of the nineteenth century took over from the Roman experience the image of successful empire and the 'duty to rule subject races' which became in time the 'White Man's Burden'. Nationalist history thus came to protect empire and racism as well as serve as a claim of ethnic and national uniqueness. History teaching has always had a central role in the propagation of official identities. In former Yugoslavia in the 1990s, different views of the history of the country over the previous fifty years, and especially radically divergent accounts of what happened in Yugoslavia during the Second World War, were used to justify each of the warring groups claims to power as well as provide the justification for 'ethnic cleansing'.[17] Longer term historical myths are used to suggest why the different peoples of Yugoslavia, who share an ethnic and linguistic heritage and who were in no meaningful way racially of different origins, but who over the last thousand years had adopted different religious and social group identities, could justify the deep-seated hatreds that they later adopted.

In the nineteenth century, European countries understanding of each other were shaped as well as reflected in history teaching. Each country evolved a national education system. That is to say, not simply an education system national in scope but also one nationalist in ideology. Taxation was committed to ensure that governments could exert control over what was taught, and uniform syllabuses were written for all pupils in French, American or Italian schools, and very often for the pupils of schools in colonies as well. National teacher training systems were made the central focus of nationalist ideas. This was especially so in what became in effect a great patriotic war fought in the classrooms of France and Germany in the aftermath of the Franco-Prussian War of 1870–71. Ernest Renan, the most celebrated historian of his day, wrote his text 'What is a Nation?'[18] for an elite audience of the teacher training and university establishment. The text was taught everywhere in France and her colonies for nearly a hundred years. It formed the basis of many French people's conception of themselves, especially for the educated middle class, at least until the collapse of the Third Republic in 1940.[19]

This concern with national self images is still significant. In both the British and the American educational systems in the 1980s there was a fierce debate over history teaching. In the US, it took the form of a contest over the 'canon' of Western literature and history, and pitted a more liberal multi-cultural view of education against a conservative Western oriented idea of what was important to teach and learn. In Britain, conservatives in education and the political world tried to control the curriculum, aiming to defeat both multi-cultural history and a more European (and less 'British') idea of history and culture. Through the manipulation of the system of schools inspection and the imposition of political control on the school curriculum, and with the active intervention of Education Minister Kenneth Baker, nationalists were able to control the ways in which young people were allowed to understand their identity. The imposition of a so-called 'national curriculum' forced schools in Britain to teach material in common, something that was commonly done in many other countries on the French model, but which was unheard of in the UK until the late 1980s. It also enforced a common view of national identity through the teaching of literature as well as of history, and in the process asserted the power of a standard 'received' idea of English language and literature over the varied literatures of Wales, Ireland and Scotland. In the early 1980s, the British film *The Ploughman's Lunch* explored the way advertising, and more generally popular culture, can be manipulated by political parties such as Mrs Thatcher's Conservatives in order to manipulate popular senses of identity, partly through nationalism but equally through racial and social exclusion.

One set of arguments about modern nationalism concerns the origins of war. Do uses or manipulations of nationalism cause wars? On the one hand, it has been argued that nationalism is a cause of war; on the other that unfulfilled aspirations to national self-determination cause conflicts which lead to war. This argument surrounds a series of debates on the origins of the First World War in particular. But other evidence suggests that both the terms of this debate and its sense of the historical evidence are flawed. International Relations scholars such as Waltz, Vasquez and Bueno de Mesquito[20] have not accepted that the causes of conflict are necessarily the causes of war. They have suggested that war is a very specific form of conflict, and that the breakdown of peace needs explanation at a number of different levels. Nationalism may contribute to the causation of wars, but it is not in itself a sufficient explanation, and most recent International Relations literature, although often seeing nationalism as potentially harmful, resists the conclusion drawn after the First World War by many idealist writers that it is in itself a primary cause of war.[21]

Nationalism as Secular Religion?

Nationalism has often been seen as a substitute for religion, or as a form of 'secular religion'. The growth of modern nationalism has been associated with the decline of religious observance (or at least of church attendance) and with the secularisation of societies.[22] This view is not nonsense, but it is also not wholly coherent. The growth of modern nationalism is only associated closely with the decline of religion in some cases. The growth of modern industrial society and of modern nationalism coincided with the decline of religion in England and the Low Countries, but religion and nationalism are identified together not only in traditional societies (Jamaica: Rastafarai; Ireland: Catholicism) but also in the United States. It is not the case that industrialism saw a decline in religion in Italy: the decline in religion occurred, but long after the growth of nationalism; it has never been a remotely relevant argument in Turkey. Northern European Marxists and their successors may have wanted to argue this case[23] and can point to some good instances, but their history is selective and shows little understanding of the social roots of popular religion. The historian Carlyle produced a study of the French Revolution which sees French nationalism as a form of secular religion sweeping irrationally but unstoppably through middle and poor classes alike.[24] This may be relevant, although it may also simplify the significance of religion in society. But it also recognises something in identity which has come to be important in late twentieth century writing again, the importance of the idea of a moral or symbolic community which operates as a powerful communicator of what is acceptable and of what is assumed, of what it is reasonable to live with and of what is unbearable.

One example of the formation of identity through the growth of links between popular politics and popular religion arises in Brazil. Brazilian nationalism is largely imposed, and often based on a (Spanish) colonial model. Popular identities amongst Black societies in cities such as Sao Paulo rest on a recovered image of a slave past. Slavery forced people from Africa and brought them to the Americas, destroying their sense of self and many of their social institutions. The ending of slavery broke up established group organisation and posed economic threats to the

Black population, who came to form the poorest and most vulnerable group in a highly differentiated and unequal society. Their positive response was through music. Since at least the start of this century, Samba teams have been organised to perform in festivals. But they have become permanent institutions, one of the main forms of popular association providing social insurance and mutual support as well as entertainment. Samba is not simply a musical form, but also a focus for social reorganisation: carnival associations in Brazil – *farvalas* – have become the basis of forms of popular culture which enable Black groups, especially Black women, to assert a distinctive identity, to compete in an arena where they can win respect and sometimes find great fame. This locus of identity has become the main organising form of popular culture and politics in the largest Brazilian city.

Nationalism and Contingency

The critical approach to modernist images of identity is made as well in Milan Kundera's novel *The Unbearable Lightness of Being* as in any 'political science' text.[25] In the aftermath of the Soviet invasion of Czechoslovakia, how were Czech identities reshaped? Two lovers – whose relationship is continuously in question – leave Prague for a day out and visit a small neighbouring town:

> . . . they pulled into the square and got out of the car. Nothing had changed. They stood facing the hotel they had once stayed at. The same old linden trees . . . when Tomas looked back at the hotel, he noticed that something had in fact changed. What had once been the Grand now bore the name Baikal. He looked at the street sign on the corner of the building: Moscow Square. Then they took a walk . . . through the streets they had known, and examined all their names: Stalingrad Street, Leningrad Street, Rostov Street, Novosibirsk Street, Kiev Street, Odessa Street. There was a Tchaikovski Sanatorium, a Tolstoy Sanatorium, a Rimski-Korsakov Sanatorium; there was a Hotel Suvorov, a Gorky Cinema and a Cafe Pushkin. All the names had been taken from Russian geography, from Russian history.
>
> Tereza suddenly first recalled the first days of the invasion. People in every city and town had pulled down the street signs; sign posts disappeared. Overnight, the country had become nameless. For seven days, Russian troops wandered the countryside, not knowing where they were. The officers searched for newspaper offices, for television and radio stations to occupy, but could not find them. Whenever they

asked, they would get either a shrug of the shoulders or false names
and directions.

Hindsight now made that anonymity seem quite dangerous to the
country. The streets and buildings could no longer return to their original names. As a result, a Czech spa had suddenly metamorphosed
into a miniature imaginary Russia and the past that Tereza had gone
there to find had turned out to be confiscated.

There is a lot in this which is relevant here. The sense of un-naming
which deprives us of identity is a common theme in much twentieth century literature. It takes a special place in Czech writing (as in Irish and
Black writing) because it is not only imagined: it happened. The sense
that language is a political structure with enormous power is crucial to
the way we talk about identity in the late twentieth century, although
there are few examples of language power quite as crude as in this example. The language of power and the language of signs overlap but are
not the same. The Czechs had scope for resistance: they could abandon
their names rather than submit to invasion unquestioningly, but they
could not choose their names. The past has been 'confiscated'; but that
past was constructed like the 'new' past. But of course the question may
be how the past is legitimately constructed and what kinds of construction indicate a more autonomous politics of identity rather than an
imposed one, rather than whether identity is 'natural' in some sense or
other or not. At this point in this book, this is just to note the existence
of themes which become of increasing importance in the whole of the
book, and are especially evident in the chapters by Youngs, Renwick and
Krause. But we should also note that there has been an on-going dialogue
between what are called here 'modernist' and 'anti-modernist' accounts
of identity, and the distinction is not always very clear or based on clearly
agreed criteria. Furthermore, some of the work usually described as
'anti-modernist' has been widely influential and is worth particular
attention here.

Imagined Communities and Multiple Identities in the Modern State

The traditional view of nationalism suggests that it is a relatively fixed,
objective force, and that the academic debate about nationalism should
focus on how far it has material or intellectual causes and whether it can
contribute to stability or instability in international relations. This debate
has not ceased. But alongside it is a more recent argument that identities
in international relations – and in all social relations – are wholly or

essentially socially constructed and have no meaningful 'objective' existence at all.

The idea of a fixed identity linked to the modern nation state is challenged by the argument that there is nothing natural or fixed about identity itself. Anderson's influential text on *imagined communities* argues that national identity is a wholly artificial or social construction, and that it follows from this that there is very little we can use to distinguish national identity and allegiance from other forms.[26] But note that Anderson does not challenge the idea that nationalism is important. Nor does he challenge the idea that nationalism is closely linked to the state. But in challenging the idea of a fixed or 'natural' sense of identity rooted in nationalism and in arguing that national identities are always constructed, Anderson not only challenges the received modernist wisdom on how identity is formed. He also undermines a set of received ideas about the state and about the relationship between the state and collective identities as a whole. If imagined communities are constructed, that is socially constructed, who has the power to shape that construction?

In mid sixteenth century France, as Emmanuel Le Roy Ladurie demonstrates in his study of popular uprising and its suppression, *Carnival in Romans*,[27] one of the main issues of conflict proved to be a contest between local, urban and artisan groups and aristocratic groups influenced from Paris for the control of the definition of identity. The destruction of local identities was a necessary part of a process of centralisation out of which the absolute monarchy of the seventeenth century emerged. Over a period of time in the 1560s and 1570s, townsmen and small merchants won political concessions which gave them a level of power against the central state, which was racked by civil and religious war. As the centre stabilised, its representatives were able to reassert themselves. In a genuine political drama, during the festivities of carnival at the start of Lent, the aristocratic faction, dressed in masks and fancy dress, organised a kind of coup in reverse in which they seized power back for the national centre, destroyed the power of the merchants, hanged their leaders, and destroyed the social and political role of their popular clubs and assemblies. This appears to be a class war, and was; but it was also a conflict between other kinds of identity, religious, regional, between 'trade' and 'land' and between different aspirations. This question of local identity is important also in international relations, although more traditional writers on nationalism have tended to ignore it, and it was important even before current conflicts such as those in Chechnya, Belgium, former Yugoslavia, Algeria and Kurdistan brought them to our attention.

The idea of a fixed identity dominated by nationalism is challenged in a different way by the ideas surrounding Anderson's work. For it suggests also that people have a variety of identities which co-exist, and that they hold multiple allegiances. Thus most individuals may feel that they belong to a town, to a region, and to a country. They may simultaneously feel equal attachment to a generational group: the VE day celebrations have reminded many people in many countries that their experience of the Second World War gave them a unique bond and a distinctive view of the world. People who remember the Woodstock festival or the 1970 Isle of Wight Festival share a common identity expressed in music as well as mythology; people twenty years younger share a common identity expressed (often) in laughing at the memories of their hippie generation elders. Sexuality, gender, ethnicity and sport, among many other things, all command allegiance and form a basis of identity; they all challenge the hegemony of nationalism among identities. A study of British responses to the bombing of civilians in 1940–41 illustrates these questions, which turn on the problem of whether we have multiple and sometimes competing senses of identity.

During the early part of the Second World War, British cities were bombed in a series of German attacks. While London and some naval towns were repeatedly bombed, some other cities were only attacked occasionally. People were asked to keep records and diaries of the experience by a government agency, Mass Observation. In the 1970s, the founder of Mass Observation, the professional anthropologist Tom Harrisson returned to these records to analyse them. They form the basis for his book *Living Through the Blitz*.[28] In the study, Harrisson asks among other things why people responded to being blitzed so differently. For in some towns they 'stuck it out'. But, despite the government propaganda of the time, in some towns people simply fled after being attacked. They subsequently lived, often in tens of thousands, in clandestine camps. Thus in 1940 people from Portsmouth fled to the nearby New Forest, where many lived until the end of the war. Harrisson found plenty of evidence to suggest that peoples' collective sense of identity explained their response to being blitzed. But the explanation did not lie in nationalism: people tended to express few nationalist sentiments and to take a deeply sceptical view of those who were overtly patriotic. What moved people was a sense of local identity and a sense of the need to help their friends and neighbours. There is a parallel argument that soldiers in the extreme of battle fight not for their image of their country but for their regiment, for their own personal survival, and often most of all so as 'not to let their mates [buddies] down'. People did not flee from Liverpool even after heavy bombing, Harrisson suggests, because of the closeness of family groups and the strength of local urban working class cultures. In Plymouth, they did not flee for the same reasons, reinforced by the particular myths and self-images of a town that had self-consciously been a naval city since the defeat of the Spanish Armada in the 1580s. But Portsmouth and some of the Midlands towns did not have the same roots. They had many more people who had recently arrived in search of the new prosperity of the English south in the 1930s, and what urban myths and bonds there were did not mean much to them. By contrast again, in Coventry, which was the target of the most devastating night of bombing of any city outside London, people fled. But most returned quickly. They needed to be able to get to work, they had close family contacts in the town, and they seemed to have wanted to defy the destruction they saw around them. But they showed remarkably little nationalism, and a contempt rather than a hatred for the Germans. Harrisson's work suggests that collective identities are very important in shaping people's responses to a crisis, but that these collective identities exist on several social and ideological levels, some of which are more consciously articulated while others are more implicit. Local and family identities are seen to be crucial, and material necessities – the need to work, the urge to stay in a damaged house and protect it from looting – work against the received wisdom either that identities are easily manipulated by state power or that nationalism or patriotism are clearly in some way 'superior' or 'prior' to other senses of identity. It also supports the view argued already here that identities, including nationalism and ethnicity, have roots which are social and historical, and that explanations which separate out as 'autonomous' either political or economic explanations of identity are inadequate and ill-conceived.

HISTORY AND IDENTITY

The Importance of Historical Specificity

In this chapter the flow of argument has been interrupted at several points in order to tell a story. There is a particular reason behind this strategy: if we cannot generalise about identity, if there is no 'big picture' which provides a context or an overview against which particular points can be judged, then we have to find other ways of managing the logic of the argument. One useful way of doing this is to set out particular cases as valid in themselves. Hence the use here of the work of Harrisson and

Ladurie, among other examples. At various times in the last century and a half, when ideas of nationalism have dominated in writing about international relations and international history, attempts have been made to generalise about it. Essentialist accounts argued that the 'essence' of nationalism was grounded in economic structures (in Marxist accounts) or rooted in a historical spirit (in Hegel) or derived from a popular resistance to central imperial power (in popular democratic thinking such as amongst Jacksonian Democrats in the US or amongst Garibaldi's followers in Italy). The discussion in this chapter so far has emphasised a central argument about identity in international relations (which continues to be explored in other chapters in this book). That argument takes the form of a debate between writers who, whether using a more explicitly 'scientific' generalising approach or a more 'historical' methodology.

One of the most used examples of modern nationalism is France. French nationalism is often seen, not only by nationalist French historians, as a paradigm case of European nationalism, where a nation state has emerged over a long period of time, characterised by a powerful hegemonic political culture linked to a powerful self-reproducing elite. French society was able to transfer legitimacy from the monarchy, the original focus of nationalism, to first the Imperial and then the Republican system. National allegiance was seen as having dominated French politics from (at least) 1789, and to have been spread as a model ideology to Italy, Spain and Germany and subsequently through much of the world. Eugene Weber[29] has made substantial inroads into the image of French nationalism as good history, although it may be that the image remained and will remain powerful. Weber's work shows that the spread of French nationalism was indeed associated with the shift to a modern industrial society, but that this only occurred in the years before the First World War. It suggests that nationalist allegiance was spread through the country where in 1850 only half the population could speak French or identified with France. The means of promoting the new forms of identity included military service, national education and the modernising influence of science, medicine and technology, including the railway system. French peasants, with their strong regional culture boosted by dialect or distinctive language and following their particular rural ways of life, resisted the 'advance' of modernisation. They were able to maintain a local identity of their own long after historians and politicians in Paris had been misrepresenting France as a united, coherent national body. Of course regional interests today are still strong in France and in many other countries, and feelings against the metropolitan centre help to underpin local identities. This remains the case, for example, in the United States as the 1994 Congressional elections illustrate. It might be possible to perceive anti-Washington sentiments apparently behind the incident in Oklahoma in 1995 when a government building was bombed resulting in considerable loss of life. If powerful nationalist models such as that of nineteenth century France or contemporary America can be shown to be all too easily over-stated in nationalist polemic, the nationalist myths and rhetorics of other societies are all the more called into question, although of course one must at the same time recognise that the myths and rhetorics have a life of their own, and that the study of identity is not an analysis of rational logics.

Foundation Myths

Within traditional and modern societies, forms of identity are not simply the result of a social process, they also contribute to social processes. They legitimate or undermine particular forms of power. They act as agencies of social communication. They have a constitutive role; that is to say that they make up and give shape to (i.e. constitute) social and political relations. Foundation myths illustrate this. If we ask where a society or a nation comes from, it will have particular answers which fulfil particular needs and reflect a collective response to the specific context. In the aftermath of the fall of Rome and the early English settlements, all of the English kingdoms claimed a common (and entirely unhistorical descent from Trojan refugees who settled in England after the end of the Trojan Wars while at the same time claimed descent from Germanic or Norse gods (usually Wodin) in their orally transmitted history of the royal line.[30] This ambiguity of identity expresses an ambiguity of circumstance, an ambiguity towards Christianity and the old gods and an ambiguity towards the Roman heritage (since the original Trojan foundation myth is that in *The Aeneid* explaining the origins of Rome, from which the English simply borrowed). Although we may want to think of contemporary societies as more rational and more based on calculation of particular interests, powerful foundation myths still shape culture and national self-images in many places. Examples where national myths shape the contemporary arts, but also popular discourse and sometimes daily political life include Finland (the Kalevala, the national epic myth), Hindu India (the Mahabarata), the French Fifth Republic (the myth of Gaullist resistance and recovery after 1940), and the communist party in the People's Republic of China (the myths of the Civil War and the Long March). Some of these myths may be more historically valid than others. The point is that as foundation myths their historicity is wholly irrelevant. The

English belief that the early kingdom of East Anglia was founded by Wodin was just as strong as De Gualle's supporters' belief in his legitimacy in 1944–5, not withstanding the *historical* 'truth' of either. The General used his radio broadcasts as a means of promoting his mythology as effectively as the court of the High King Raedwald used the potent symbols of power and wealth now labelled in the British Museum as the Sutton Hoo treasure. In both cases, identity is shaped by forces of social communication which were effective at the time. In both cases the myth making did not involve anything as simple as a lie. But in neither case did it embody very much literal truth. In both cases, we cannot simply say that people were merely manipulated: the propaganda was effective because people wanted to belong, wanted to believe and wanted to exclude others from the community they identified with.

Among the most subtle forms of communicated identity in this sense is that to be found in the work of the Irish poet Seamus Heaney.[31] In the 1970s, it was fashionable in Irish Republican circles to denounce Heaney because his work was seen as not being overtly political and because for many years he appeared to avoid writing about current political issues. Yet now Heaney is recognised as the greatest national voice after only Yeats and Joyce. His work has continued to explore Irish identity and its history through a series of explorations of his own experience, his relations with landscape and place and farming and the images of home and exile. Heaney expresses in his poetry aspects of identity which are uncertain and hard to define and which nonetheless have a distinctive Irishness without resort to bog Irish parody (as in Synge), self-conscious political extravagance (Behan) or aloof exiled abstraction (Beckett). The influence Heaney has had on organised Irish political nationalism is limited. The influence he has had on literature is enormous; but so too is his influence on the ways in which Irish *and* non-Irish people define themselves. This is broader than in narrowly political terms, encompassing cultural and social community, with rights as well as with identity. Yet he is quite entitled to insist that all of his work is political.

The Reconstruction of the State: Capitalism and Globalisation

If it is generally accepted that modern nationalism has evolved in parallel with the emergence of the modern state and the formation of a particular structure of international relations, the modern states system, then fundamental changes in the state and the states system logically must either reshape or transform identity. If the identity of modern states is a product of capitalist economic development, then a fundamental restructuring of capitalism represents a fundamental challenge to identity. If the self-defined identity of a society is grounded in fundamental beliefs and cultural practices, the transformation of those beliefs and practices equally represents an undermining of identity.[32] There are challenges of this sort as international relations step towards the twenty-first century, particularly from the processes of globalisation and the reassertion of local or regional identities, from the break-up of established patterns of work and the growth of new patterns of political and social communications associated with mass media, computer networking and global communications corporations, and from the transformation of nation states in the face of the growth of regional blocs (such as the North American Free Trade Association) and the uncertainties of a post-superpower post-Cold War world. These issues are explored – and criticised – in successive chapters in this book. In the post-Cold War world, questions of identity have become a major issue on the agenda of International Relations, and there are a wider range of questions about identity which have to be addressed. This makes them all the more important, but it makes the potential answers more complex and less certain.

CONCLUSION

This chapter has tried to make four central points which introduce themes developed in the book in subsequent chapters:

i) Conceptions of identity, including nationalism, nationality, ethnicity and race among others, have been understood in a long-standing literature as a central focus in International Relations which links the growth of nationalism with the distinctive patterns of modern society. In the chapter, this has been shown to be an important argument but one which is open to criticism. There is a link between conceptions of nationalism and the emergence and development of the 'modern' but it cannot be taken for granted or used as a whole explanation, and pre- or postmodern (in Giddens language 'late-modern') societies cannot be understood without looking at how they are shaped (but also constituted, haunted and self-obsessed) by national and by other identities.

ii) Explanations of the origins and character of identity based on single factors are at best incomplete, and we cannot usefully continue to talk, for example, as if 'political' and 'cultural' or 'economic' nationalism were clearly distinct, or that one is found in one country and another elsewhere.

iii) Identities are assumed by groups of people for reasons which are not wholly explicable in terms of calculations of interest, or even in terms of rational responses to threats or outside pressures. Identities are always historically, socially and materially grounded, but they cannot be reduced to these elements. They retain distinctive features of which the most important, in the view of this chapter, are the links between political, cultural and social processes and the importance of the historical specificity and particular experience of identities in particular cases and situations.

iv) Identity in International Relations has tended to be associated with the study of nationalism. There were good reasons for this, and nationalism has certainly not disappeared or become less important or less controversial. But other forms of identity have become of increasing significance alongside concerns with nationalism, and at the same time the definitions of nationalism have become necessarily broader and more difficult to separate from other forms of identity.

Notes

1.   A. Storr, *The Integrity of the Personality* (Harmondsworth, Middlesex: Penguin, 1960).
2.   R.D. Laing, *The Politics of the Family* (Harmondsworth, Middlesex: Penguin, 1976).
3.   L. Greenfeld, *Nationalism: Five Roads to Modernity* (Cambridge, Mass.: Harvard University Press, 1992); J. Hutchinson, *Modern Nationalism* (London: Fontana, 1994); A. Smith, *Theories of Nationalism* (London: Duckworth, 1973); C. Tilly, 'Reflections on the history of European state making', in C. Tilly (ed.), *The Formation of Nation States in Western Europe*, (Princeton, NJ.: Princeton UP, 1975); W. Bloom, *Personal Identity, National Identity and International Relations* (Cambridge: CUP, 1990).
4.   E. Kedourie, *Nationalism* (Oxford: Blackwell, 4th ed., 1993, K. Minogue, *Nationalism* (London: Batsford, 1967); see discussion in Smith, A. *op. cit.*
5.   E. Burke, *Reflections on the Revolution in France* (Harmondsworth, Middlesex: Penguin, 1969).
6.   I. Duchacek, *Nations and Men* (Lanham: University of America Press, 1982, 3rd ed.).
7.   C. Navari,'Diplomatic structure and idiom', in J. Mayall (ed.), *The Community of States* (London: Allen & Unwin, 1982), pp. 15–33.
8.   R. Purnell, *The Society of States* (London: Weidenfeld & Nicolson, 1973).
9.   A. Wolfers, *Discord and Collaboration* (Baltimore and London: Johns Hopkins Press, 1962).

10. A. Cobban, *The Nation State and National Self Determination* (London: Collins, 1969, revised edition).
11. A. Smith, *Theories of Nationalism* (London: Duckworth, 1973).
12. A. Giddens, *The Consequences of Modernity* (Cambridge: Polity Press in association with Blackwell, 1990).
13. Purnell, *op. cit.*
14. E. Hobsbawm, *The Age of Revolution* (London: Abacus Books, 1977).
15. A. Giddens, *op. cit.*
16. Purnell, *op. cit.*
17. M. Glenny, *The Fall of Yugoslavia* (Harmondsworth, Middlesex: Penguin, 1992); T. Garton Ash, *We The People* (London: Granta Books, 1990).
18. H. Kohn, *Nationalism and Realism 1852-1879* (New York: Van Nostrand, 1968).
19. H. Kohn, *The Making of the Modern French Mind* (New York: Van Nostrand, 1955).
20. K. Waltz, *Man, the State and War* (New York: Columbia University Press, 1959); B. Bueno de Mesquito, *The War Trap* (New Haven: Yale UP, 1981); J.A. Vasquez, *The War Puzzle* (Cambridge: Cambridge University Press, 1993).
21. B. Porter (ed.), *The Aberystwyth Papers* (Oxford: OUP, 1969).
22. Llobera, J.R. *The God of Modernity* (Oxford: Berg, 1994); Hobsbawm, *op. cit.*
23. *Ibid.*
24. T. Carlyle, *The French Revolution* (London: Collins, 1920) (2 vols).
25. M. Kundera, *The Unbearable Lightness of Being* (London: Faber & Faber, 1984).
26. B. Anderson, *Imagined Communities* (London: Verso/New Left Books, 1983).
27. E. Le Roy Ladurie, *Carnival in Romans* (Harmondsworth, Middlesex: Penguin, 1984.)
28. T. Harrisson, *Living Through the Blitz* (London: Collins, 1976).
29. E. Weber, *Peasants into Frenchmen* (London: Chatto & Windus, 1977).
30. M. Whittock, *The Making of England* (London: Allen & Unwin, 1978).
31. S. Heaney, *Seeing Things* (London: Faber & Faber, 1990).
32. Giddens, *op. cit.*; Smith, *op. cit.*

2 Beyond the 'Inside/Outside' Divide
Gillian Youngs

INTRODUCTION

The state has been under siege in the study of global relations[1] both substantively and theoretically. The strain has increased with time, particularly in the post-1945 period[2] with the transnational destructive capacities of nuclear weapons[3] the growth of the international market, most recently in 'invisible' goods such as services and finance[4] and the global reach of sophisticated communications networks.[5] The collapse of the binary world division between East and West and the apparent increased fragmentation and instability have left analysts challenged by the need to understand the violent uncertainties now produced[6] or anxious to develop comforting theories of a new unified global age of liberal capitalism.[7] The bottom line with regard to the state has been the degree to which it can be considered a suitable and concretely appropriate unit of analysis in international, or what I prefer, in the contemporary context, to call global, relations. Also, how does it divide *the national domain* 'inside' from *the international domain* 'outside' and what are the meanings of such divisions?[8]

This chapter argues that these issues are fundamental to our ability to address the question of identities, and that we need to begin by both negotiating the framing of the dominant state-centric tradition of thinking about the international, and understanding recent complex theoretical challenges to it. There is no doubt that political identity in any widespread sense has been absent for too long from agendas in the field. This forceful message is communicated in a wealth of new material in gender analysis[9] and other critical writing attacking, on various bases of theory and practice, state-centric traditions.[10] As well as discussing relevant aspects of this work, the approach adopted here is in keeping with the spirit of the critical theme characteristic of the vast majority of it. As such, it totally rejects any claim that theory can be regarded as divorced from practice and asserts that we must rather look at all times for the ways in which they are related.[11]

Explorations of the theory/practice relationship are all the more problematic when the realm of 'practice' under consideration is of an
abstract nature. Such is the case when we are dealing with identity in global relations. On the theory side we have the state-as-unit-of-analysis
means of interpreting the world. On the practice side we have nationalism[12] the category usually taken to incorporate issues of identity in this
context. The central argument of this chapter is that this theory/practice
marriage, rather than opening up consideration of political identity, has
blocked it from analytical view. In order to understand why and how this
has happened we need to consider the mutual reinforcement of the theoretical abstraction of state-centrism and the concretely[13] abstract qualities of nationalism as a socio-historical and psychological influence.[14]

In three major ways this mutual reinforcement has largely *removed*[15]
the very notion of the individual political subject from consideration.
First, the whole idea of individuality and the acting subject is abstracted
and contained within the 'state-as-actor' approach[16] and the well-established and by now over-familiar perspectives of *the world as a stage* or *the
international arena*. These are such commonplace analogies, heard every
day in the media, that the powerful influence of their 'metaphysical'[17]
connotations can be easily overlooked. These indicate an unquestioned
predisposition to view global relations within such strictly defined state-
centric parameters. We will discuss how this influence has been reinforced through the dominant theories of realism and neorealism[18] and
how approaches to nationalism have embellished further the abstractions which these schools of thought have championed. Second, the form
of these abstractions has encouraged a static rather than a dynamic view
of politics, that is, one which fails to recognise politics as process. The
work of Rob Walker[19] has gone furthest to present detailed challenges to
the static orientations of this view of politics, and thus to make the acting
political subject analytically *present*.[20] Third, a root orientation of the
abstractions has been the inherent *separation* of politics from economics,
the overriding identification of politics with the state and economics
with the market, and the designation of politics as the realm of value-
choice[21] and economics as the domain of rationalistic imperatives.
While this is, in some respects, paralleled by the separation of political
and economic nationalism, the focus on nationalism has concentrated
on its political manifestations and this will be reflected in the following
discussion.

These three forms of abstraction – the 'state-as-actor' approach, a
resulting static view of politics, and a *separation* of politics and economics – have worked to significantly identify political presence and action

in global relations with 'unitary' states[22] and thus to severely constrain considerations of political subjectivity in a broader sense.

MAKING THE POLITICAL SUBJECT RE-APPEAR

Dominant realist and neorealist perspectives of global relations have, through their particularistic[23] preoccupation with a state-centric world view, effectively erased the political individual from the analytical terrain. The state has been continually identified as key *actor*, as the *individual entity* that counts in interpretations of international affairs. This stance is much more than a statement of the importance of the state, or of its vital role in the determination of those affairs. As a number of critics have identified, it offers a 'particular', delimited and, in many respects, distorted view of those affairs.[24] It is ontological in the sense that it locates the essence of those affairs in the interests and activities of state actors and particularistically defines those interests and activities; that is, the very nature of states *as* actors.[25] It is epistemological in that it identifies the state-centric 'prism'[26] as the means of gathering knowledge about how that world works, what influences shape it, and, perhaps most importantly, how it may change.[27] It is methodological in the way it utilises this state-centrism as a means of avoiding the complexities of the operation of social relations within *and* across state boundaries.[28] It locates political identity, to the degree that it is considered important in global politics, at the level of the state.[29] On this basis, political essence and individuality are located at this level too. The state is articulated as the collective personification of political presence on *the international stage*. The central imagery of the foundational realist text *Leviathan* by Thomas Hobbes[30] is a perfect illustration of this point, as is *Man, the State and War* by Kenneth Waltz.[31]

Sovereignty is a key concept here, infusing the notion of the state as *political actor* with the symbolic power of authoritative existence. That power conveys the imagery of the state as the collective personification of political presence and intrinsically a 'unitary' actor,[32] coherent and bounded.[33] Thus the state is identified as the focal point of political rationality: the locus of order in an otherwise chaotic world. Sovereignty embraces a notion of successful control over the bounded political domain of the state in order to achieve *recognition on the international stage*.[34] What needs to be understood is the degree to which state-centrism and the key concepts of sovereignty, order and anarchy closely associated with it are directly concerned with what is *visible* in analyses of world politics. The ontological, epistemological and methodological means that prioritise interpretation through the state-centric 'prism' endow the 'state-as-actor' with particular symbolic qualities which firmly locate political individuality and presence at the level of the state. The implications are profound for investigation of politics on any other level. They lead, in terms of *individual* political identities, that is, the identities of the subjects[35] of states, to the symbolic substitution of them by the 'state-as-actor' as a *collective* and, equally important, authoritative representation of them. Questions about the nature of those subjects, their differences of status, their relevance or roles, are restricted by this theoretical disposition. The restriction follows the lines of the logic of state-centrism and the concept of sovereignty. Interest in the subjects tends to be limited to the ways in which they support or challenge the existing state order either at a state or international level.[36] The *black box* view of the 'state-as-actor' obscures individual subjects, effectively *removing* them from the analytical horizon.[37]

While nationalism clearly concerns individuals within a national society, it is essentially a collective concept which addresses the ways in which those individuals can be understood to be identified with, or to identify themselves with, a national entity. Thus it parallels the concept of sovereignty and the idea of a unitary state. The symbolism of collective political representation conveyed by sovereignty is consistent with the collectivising qualities assigned to nationalism. Nationalism in the study of world politics is also placed in similar relation to questions of international order. It may be seen as a social force for cohesion within national polities, endowed with relatively positive characteristics. In this sense it is not necessarily disruptive to international peace. However nationalism may be one of the forces mobilising or used to mobilise populations toward direct or indirect conflict or oppression either within or between national societies. In such circumstances nationalism is understood as a direct threat to, or contributory cause of, disorder. The complex role of nationalistic facets of Nazi ideology and their racial emphasis in the extermination of Jews and other *identified non-persons* during aggressive German expansionism in the build-up to and outbreak of World War Two remains one of the most extensively investigated examples.[38] Recent conflicts, particularly in former Yugoslavia, have prompted widespread discussion of 'ethnic nationalism' and the nature of ethnicity when related to nationalism (see also chapter in this volume by Davies).[39]

Despite the intricacies of various forms of analysis of nationalism, it remains a collective concept, and, in dealing with collectivities, whether within or between national societies, places its explanatory focus at the

level of the collective, however it may be defined. It is seeking explanations of how such collectives come to exist with apparent yet varying
degrees of unity.[40] Emphases on nationalism and the 'unproblematic
unity' of the 'state-as-actor' approach[41] mutually reinforce one another in
removing political subjects from analytical attention.[42] Bringing these
subjects back into the picture is not a straightforward matter, as indicated by the complexity of critical work[43] which has endeavoured to do
so.

It is not simply a case of opening the black box of the state- as-unitary-
actor concept. Or at least it has been recognised that the process of opening that box and keeping it open presents enormous challenges. The most
basic is re-establishing the understanding of interconnections between
theory and practice which positivist separations have so effectively disrupted.[44] This has been addressed, in broad terms, by analysis which
emphasises two important and related factors. The first is that a high
level of abstraction, such as that achieved in realist and neorealist formulations of the state-as-actor approach, allows for ahistorical universalisa-
tions.[45] The second is that spatio-temporal definitions are themselves
political, that is, representative of certain interests triumphing over other
competing but less powerful interests. With regard to both factors we
need to take seriously the power/knowledge relationship[46] and recognise
that descriptions of the world, whether designated theoretical or otherwise, are not abstracted from it but are dimensions of its socio-historical
processes. When we consider the ahistorical and universalistic abstractions associated with the state-as-actor mode of interpreting world politics, sovereignty is high on the list. But there are others. John Maclean
has discussed the timelessness of concepts such as 'justice, obligation
and rights'.[47] Maclean[48] and Rob Walker,[49] in particular, have emphasised the importance of the continuities between political theory and
international theory in this respect.[50] These continuities have worked to
maintain the analytical gaze through the state-centric 'prism'.[51] As
Maclean has forcefully put it:

> The territorial state is still seen as both the basic unit for analysis and
> the theoretical boundary for the conception of the whole. This is not
> to deny that other entities besides the state are studied (political par-
> ties, pressure groups, trade unions and bureaucracies, for example),
> *but rather to assert that they are studied within the context of extant terri-*
> *torial states, theoretically as well as concretely separated.*[52] [my emphasis]

Rob Walker's[53] 'inside/outside' discussion of the characteristics of the
state-centric disposition, and its formulations and reformulations over

time in political theory and international theory, demonstrates the degree to which they are concerned with linkages between political (that is, state) and individual identity, authority and security.[54] Walker's analysis looks deep inside the black box and reveals it for what it actually is: a political space where the maintenance of central authority is directly associated with the definition of bounded territoriality as the crucial divide between internal *security and order* and external *insecurity and chaos.* His arguments are developed in the context of the nature of 'modernity' and its universalising tendencies.[55] The role of binary divides of presence and absence in traditions of Western dualism (order/chaos, rationality/emotion, man/woman, science/nature), the reinforcement of each of these divides by the others, and their importance to the maintenance of power relations are central to this kind of argument[56] There is an attempt to move away from static notions of the state which the extremely abstract drive of state-centrism has entrenched. An emphasis is placed on politics as practice. For Walker[57] sovereignty is about 'practices' and this applies to international theory as much as to 'the routines of state-craft'.

POLITICS AS PROCESS: INTRODUCING POLITICAL SUBJECTIVITY

Understanding the politics of 'state-craft' in a dynamic rather than a primarily abstract fashion directs our attention to the ways in which power relations operate over time. Doing so on the basis of a recognition of the relevance of the 'inside/outside' definition to the maintenance of those relations links centralised state authority to those over whom it is exercised. It facilitates an historical rather than an abstract approach to security, a concept which has been central to the shaping of the study of international relations.[58] It demonstrates that notions of security are strongly associated with identity and that the 'inside/outside', state/international, order/anarchy sets of oppositions reflect the political processes through which states secure an identity. Crucially, they emphasise the direct involvement which individual subjects have in those processes and the ways in which these integrate questions of secure individual identity with secure state identity.[59] Thus they introduce political subjectivity into the picture. Political subjectivity incorporates an understanding of the constant and varied interactions of individuals with their environment over time, and signals that achieving security, including security of identity, is a continuing aspect of this interaction, which will vary in intensity for reasons including the degree to which threats are perceived, or exist, on economic, political, social or personal grounds. As indicated above, one of the main issues here is the idea of a secure unitary being and the binary oppositions which are mobilised in dualistic thinking (related to theory *and* practice) to achieve the conviction of its possibility.[60] Richard Ashley[61] has explained this 'logic of representation' as:

> ... a practical logic that pervades every aspect of modern culture and that is intimately involved in the constitution and empowerment of the institution of the sovereign state as a centre of law, rational administrative resources, and legitimate violence... It is a territorialising logic. It presupposes and never questions the existence of exclusionary boundaries between inside and outside: between those domains where meaning, truth, and authority originate in a state of pure *presence* and those external domains where they are *absent* and need to be represented. This pervasive logic of representation is intrinsically paradoxical. The boundaries presupposed are never simply there; they are always in the process of being imposed, transgressed, undone, and imposed anew.[62]

The writings of Richard Ashley and Rob Walker, in complementary as well as contrasting ways, have explained in detail why political identity should not be considered in an abstract manner. The formation and reformation of this identity occurs within a particular political space defined in specific ways over time. For citizens, and their experience varies depending on the amount of power and freedom they possess, the central defining category is the bounded state. State-making practices fix identity at the level of the state. The symbolism of sovereignty reflects the security of individual identity in the security of state identity, providing a rationale for centralised state authority. Hence Walker's[63] belief that the 'rethinking' of democracy and 'the principle of state sovereignty' are inseparable.

In terms of political identity, in 'modernity' the individual's link to humanity comes via the state and a world view of 'a realm of particular states', he explains.[64] Questions of citizenship illustrate some of the important complexities of this position. The *universal* principles of citizenship, when put into practice, are a hard demonstration of the contrasting degrees of political existence accorded by states to separate categories of individuals. Once again, this is a contingent situation. Changing political, economic and social pressures affect its practices, as recent work on migration and the 'Fortress Europe' phenomenon has revealed.[65] The various causes of migration, as well as the fate of refugees, whose citizenship may effectively be suspended indefinitely when they are confined to camps[66], are a forceful reminder of the misleading nature of abstract universalised images of the state and idealised notions of its guarantee of security for individual political identity. Refugees often risk death, danger and extreme insecurity in pursuit of the economic and/or political security of which they are deprived in their home state for one reason or another. The movement or anticipated movement of people, particularly on a large scale, produces efforts to reassert or redefine the systems of inclusion and exclusion which are a basic element of inside/outside state practices.

Once we are considering such practices, ideal notions of secure political identity are quickly shifted sideways. Inequality of such security is most evident. We do not have to recall *major* phenomena, such as the oppressive characteristics of the former apartheid system in South Africa, to illustrate the point. Certainly political security is dependent on the nature of the state you live in and the times you live in: as the South African case makes clear, change can come, although not overnight.[67] In all states and at all times, however, gender, sexuality, personal and socio-economic background and circumstances influence how secure individuals may consider their political identity to be, even if they strongly support the political system in question. The *ideal* of a secure political identity belongs, in fact, to the very few. The majority live in relative inclusion and exclusion across the different activities and relationships of their daily lives. The so-called 'marginal times and places... where power is conspicuously at work'[68] are all around us. But realist and neorealist state-centrism continually draws us away from such understandings with the lure of the ultimate security of unitary state presence. As Ashley[69] has put it:

Realist power politics is ... an art of the inscription of the dangerous, the externalisation and totalisation of dangers, all in the name of a social totality that is never really present, that always contains traces of the outside within, and that is never more than an effect of the work of art by which differences between inside and outside are marked and total dangers inscribed.[70]

Ashley communicates in such explanations the force of processes affirming boundaries through differentiations between 'inside' and 'outside'. Thus his work develops our understanding of the deeper materiality of boundaries. Superficial notions of them as mere lines of division, or demarcations of territory, signal to us little of their implications as part of the practices of power in particular socio-historical circumstances.

These implications relate to the deeper materiality of boundaries and their vital role as political points of reference which help to assert the power over a defined domain through representational oppositions locating safety within and danger without. The important analytical linkages which Ashley and Walker have highlighted in this respect are between time, space and the exercise of political power.[71] Their work has made the black box of the state transparent, so that we can see inside it and understand the ways in which its continued existence or sovereignty is directly associated with the shaping of the view of the outside from the inside. Political authority becomes thus a much less abstract quality in international relations; we can more easily see that it would not exist without the relative success of identifications of security among those subjected to it. Part of the proof of this success on a general level is the problem as termed by Walker:[72] '. . . states have become (second) nature, and come to seem inevitable'. A crucial basis for this apparent inevitability is the abstraction of the state as the prime definitive category of national and international political life, and the conceptual and theoretical separation of politics and economics which this has entailed.

POLITICAL SUBJECTIVITY AND POLITICAL ECONOMY

The development of a complex understanding of political subjectivity inevitably implies recognition of the influences of political economy. Gender analysis in particular has emphasised the degree to which political and economic factors cannot be easily separated when addressing issues of subjectivity and power. This is a clear message which V. Spike Peterson and Anne Sisson Runyan[73] have communicated in their powerful text *Global Gender Issues*, which highlights the distinctively strong purchase which gender critiques of international relations retain on the relationship between theory and practice, between ways of knowing and analysing and what is understood to be worthy or important as subject matter. The straightforward idea of 'the gender lens' communicates numerous and far-reaching challenges in these two key relationships: politics and economics, theory and practice. The following captures this dual strength:

> The amassing of global data reveals the extent and pattern of gender inequality: Women everywhere have less access to political power and economic resources and less control over processes that reproduce

this systemic inequality. Moreover, our knowledge of the world of men and the politics they create is incomplete and inaccurate without knowing how men's activities, including their politics, are related to, even dependent upon, what women are doing – and why.[74]

Political economy enables us to investigate the ways in which identity is influenced by a mix of political and economic factors which span the public and private realms and which cross, either directly or indirectly, a vast range of social, political and economic *boundaries*. Our interest in boundaries, in this regard, relates to those which work to define a whole range of public and private activities and relations. It can certainly not be restricted to state boundaries, important though they may still be.[75] Political economy facilitates a move away from abstract ideas of unified identities. It recognises that individuals do not live as a coherent whole. Their involvement in the world is in the form of frag-mented activities which feature continuities and discontinuities and are rarely without contradictions within and across them. Their subjectiv-ities are formed and reformed through these engagements and the ways in which these impact on, affirm or challenge existing under-standings of identity. The dynamics of human existence concern time and space. At different times and in different places we may be engaged in practical or theoretical endeavours of an intensely public or private kind which involve a range of historical influences, social tensions, and forces for change and stability. It is possible to argue that the separation of politics and economics predominant in the study of 'inter-national relations'[76] has, more than any other factor, inhibited investigation of the complexities of these dynamics and aspects of inter-subjectivity relevant to them.[77] It is fair to say that the struggle to integrate politics and economics in the study of global relations has, in profound senses, only just begun, and many have focused on the kinds of ontologi-cal, epistemological and methodological concerns discussed above as integral to it.[78] The linkages between political and economic activities and relationships are directly concerned with specific times and places. Our understanding of them cannot be separated from those. But the pre-dominant conceptual and theoretical disposition has been to do just that via the abstractions outlined above, with, of course, the separation of politics and economics being among them.[79] The development of new and more open analytical perspectives on time/place significance is enormously difficult for those working in a field where the dominant theoretical schools, realism and neorealism, have been so closely aligned with the practices of states.[80] The continuing

importance of the state as a definitive political category in practice and
the state-centric obsession in theory interact to reinforce one another.

For this reason, among others, it is difficult for us to move toward the
kind of theory that allows us to deal seriously with political identity/ subjectivity. We are still a long way from the kind of theory that integrates
issues of political *and* economic identity and subjectivity. It is not surprising that work related to globalisation in the areas of social theory and
cultural studies,[81] and political, economic and cultural geography[82] have
done much to prompt thinking in this direction, for these fields, in one
way or another, have particular purchases on spatiality and related time/
space/power linkages.[83] Anthony Giddens' *The Consequences of Modernity*[84] provides an extremely clear explanation of the ways in which our
experience of time and space, and the relationship between them, is
being altered by global communications and media systems which help
to shape the character of, as well as themselves forming part of, global
capitalist processes. However, we need to keep firmly in mind the
inequalities embedded in these processes. Such explanations risk the
danger of universalising in global rather than state-centric mode and we
must guard against this.[85] This is particularly important in the case of
political identity/subjectivity, which, as underlined above, vary within as
well as across national settings. In this respect, the importance of culture
when considering identity, nationalism and globalisation has been
emphasised. Analysis of globalisation identifies transnational as well as
nationally-defined cultural influences and addresses global power relations through concepts such as 'cultural imperialism.'[86] Technology,
notably in the broad area of communications, is central to considerations
of contemporary globalised cultural factors, grounding such issues
firmly in political economy.[87]

CONCLUSION

Recent critical work in international theory and fresh examinations of
time/space relationships in the study of globalisation provide us with
sound bases to develop our analysis of political identity/subjectivity in
dynamic and concrete ways. We must leave behind the high degree of
abstraction and reductionism with which the state-centric 'prism' presents us. It assists us little with identification or investigation of the range
of processes through which subjectivities are formed and reformed – processes which are not neatly contained within state-defined packages but
which operate in a global context. Some of them may be understood

within specific national settings but many cannot. We need to take account of linkages between various local/local and local/national contexts both within and across states. In this chapter, parallels have been drawn between abstract interpretations of nationalism and political analysis predicated on the division of the world into bounded states. We cannot underestimate how problematic nationalism remains as a concept. It too needs to be freed of the conceptual bonds of state-centrism. While nationalisms continue to exist, some of them in new as well as more established forms, we cannot assume in either case that they are unaffected by the workings of global capitalism, which continues to expand its technological reach. In the diversified global market place, inequality of access and ability to buy, especially in the advanced communications technology sector, contributes significantly to senses of identity in relation to that realm of exchange. In political economy, we are still confronted with fundamental survival issues – poverty, starvation and disease. But the scope of economic inequalities is growing and not all of them can be articulated on the basis of old-fashioned material goods. The rise in service and financial products, closely bound to technological developments, is offering new possibilities for definitions of lifestyle to those, as always, who can afford them. These patterns of inequality cut across as well as along state boundaries. This is the case too with the impact of changes in global production, which are redefining the nature of work and its rewards, and destabilising communities in a range of ways across the world. Migrations, in part linked with such changes, severely disrupt notions of states as unitary entities, politically or culturally, and remind us that political subjects come in many varieties. Not only are they diverse in terms of their own socio-cultural background and heritage, but, often related to these factors, state definitions of their subject-hood differ. There are grades of citizenship and it matters which one you possess.

Recent critical discussion in International Relations suggests that we will keep coming back to the state, certainly as long as the weight of its role in practice continues to be as heavy as it is today. We should not be surprised, then, that theory may retreat to what appear to be simplified representations of state power, symbolic as well as material. Critical work on state-centrism usefully highlights the importance of this symbolism and has uncovered the way in which security of identity has come to be framed in mainstream Western thinking. The 'inside/outside' metaphor has a strong psychological hold. It will not be overturned by wishful thinking. Political discourses of state-making work to reaffirm it

34   *Beyond the 'Inside/Outside' Divide*

continually in theory and practice. We can but take their repercussions
seriously and then our challenges may be serious too.

Notes

1.   Traditionally, the area referred to here is known as international relations.
     The use of the term global is intended primarily to refer to recent
     emphases on globalising processes and globalisation.
2.   The debate is a longstanding one, however. One of the best illustrations is
     E.H. Carr, *The Twenty Years Crisis* (London: Macmillan, 1946, 2nd ed.) first
     published 1939.
3.   See J.H. Herz, 'Rise and Demise of the Territorial State', *World Politics* 9:
     473–93, 1952 and J.H. Herz, 'The Territorial State Revisited', *Polity* 1(1):11–
     34, 1968.
4.   See S. Strange, *States and Markets*, 2nd ed. (London: Pinter, 1994) and R.
     Stubbs and G. Underhill, *The Political Economy of Global Change*
     (London: Macmillan, 1994).
5.   See C. J. Hamelink, *The Politics of World Communication* (London: Sage,
     1994).
6.   See J. N. Rosenau, *Turbulence in World Politics* (Hemel Hempstead: Har-
     vester Wheatsheaf, 1990).
7.   The most noteworthy example of this reaction is Francis Fukuyama's 'end
     of history' thesis in F. Fukuyama, *The End of History and the Last Man*
     (London: Penguin, 1992). See also G. Youngs, *From International to Global
     Relations; A Conceptual Challenge* (Cambridge: Polity Press, 1996) and
     Youngs, in G. Youngs and E. Kofman, *Globalisation; Theory and Practice*
     (London: Pinter, 1996).
8.   See R. B. J. Walker, *Inside/Outside: International Relations as Political The-
     ory* (Cambridge: Cambridge University Press, 1993).
9.   See chapter by Krause in this volume.
10. See J. Mclean, 'Political Theory' International Theory as the Politics of
     Ideas', *Millennium*, vol. 10, no. 2, 1981.
11. It should be noted here that despite shared concerns with theory/practice
     issues, the theorists cited come from contrasting 'schools of thought', for
     example Maclean from a Marxist tradition and Walker, Ashley and Weber
     from the broadly postpositivist group of thinkers.
12. A useful overview of different approaches to nationalism is J.G. Kellas, *The
     Politics of Nationalism and Ethnicity* (London: Macmillan, 1991).
13. The use of the term 'concrete' here is intended to emphasise the problems
     involved in examination of social forces which are highly abstract while
     having *real* influence.
14. One of the best known motifs of recent studies of nationalism has been
     Benedict Anderson's notion of 'imagined communities'. See B. Anderson,
     *Imagined Communities: Reflections on the Origins and Spread of National-
     ism* (London: Verso, 1991).

15. J. Maclean, 1981, *op. cit.*
16. K. Richard Ashley, 'The Poverty of Neorealism', *International Organization* 38(2) pp. 225–86, 1984.
17. *Ibid*, p. 239.
18. See D. Baldwin, *Neorealism and Neoliberalism: The Contemporary Debate* (New York: Columbia University Press, 1993).
19. R.B.J. Walker, 'Sovereignty, Identity, Community: Reflections on the Horizons of Contemporary Political Practice', R.B.J. Walker and S. Mendlovitz (eds.), *Contending Sovereignties: Rethinking Political Community.* (Boulder, Col.: Lynne Rienner, 1990).
20. See R.K. Ashley, 'Three Modes of Economism', *International Studies Quarterly* 27: 463–9, 1983; Ashley 1984 *op. cit.*
21. The emphasis here is broadly on democratic ideas of politics.
22. R.K. Ashley and R.B.J. Walker, 'Reading Dissidence/Writing the Discipline: Crisis and the Question of Sovereignty in International Studies', *International Studies Quarterly* 34(3) pp. 367–416, 1990.
23. On particularism see Ashley, 1984, *op. cit* p. 268.
24. See Ashley, 1984, *op. cit*, Maclean, 1981, *op. cit.* and Maclean, in *Millennium*, vol. 17, no. 2, 1988.
25. The most detailed realist statement can be found in H.J. Morgenthau and Kenneth W. Thompson, *Politics Among Nations*, 6th edn. (New York: Knopf, 1985) and the neorealist position is best explained in K.N. Waltz, *Theory of International Politics* (New York: McGraw-Hill, 1979). See also Ashley, 1984, *op. cit.* pp. 239–42
26. See Ashley, 1984, *op. cit.* p. 239.
27. See Walker, 1993, *op. cit.*
28. See Ashley, 1984, *op. cit.* p. 239–40.
29. See J.D. Singer, The Level of Analysis Problem in International Relations' in K.L. Knorr, and S. Verba (eds), *The International System: Theoretical Essays* (Princeton: Princeton University Press, 1978).
30. T. Hobbes, *Leviathan* (Oxford: Clarendon Press, 1909) (first published 1651).
31. K.N. Waltz, *Man, the State and War* (New York: Columbia University Press, 1959).
32. Ashley, 1984, *op. cit.* p. 238.
33. Walker, 1993, *op. cit.*
34. H. Bull, *The Anarchical Society* (London: Macmillan), 1977.
35. A *universal* perspective on political subjects is not suggested here.
36. *Survival.* Issue on Ethnic Conflict and International Security, 35(1), 1993.
37. Rob Walker, 1993, p. 125.
38. Mosse, 1993, *op. cit.*
39. See Ignatieff, *Blood and Belonging. Journeys Into the New Nationalism* (London: BBC Books, 1993).
40. Gender critiques of nationalism have challenged notions of *unity* in such circumstances. See chapter by Krause in this volume.
41. Ashley, 1984, *op. cit.* pp. 238–9.
42. It is interesting to note how realist interpretations can include nationalism as a dimension of state power. See Morgenthau and Thompson, 1985, *op. cit.*

43.   W. Connolly, *Identity/Difference: Democratic Negotiations of Political Paradox* (London: Cornell University Press, 1991).
44.   A range of theoretical approaches has been referred to above as attacking this separation of theory and practice. I was initially, and continue to be, assisted in this difficult area by Maclean 1981.
45.   J. Rosenberg, *The Empire of Civil Society. A Critique of the Realist Theory of International Relations* (London: Verso, 1994).
46.   My own understanding of this relationship has been most influenced by the work of Michel Foucault. See, for example, M. Foucault, *Les mots et les choses* (Paris: Editions Gallimard, 1966). Trans. as *The Order of Things* by A.S. Smith (London: Tavistock Publications, 1970).
47.   See Maclean's 1981: 111 for a fuller discussion of this point.
48.   Maclean, 1981 and 1988, *op. cit.*
49.   Walker, 1993, *op. cit.*
50.   There is not space to discuss Maclean's interesting analysis of ideology and theory. See Maclean, 1981.
51.   Ashley, 1984, *op. cit.*, p. 239.
52.   Maclean, *op. cit.*, p. 103.
53.   Walker, 1993, *op. cit.*
54.   Ashley, 1991, *op. cit.*
55.   Walker, 1993, *op. cit.*, p. 12.
56.   Ashley, 1989, *op. cit.*
57.   Walker, 1993 *op. cit.*, p. 13
58.   See B. Buzan, *People, States and Fear: An Agenda for International Security in the Post-Cold War Era* (Hemel Hempstead: Harvester Wheatsheaf, 1991).
59.   Ashley, 1989 and D.U. Gregory, Foreword, in Der Derian and Shapiro, 1989.
60.   Walker, 1993 *op. cit.*, pp. 152–3.
61.   Ashley, 1991, *op. cit.*, p. 38.
62.   *Ibid*, p. 38.
63.   Walker, 1993, *op. cit*, p. 154.
64.   *Ibid*, p. 154.
65.   See R. King, *Mass Migration in Europe. The Legacy and the Future* (London: Belhaven Press, 1993) and E. Kofman and R. Sales, 'Towards Fortress Europe?' *Women's Studies International Forum* 15(1):129–40, 1992.
66.   This has been the case, for example, with large numbers of Vietnamese refugees.
67.   See K. Booth and P. Vale, 'Security in Southern Africa: After Apartheid; Beyond Realism', *International Affairs* 71(2):285–304, 1995.
68.   Ashley, *op. cit.* 1991, p. 60.
69.   *Ibid*, p. 67.
70.   See Ashley's analysis of the paradoxical nature of 'the territorial state of the discipline', which is a central theme of the essay referred to.
71.   See in particular chapters three, six and seven in Walker (1993).
72.   Walker, 1993, *op. cit.*, p. 179.
73.   V.S. Peterson, and A.S. Runyan, *Global Gender Issues* (Boulder, Col.: Westview Press, 1993).
74.   *Ibid*, p. 12.

75. J.J. Pettman, 'An International Political Economy of Sex?' in Kofman and Youngs, 1996.
76. See note 1. See also Peterson, 1992.
77. V.S. Peterson, 'Shifting Ground(s): Remapping in the Context of Globalisation(s)'. In Kofman and Youngs 1996.
78. C.N. Murphy and R. Tooze, *The New International Political Economy.* (Boulder, Col.: Lynne Rienner, 1991).
79. R. Tooze, 'Conceptualizing the Global Economy', in A. G. McGrew and P. Lewis (eds), *Global Politics: Globalization and the Nation-State* (Cambridge: Polity, 1992).
80. C. Hill and P. Beshoff (eds), *Two Worlds of International Relations. Academics and Practitioners in the Trade of Ideas* (London: Routledge, 1994).
81. Giddens, 1991 *op. cit.*, and M. Featherstone (ed.) *Global Culture. Nationalism, Globalisation and Modernity.* (London: Sage, 1990) and R. Robertson, *Globalization: Social Theory and Global Culture* (London: Sage, 1992).
82. D. Harvey, *The Condition of Postmodernity: An Enquiry into the Origins of Cultural Change* (Oxford: Blackwell, 1989).
83. Giddens, 1991.
84. *Ibid.*
85. G. Youngs, 'Dangers of Discourse: The Case of Globalisation' in Kofman and Youngs, 1991, and J. Tomlinson, *Cultural Imperialism* (London: Pinter, 1991).
86. G. Youngs, 'Culture and the Technological Imperative: Missing Dimensions', in M. Talalay, C. Farrands and R. Tooze (eds), *Technology, Competitiveness and Culture in Global Political Economy* (London: Routledge, 1996).
87. *Ibid.*

3 Globalisation and Collective Identities
Jan Aart Scholte

In 1960, as the process of globalisation began to move into historical
high gear, seventeen new members entered the not coincidentally named
United *Nations* Organisation.[1] Reflecting on the worldwide process of
decolonisation unfolding around him, the Harvard professor Rupert
Emerson in the same year dubbed the nation the 'terminal community';
nationhood was the locus of group identity and solidarity that invariably
prevailed 'when the chips are down'.[2] In the world of 1960 the nationality
principle did generally rank above, and override, alternative potential
constructions of collective identity, e.g., in terms of smaller-scale locality,
larger-scale region, religious faith, class, race, gender, sexual orientation,
age and so on. These other touchstones of self-other relations also operated thirty-five years ago, and indeed often affected the particular shape
and direction of a given national project. However, for the most part they
were decidedly subordinate to that primary framework of 'us-ness', the
nation. Thus women's movements, ethnic associations, labour movements and religious campaigns were generally organised on national
lines and usually rallied to 'the national interest', while generation politics and open collective expressions of lesbian and gay identities rarely
surfaced at all. In 1960, forging group solidarity in the world system nor-
mally entailed, above anything else, identifying a territorial homeland
and emphasising the national distinctiveness that was associated with
that country. World social relations were in this light suitably defined as
'inter-national' relations. Other principal social structures of the day –
including industrialism, corporate capitalism, the sovereign state, militarism and patriarchy – generally reinforced the position of the nation
as the foremost structure of collective identity. Governance in the first
place meant the *national* state, production was organised primarily
around *national* economies, geography focused on *national* environ-
ments and emancipatory strategies centred above all on the pursuit of
national self-determination.[3]

Today, after four decades of spreading, deepening and generally ac-
celerating globalisation, the organisation of group affiliations in the
world system has become less clear and less fixed. An upsurge of ident-

ity politics since the 1960s has disturbed and in some ways eroded the pre-eminence of the nationality principle that seemed complete and irreversible thirty-five years ago. Across the continents there have been increases in gender awareness, youth culture, religious revivalism, ethnic consciousness of minority populations, regionalism, 'coming out' of lesbians and gay men, and self-assertion of indigenous peoples. Each of these alternative forms of collective identity often bypass, if not directly challenge, the nationality principle. Such developments have prodded the discipline of International Relations (IR) to elevate questions of identity on its research agenda in the 1990s. Some might even argue that, in the changing historical circumstances, the field wants a new name.

The present chapter explores the relationship between globalisation (understood as a still-ongoing process whereby the world is in many respects becoming one relatively borderless arena of social life) and the construction of collective identities. It assesses how, and how far, moves in the late twentieth century towards 'the crystallisation of the entire world as a single place'[4] have dislocated and rearranged patterns of self-other identification. The discussion first considers how, over the longer term, international relations have been constitutive of national identities. The second section of the chapter elaborates a distinction between 'global' and 'international' relations and observes that contemporary globalisation has disrupted previously dominant territorial bases of identity construction. Subsequent sections link globalisation to recent tendencies of homogenisation, localisation and deterritorialisation of collective identities in the world system. The sixth section emphasises that globalisation has also frequently encouraged powerful reaffirmations of nationalism. These manifold and often contradictory attempts to reconstruct home in the present-day globalising world have brought greater fluidity, multidimensionality, uncertainty and perplexity to notions of self and community. The chapter's concluding section makes some general suggestions for coping with this confusion in creative and non-violent ways.

'INTER-NATIONAL' RELATIONS

The construction of identity, personal and collective, is a pervasive and crucial aspect of social life. Identity figures in all human interests, activities, norms and social structures. The historical record is replete with instances where people have killed and been killed in the assertion of their sense of self. The need for recognition – to define oneself (or who one wants to become) and to have that identity acknowledged by others – is a first-order preoccupation in social relations. The pursuit of identity ranks alongside, and is deeply interconnected with, quests for subsistence, power, communion and knowledge. At its core human existence is, amongst other things, a process of forging identity.

In spite of this significance, the construction of corporate identities has until recently received little attention in international studies. IR has concentrated on the hows and whys of war, diplomacy, commerce, integration, law and human rights. Although questions of collective identification are deeply implicated in each of these issues, students of world affairs have generally regarded identity as an unproblematic aspect of international life. Researchers in each of the principal traditions in the discipline – realism, liberalism and Marxism – have presumed that ambiguous and fluctuating identities arose only at the levels of individuals and small-scale communities. As a 'personal' or 'domestic' matter, problems of identity were a concern for Psychology and Sociology rather than IR. When it came to social relations on a world scale (so the prevailing supposition went) identity boiled down to nationality and loyalty to the corresponding territorial state. The very name of the discipline – 'International Relations' – implied as much. Articulating this consensus, the early realist Reinhold Niebuhr declared sixty years ago that the nation was 'the most absolute of all human associations'.[5] At most, an occasional writing in IR investigated the causes and consequences of nationalism, or competition between contending constructions of nationality.[6] However, such discussions gave little if any consideration to possible alternative frameworks of collective identity. Prior to the 1970s, only an incidental and little-read publication (in IR or any other field) explored transnational racial, gendered, religious, generational, ethnic, sexual or professional identities.[7]

This fixation on nationality, and the corresponding neglect of other identity forms, is somewhat curious given that nationhood is a comparatively recent historical phenomenon. True, many contemporary nations have developed from premodern antecedents, and various labels such as 'Vietnamese' and 'Flemish' already served to distinguish certain groups many centuries ago.[8] However, this was not a fully-fledged sense of national identity: deeply rooted in and constantly at the fore of consciousness; spread across all provinces, classes and religions in a country; and central to political organisation and aspirations. Such national*ism* did not consolidate anywhere in the world before the second half of the nineteenth century. Even the population of France, often depicted as the birthplace of the national idea, was not comprehensively 'nationalised' until this relatively recent historical juncture.[9] Nations have been timeless and 'natural' only in the imaginations of those who insist, against all contrary evidence, on inventing an immutable primordial community for their sense of security in the modern, international world.

What was it about the latter half of the nineteenth century that ushered in a period of nationalism? Social-structural causes might be found in the concurrent deepening of industrial capitalism, the state, militarism, patriarchy, secularism and the policing of sexual behaviour. The impacts of such forces have been extensively explored in other historical–sociological research.[10] In addition, however, the formation of national identities can be explained in geographical terms as a consequence of the unprecedented compression of social space that occurred across the world from the middle of the nineteenth century onwards. Before that juncture, collective identities derived chiefly from relatively small-scale, comparatively isolated, and more or less autonomous localities. Although various long-range empires, periodic booms in long-distance trade, and several religions with universalist pretensions existed in these earlier times, social relations were in the main heavily focused on the immediate territorial vicinity. Only very small proportions of populations (e.g., certain clerics and aristocrats) regularly acted in a larger realm and identified themselves with widely dispersed groups of people. However, after the mid-nineteenth century the spread of mechanisation, the expansionary tendencies of capitalism, the proliferation of large-scale bureaucratic organisations and the growth of this-worldly as against spiritual orientations together encouraged (and at the same time were also encouraged by) an unprecedented intensification of long-distance exchanges and interdependencies in the world system. In combination with those other developments, the reconfiguration of social geography – this major (though by no means complete) transcendence of the local – disrupted previously dominant patterns of group identity centred on frequent face-to-face contacts. The resulting searches for new frameworks of collective self-definition generally came by one or the other path to the nationality principle. Nations were territorial identities of a larger scope, the cultural aspect of the merger of districts into country units of previously unknown proportions.

National identity and solidarity were and remain very much a product of, amongst other things, 'inter-national' relations.[11] Historically, national distinctiveness (in terms of language, customs, sensibilities, race, religion, heritage, shared destiny or whatever) was not accentuated and insisted upon until *internationalisation* set in train processes of reciprocal national self-definition. It is no coincidence that most of the numerous national projects across the world consolidated more or less simultaneously (albeit to varying degrees) during the same hundred-year period after the middle of the nineteenth century. Identity is constructed in relation to difference, and the rise of nationhood depended on an awareness of differences spread over distance that could only be perceived in the context of wide-ranging and extended close encounters with other nations. For example, Acton's quip that 'exile is the nursery of nationality' suggests that immersion in the land of 'outsiders' has produced some of the deepest national consciousness and affections.[12] Many an immigrant, tourist, trader, exchange student and diplomat will concur.

In another of their inter-national attributes, national groupings have been constructed as much from without as from within. For instance, it was 'foreigners' who in the 1850s first applied the label of 'Indonesian' to the populace of the South East Asian archipelago.[13] Most nationalist strivings have enjoyed significant support from outside, whether in the case of Napoleon III in Italian unification, the Bolsheviks in Central Asia, Wilson's Fourteen Points in respect of Eastern Europe, or the United Nations in post-1945 decolonisation. Indeed, in such scenarios one group has arguably sought to confirm its national self in part by encouraging the construction of the other in similar, national terms.

Nations have also been intrinsically inter-national insofar as they have frequently taken shape and been sustained through acts of collective self-protection of the 'homeland' against intrusion from 'outside'. The articulation of external dangers has been pivotal to forging and sustaining many a nation. In this vein Michael Howard has suggested that 'it is in fact very difficult to create national self-consciousness *without* a war',[14] while Silviu Brucan has argued that a nation's existence has depended on struggles in the international realm 'either to maintain or to expand its common language, territory, economy and culture'.[15] For Terry Eagleton, 'the need for national definition is felt more by the underdogs, who have to define themselves against the dominant forces'.[16] Accelerated internationalisation, especially from the mid-nineteenth century onwards, threatened established – localised – group identities. These small-scale collectivities generally lacked the means for effective self-assertion against 'foreign' states, companies, armies, mass media, languages, churches and so on. However, localities could attempt to resurrect self-determination by bonding together in a nation, with their own national government, national currency, national schools, national symbols, etc. Paradoxically, of course, the resulting processes of state-building, industrialisation, secularisation and the like generally further undermined pre-existent 'traditional' cultures, but the reconstructed sense of distinctiveness and autonomy gave comfort nevertheless. At the same time as defending the self, national projects have very often involved inter-national violence towards the other. Nation-building has on the whole not been an exercise in cross-national empathy and co-operation. James Der Derian has in this vein highlighted 'the traditional gambit of defining and unifying a national identity through the alienation of others'.[17] Nationality has been a question of privilege within the world system. 'Insiders' have enjoyed certain entitlements that have simultaneously been denied to 'outsiders', for example, in respect of residence, passport, suffrage, welfare provisions, etc. Discrimination of this kind has not only operated between citizens of different countries, but has also often extended to 'strangers' within, including racial, linguistic and religious minorities, indigenous peoples, women, homosexuals and the disabled. At its most brutal, this dynamic of nationalist exclusion has manifested itself in Nazi exterminations, 'ethnic cleansing' in the Balkans, 'pacification' in East Timor and other genocides. Nationhood has thus generally involved complementary assertions and suppressions of identities, whereby the elevation of one construction of the self has entailed the marginalisation and silencing of others.

In sum, then, the consolidation of nationalism after the mid-nineteenth century might be understood broadly as an attempt to secure a sense of place, communal solidarity and control of destiny at a time when an unprecedented compression of social space – together with the advance of secularism, industrialism, large-scale capitalism and anonymous bureaucracy – greatly undermined constructions of being, belonging and autonomy centred on locality. The process of nationalisation developed so far that, in the twentieth century, it has been almost a requirement in order to participate effectively in long-distance social relations that people organise themselves in terms of national identities, however shallow and fragile they may be, and however unhappy the frequently violent consequences.

GLOBALISATION[18]

As implied in the discussion so far, the construction of collective identities has historically been closely bound up with place. Defining *who* 'we' are has simultaneously in large part been a question of *where* persons are in the world. Location has conventionally been plotted in a three-dimensional space of longitudes, latitudes and altitudes. People have correspondingly mapped their collective self-identifications mainly in relation to places on this traditional geographical grid. In this way identities have maintained a prominent and on the whole overriding territorial character. Even communities rooted in kinship have generally linked their common blood to a (perhaps distant) shared homeland. With increasing compression of social space over the centuries, notions of group affiliation expanded territorially until, with intense internationalisation of the last hundred and fifty years or so, identity came to centre primarily on large-scale country units and associated national populations.

Accelerated globalisation of recent decades has produced a fundamental rupture in this long-term trend. As it is conceived here, globalisation refers to the introduction and spread of a fourth dimension of social space. 'Global' relations are place-less, distance-less, borderless interactions and interdependencies between persons: they unfold in *the world as a single place.*[19] This quality of what might be called 'supraterritoriality' distinguishes global from international circumstances; hence globalisation is not the same thing as internationalisation.[20] *International* exchanges take place over considerable distances and require fairly long time intervals to complete. In contrast, *global* conditions are situated in a space where distance can be covered in effectively no time. The international realm is a patchwork of countries, while the global sphere is a web of flows. Global circumstances can surface simultaneously at and move instantaneously between any spot on the planet. Manifestations of supraterritoriality include electromagnetic broadcasting, telecommunications, computer networks, electronic financial transactions, certain ecological problems like ozone depletion and the greenhouse effect, a host of consumer goods, remote sensing, and countless commercial and regulatory agencies. None of these conditions can be pinned down in three-dimensional space. Although global phenomena 'touch down' at specific places, they are in no way bound to those locations.

Various contemporary social theorists have highlighted the rise of supraterritoriality, even if they have used different vocabulary to describe the trend. For example, thirty years ago Marshall McLuhan announced the creation of a 'global village' and referred, somewhat obscurely, to conditions of 'allatonceness [where] "time" has ceased, "space" has vanished'.[21] More recently, Manuel Castells has distinguished a new 'space of flows' alongside the old 'space of places', while Joshua Meyrowitz has highlighted a growing detachment of social place from physical place.[22] In 1984 the science-fiction writer William Gibson introduced the term 'cyberspace' to describe a microelectronic social world within and between computers.[23] On like lines other authors have recently coined academic sound-bites concerning 'hyperspace', heightened 'time-space distanciation', 'pace displacing space' and a 'nonterritorial region'.[24]

True, supraterritoriality is not completely new to the last decades of the twentieth century. Electrical communication first appeared in the nineteenth century, scheduled short-wave radio programmes emerged in the 1920s, and film distribution on an intercontinental scale reached considerable proportions by the 1930s. Already in the 1850s Karl Marx anticipated 'the annihilation of space by time' as 'capital by its nature drives beyond every spatial barrier' to 'conquer the whole earth for its market'.[25] English speakers acquired a habit of using the word 'global' to mean 'worldwide' (as opposed to 'spherical') in the 1890s, while the terms 'globalise' and 'globalism' were first coined fifty years ago.[26] Likewise, Martin Heidegger at mid-century described the advent of 'distanceless-ness' and an 'abolition of every possibility of remoteness'.[27]

Yet before the 1960s talk of globalisation remained largely futuristic. Relatively few people in these earlier times had radios, let alone televisions. In 1942 a recently defeated candidate for the US presidency was well-nigh alone in his experience of 'one world' by flying round the planet in 160 hours.[28] The first digital computer was not assembled until 1946, the first submarine telephone link was not laid until 1956, the first broadcast satellite was not launched until 1962, and the first computer network only came on-line in 1969. Before 1960 distanceless exchanges emerged for the most part slowly, amongst small and restricted circles of people, and at the margins of daily life. During the past four decades, however, globalisation has shifted into overdrive, bringing unprecedented growth in the number, variety, intensity, institutionalisation, awareness and impact of supraterritorial phenomena. In the mid-1990s each day brings over a trillion dollars in Eurocurrency dealings across the planet. More than 800 million television screens and in excess of 700 million telephone connection points link the world as a whole. Electronic newscasts report simultaneously to audiences at every longitude and latitude, blue jeans appear in clothing piles worldwide, and socially produced global climate change is in prospect if not already ongoing. Supraterritorial space has become significant in the everyday routines of the greater part of humanity.

That said, globalisation should not (as so often happens) be exaggerated or oversimplified.[29] The process has *not* touched every person, location and sphere of activity to the same extent. It has *not* been inevitable, linear, irreversible or completed. Globalisation has *not* constituted the sole or primary motor of contemporary history. Place, distance and territorial borders have *not* ceased to be important in the present time of globalisation. The rise of supraterritoriality has thus far *not* heralded the end of the state. Everyone has *not* enjoyed equal access to, an equal voice in and equal benefits from the nonterritorial realm. Globalisation has to date *not* created a world community with universal prosperity, planetary democracy and perpetual peace. Nor – as will be elaborated in later sections of this chapter – has the process removed cultural differences from the world system. However, while acknowledging and emphasising these qualifications, it can still be affirmed that a large-scale, wide-ranging and deeply penetrating shift in the spatial character of social relations has been unfolding in recent times. Globalisation has thus of late rightly become a focus of burgeoning research.

One prominent theme in this proliferating literature is that globalisation has unsettled long-dominant territorially based constructions of collective identities, including in particular the nationality principle. As geographer Doreen Massey notes, contemporary growth of supraterritoriality has bred 'an increasing uncertainty about what we mean by "places" and how we relate to them'.[30] In the words of sociologist Zdravko Mlinar, globalisation has radically altered experiences of proximity and social connectedness, shaking 'traditional territorial identities based on *contiguity, homogeneity,* and clearly (physically and socially) identifiable *borders*.'[31] Planetary instantaneity has given people a substantial degree of intimacy with previously absent parts of humanity. Direct-dial telephones, nuclear fallout, global corporations and the like have brought the 'outsider' to the 'inside' as never before.

Yet how and how far, more precisely, has globalisation transformed affective geography in the world system? In what ways, if any, has the process disrupted and changed relations of 'closeness' and 'remoteness', 'stranger' and 'neighbour', 'home' and 'away', 'them' and 'us', 'friend' and 'foe'? Have supraterritorial social relations fostered fundamentally different kinds of self-identification and collective solidarity? Is the expansion of global space so redefining the nature of boundaries that the age-old formula of distinguishing self and other along territorial lines is being superseded? In particular, does globality spell the demise of nationality? How are collective attachments to be forged in the world system if not through place?

Such questions have received greatest academic attention from sociologists, social anthropologists and human geographers;[32] however, during the past decade globalisation has also helped prod students of International Relations to produce an unprecedented quantity and quality of research into the construction of collective identities.[33] Indeed, by 1995 it was seen fit to include a chapter on questions of identity in a textbook of IR theory.[34] In the same year the annual convention of the International Studies Association included more than a dozen panels specifically dedicated to the identity problematique.

As with various other new issues in the discipline, followers of realist paths have made little if any contribution of note to the unfolding IR investigations of identity formation. Indeed, their statist and materialist dispositions largely preclude them from entering the debate. At most, realists have asked how 'cultural differences' (by which they usually mean ethnic and national characters) affect interstate conflict and cooperation. For the rest these traditionalists have not seen identity as an issue. Following the example of Hans Morgenthau, they have tended to collapse the concept of 'nation' into that of 'state'.[35] Realists have not explored the socially constructed and historically contingent character of nationhood and have neglected other dimensions of identity including gender, race, class and so on.

Blindness to the multifaceted and fluctuating nature of identities has also afflicted many liberalists in IR. Researchers working within this paradigm tend to take national identities for granted and frequently depict the achievement of national self-determination through a liberal-democratic state as 'the end of history'. Like realists, liberalists have often inadequately distinguished nationhood (a structure of collective identity) from statehood (a structure of governance). Many liberalists also take it as an article of faith that globalisation will automatically yield a worldwide community of nations through institutionalised interstate co-operation. On the other hand, more questioning liberalist investigations (for example, of so-called 'transnationalism') have acknowledged that people may construct collective identities in other-than-national terms.[36]

However, the most extensive, probing and innovative studies of the construction of group identities in globalising social relations have emerged from recent new directions in IR scholarship, including feminist perspectives, ecological approaches, critical theory and poststructuralism. Researchers in these circles have shown the greatest readiness to problematise space and to assess the implications of a rise of supraterritoriality for fundamental change in the contemporary world system. The following observations concerning homogenisation, localisation, deterritorialisation, renationalisation and fragmentation of collective identities under conditions of globalisation draw inspiration (both appreciative and critical) chiefly from these alternative approaches.

HOMOGENISATION

Long before the contemporary acceleration of globalisation, many a theory of history expected that time–space compression would progressively eliminate place-bound differences and create the conditions for a single, homogeneous worldwide human community. Such an assumption was fairly explicit in the work of several nineteenth-century pioneers of modern social science, including Comte, Mill and Marx. Likewise, when Reiser and Davies invented the verb 'globalise' in 1944, they took it to mean 'universalise' and foresaw 'a planetary synthesis of cultures' in a 'global humanism'.[37] Modernisation theorists of the 1960s and neoliberals of recent years have reiterated this equation of globalism with universalism.[38]

By effectively removing territorial separations between people, globalisation has indeed facilitated certain tendencies towards cultural convergence. Phenomena such as global markets, electronic mass media and cyberspace have helped to give planetary currency to a host of objects, ideas, symbols, words, weights and measures, rules and habits. Across the continents one encounters pop music, cigarettes, traffic signals and 'stress' (the word has in the past several decades surfaced in all languages from Tagalog to Swedish).[39] 'Global English' – the language stripped of its various patois and local accents – increasingly serves as the linguistic medium for worldwide interchange.[40] The spread of supraterritoriality has promoted (and largely depended upon) the adoption across the continents of broadly similar methods of transport, communications, information processing and organisational management. The process has also produced (and required) significant, albeit by no means complete, world-scale convergences of legal and ethical principles. For instance, the discourse of 'human rights' has taken root well-nigh everywhere on earth, even if a consensus on the specific nature of those universal entitlements remains elusive. Meanwhile global governance agencies such as the International Monetary Fund have propagated universalistic macroeconomic policies. In addition to this more immediately observable evidence of homogenisation, the rise of supraterritoriality has facilitated the rapid dispersal and reinforcement throughout the contemporary world of broadly similar shifts in social structure, such as the growth of consumer capitalism, the retreat of state-supplied social security or the spread of religious resurgence. Experiencing this world-scale convergence of symbols, actions, norms and social changes, people who have been pulled furthest into the maelstrom of globalisation (e.g., numerous managers, academics and artists) have often found territorially constructed distinctions of self and other to be increasingly artificial and unsatisfactory. We can wonder whether a parallel might be emerging with a previous era when nationalist sentiment was first mainly restricted to the up-and-coming bourgeoisie of that time.

Yet this is not to affirm that cosmopolitanism is winning the day with contemporary globalisation. True, photos of the planet from outer space, round-the-world broadcasts and global ecological concerns have created a greater consciousness of Earth – and not just one or the other of its many plots of land – as home. In addition, worldwide appeals for disaster relief and humanitarian intervention have since the 1970s elicited popular and governmental responses on a much larger scale and with much greater frequency than prevailed previously. Nevertheless, universalist sentiments and acts of solidarity with humanity as a whole remain for the most part secondary and fleeting in everyday life at the end of the twentieth century. Human affiliations and loyalties are still heavily influenced by a person's particular location in the 'global village', whether in terms of place, age, sexual orientation, nationality or other shared experience.

Moreover, celebrations of universality often overlook the fact that, insofar as globalisation has encouraged homogenisation, the process has frequently gone hand in hand with a suppression and even extinction of identities. Particularisms dependent on territorial isolation have been most vulnerable. For example, radio made little time for the 'long songs' of the Dayak and recently obliterated this age-old cultural form in less than twenty years.[41] Disney has not accommodated 'tradition' except insofar as it can be, to take a phrase from Robert Cox, 'assimilated as folklore in a global entertainment industry'.[42] Computer fonts are unavailable for many localised languages, some of which have also been annihilated in a deluge of global audio-visual productions. Many observers have thus worried that globalisation is crushing cultural diversity along with biodiversity.

Such worries appear well-founded in the light of the above evidence; however, they seem over pessimistic when other developments are also taken into account. Although globalisation has contributed to the retreat and elimination of some territorial identities, the 'space of flows' has been absorbed with limited disruptions at other locations. Indeed, in numerous further instances the rise of supraterritoriality has helped to produce new diversities and alternative forms of self-other differentiation. As the following comments concerning localisation, deterritorialisation, renationalisation and fragmentation of collective identities indicate, globalisation of recent times has been an occasion for heterogenisation as well as homogenisation.[43] The shrinkage of the world has both undermined and enhanced pluralism: decreasing diversity through cultural extinctions but also increasing it by loosening the hold of the state (historically a major promoter of national identities) and by unleashing new dynamics of differentiation both around and beyond the nationality principle. In this light Roland Robertson is right that contemporary globalisation involves 'the particularization of universalism (the rendering of the world as a single place) *and* the universalization of particularism (the globalized expectation that societies . . . should have distinct identities)'.[44]

LOCALISATION

For one thing, globalisation has by no means eliminated diversity between local sites. On the contrary, the process has on numerous occasions encouraged a reinvigoration of substate territorial identities, for example, amongst indigenous peoples and other ethnic groups. To this extent globalisation and localisation have often unfolded in tandem, although their interconnection in 'glocalisation' has frequently involved significant friction.

The local co-exists with, is not wholly subordinate to, and indeed shapes the global at the same time that it is shaped by the supraterritorial realm. What might be called 'globalist' analyses wrongly suppose, in reductionist fashion, that one dimension of social space (the global) determines conditions on all other planes (international, country, district, household, etc.). In practice, however, locality has survived alongside globality. Supraterritorial phenomena are mediated through and translated into an immediate territorial context at the same time that the 'space of flows' intervenes in and remoulds local circumstances. For example, global capitalism has taken different forms in Asian, Anglo-Saxon and continental European contexts. Largely due to diverse local situations, structural adjustment policies formulated in global governance organisations have had varying consequences between, say, Argentina and Zaïre. The impacts of global environmental change are felt in specific places and in each case elicit a particular local response. Reception research has shown that mass media productions are often appreciated quite differently, and with correspondingly varying effects, by different parts of a global audience.[45] Direct satellite broadcasters have discovered, at a considerable cost in lost profits, that they need to cater programming to a diversity of local tastes. Other global products, too, may be put to disparate uses according to the terrestrial receiving point. Thus, for instance, marketers of Coca-Cola have stressed the need to be 'multilocal', and a recent Nike corporate mission statement declares that 'the company that succeeds on a global scale learns to delicately balance... a single, identifiable global identity... and performance needs that vary widely from country to country'.[46] With more positive intent, cultural preservationists have on various occasions exploited the technologies of globalisation to reinvigorate otherwise declining or dormant local identities. For example, recent years have seen video contribute to a revitalisation of Bedouin identity in Egypt, while television has fostered local solidarities amongst Aborigines in Australia and amongst Catalans in Spain. Satellite broadcasts have furthered the survival of the Inuktituk language in the Canadian Arctic, and radio has fuelled Maori identity politics in New Zealand.[47]

Globalisation has encouraged reassertions of indigenous identities across the world in other ways, too.[48] In some instances these activities have, much as in the construction of national identities described earlier, constituted a self-protective response to intervention from 'outside'. Thus, for example, global tourism has intensified native Hawaiian sensibilities, global deforestation has triggered indigenous activism in Amazonia, and the formation of the North American Free Trade Association sparked armed rebellion in pursuit of aboriginal rights in Chiapas State at the beginning of 1994. In addition, globalisation has transferred some power away from the territorial state,[49] which in the past often repressed native peoples in the name of nation-building. At the same time, various global governance agencies and global social movements have deployed some of their increased influence in support of aboriginal groups. For instance, United Nations bodies have promoted the recent codification of indigenous peoples' rights in international law and declared 1993 to be the International Year of the World's Indigenous People. Meanwhile the nongovernmental Unrepresented Nations and Peoples Organisation has since its creation in 1991 promoted the causes of more than forty member communities.[50] Since several global gatherings in the mid-1970s, a number of movements for the advancement of indigenous peoples have strengthened their respective campaigns by means of intercontinental mutual support. Air, telephone and computer networks have allowed Navajo to aid Saami and Cree to assist Miskito to extents that were previously not possible. Concurrently, global mass media have helped to turn the Zapatistas of Chiapas, the Movement for the Survival of the Ogoni People (MOSOP) in Nigeria, the Free Papua Organisation (OPM) in Indonesia and other strivings for the rights of indigenous peoples into world-scale *causes célèbres*.[51] Thus the growth of supraterritoriality has in multiple cases given the descendants of the earliest known inhabitants of conquered lands an occasion to reaffirm their local ways of being. Globalisation has not been the only force behind these asser-tions of so-called 'fourth world' identities; indeed, the process seems to have played little role in other instances, such as the long-running struggles of various hill peoples in South Asia. However, much contem-porary indigenisation can be understood in part as a form of localisation under conditions of globalisation.

Connections between expanding supraterritoriality and the construc-tion of collective identities on a reduced scale can also be drawn in respect of other ethnic revivals that have proliferated across the planet since the 1960s. In these cases localised groupings who were previously overwhelmed in a larger national project have resurrected their linguis-tic, racial and/or historical distinctiveness, often in the process demand-ing secession from the national state that has ruled over them.[52] Indeed, such reinventions of purportedly primordial identifications have been instrumental in effecting the segmentation of several states: with interna-tional recognition in the cases of the former Soviet Union, Yugoslavia and ex-Czechoslovakia; and *de facto* in the cases of Angola, Cyprus, Liberia, Sierra Leone, Somalia and Sudan. Ethnic revivals have also prompted major constitutional reforms in Spain (1978) and Belgium (1993) as well as proposed changes rejected by the Canadian electorate in 1992. Largely owing to the plethora of neo-traditionalist rebellions across Africa, Europe and Asia, states in the late twentieth century have more often turned their military machines inwards against minority populations than outwards against other states.[53] Ethnic conflicts lay at the heart of eighteen of the twenty-three wars being fought in 1994 and eight of the thirteen then-ongoing United Nations peacekeeping opera-tions.[54] In sum, the time of globalisation has also been a time of growing 'tribal' consciousness.

As in regard to indigenous peoples' movements, it would be over sim-plistic to attribute ethnic revivalism solely to globalisation; however, the concurrence of the two trends is more than coincidental. Like indigen-ism and old-style nationalism, contemporary resurgences of ethnic iden-tities have unfolded in part as defensive reactions against intrusions of the other who threatens to erase the self. In the late twentieth century these apparent dangers have often emanated from the supraterritorial realm, in the form of global capital, global governance, global television, global ecological degradation and the like. In addition, many ethnic revi-vals of recent times have reproduced the exclusionary character of nationalism, seeking with an insistence or desperation that readily turns violent to demarcate boundaries and bar trespassers. The perceived intruders might include the ruling state insofar as it comes to be seen less as a protector of domestic interests and more as a collaborator with 'outside' exploitative global forces. Such a dynamic has apparently operated in recent decades amongst, for example, the Moros, the Québecois and the Scots in their relations with the Philippine, Canadian and British states, respectively.

In several ways, then, the last thirty years have witnessed an intertwining of processes of globalisation and the promotion of substate territorial identities. To paraphrase Raimondo Strassoldo, this 'new localism' can be appreciated in one sense as a search for enclaves of familiarity and intimacy at a time when globalising technologies have exposed the self to an infinity of locations, persons, things and ideas all at once.[55] To this extent the global has, far from erasing parochialism, in fact often given the local new life and legitimacy.[56] David Harvey suggests that place-bound identities might actually have become *more* rather than less important in a world of diminishing spatial barriers.[57] Liberal-universalist convictions that the good society lies in a cosmopolis beyond the local neighbourhood and the state are clearly not shared by all. At the risk of overgeneralisation, it might be suggested that, whereas between the mid-nineteenth and mid-twentieth centuries internationalisation brought an erosion (but not elimination) of local identities, more recently globalisation has created conditions that favour the renewal of collective solidarities on a smaller scale.

DETERRITORIALISATION

Yet that smaller scale – the 'locality' – need not be territorial in character. Indeed, to the extent that many present-day social relations transpire on the supraterritorial plane of telecommunications, electronic mass media and the like, it is not surprising to witness growth in self-identifications and communities that lack a specific territorial grounding. As distance-lessness has become an increasingly widespread and primary social fact, more and more persons have situated important aspects of their identity in global as well as (and to some extent instead of) three-dimensional space. The last thirty years have seen significant increases in assertions of identities and solidarities that are largely disconnected from place, for example, related to religious faith, (managerial) class, race, gender, youth and sexual orientation. In addition, computer bulletin boards, telephone help lines and the like have encouraged the development of supraterritorial communities of the disabled and other special-interest groups.[58]

National identities, too, have in some instances undergone a degree of deterritorialisation. Insofar as most of these constructions link collective identity with shared experiences of injustice, they have fostered the development of supraterritorial politics of emancipation.

Religious Identities

On the one hand, then, contemporary globalisation has on various occasions promoted the growth of confessionally based supraterritorial collective identities. The last quarter of the twentieth century has witnessed a world-systemic religious resurgence encompassing Hindu, Buddhist, Judaic, Christian, Islamic, Sikh, Baha'i and various so-called New Age faiths.[59] The greatest significance of these movements – particularly those of a revivalist (or, to use the more pejorative term, 'fundamentalist') character – probably lies in their challenge to prevailing techno-scientific rationalist knowledge.[60] However, the trend has also involved some reconstruction of collective identities on a nonterritorial basis. True, the heart of these putative communities may be located at a particular place: *Eretz Yisrael* for many fundamentalist Jews, Ayodhya for the Bharatiya Janata Party (BJP), and so on. Moreover, many nationalist campaigns have focused on religious differences as a primary basis for drawing boundaries between countries. However, much recent religious revivalism gives a definite priority to shared faith over common territory and nationality. Thus Ayatollah Ruhollah Khomeini declared that his return to Tehran in 1979 after prolonged exile evoked no special emotion; his 'homeland' was Islam.[61] The ensuing revolution in Iran found echoes worldwide at greater speeds and (non)distances than in any previous Muslim revivalist movement.[62]

Like the other nonterritorial identities discussed below, collective self-consciousness as a supranational, religiously based 'civilisation' is not new to the late twentieth century, but accelerated globalisation has given considerable stimulus to such constructions.[63] Today, when the whole world is a day away, aeroplanes take the Pope anywhere and draw *haji* from everywhere. Worldwide mass media and publishers instantly made the Rushdie affair a global event in 1989. Satellite broadcasts have enabled televangelists to preach global sermons. The Organisation of the Islamic Conference, set up in the early 1970s, has taken part in global governance. Global money from expatriates in Britain, Canada and the USA has funded Sikhist activism in the Punjab. The Isnet (Islamic Network) has carved out a Muslim place in cyberspace, while the leading mullah in Tajikistan communicates by fax and cellular telephone.[64] Ideas of the *umma* or the universal church can be put into practice as never before.

At the same time as being pursued through global channels, the contemporary upsurge of identities rooted in religion has, like ethnic revivalism, often also been in part a defensive response to lost senses of place, community and self-determination through globalisation. Recent religious revitalisation has frequently waxed into a kind of nonterritorial protectionism, suffused with exclusivist claims and politics of violence. Indeed, certain cold warriors have, in their search for a new manichaean planetary rift to replace the East-West divide, seized upon these tendencies to promote the thesis that inter*civilisational* antagonism is replacing inter*national* conflict as the predominant motif of world politics.[65] Although this analysis is no less simplistic and potentially dangerous than the earlier Cold War mindset, it highlights one important way that collective identities have deviated from the nationality principle in the present time of globalisation.

Borderless Class Identities

Meanwhile, other supraterritorial collective identities have developed along class lines. Like religious identities, these constructions of group affiliation and allegiance are not yesterday's invention. Already in the last quarter of the nineteenth century, the First and Second Internationals gave expression to a nonterritorial unity of workers. Twenty-seven international trade secretariats operated as of 1914, and several years later the Bolsheviks obtained a notable intercontinental response to their proclamation of a world proletarian revolution.[66]

In contrast, globalisation of the late twentieth century has if anything seen a decline in supraterritorial working-class consciousness and solidarity. In the 1990s even most political parties of the purported left have refused a discourse of socialism. Hypermobile capital of the present day, together with changing labour practices and structural unemployment, has more often tended to set wage earners of the world in competition against each another. Lacking a well-developed sense of placeless solidarity, and therefore generally neglecting one-world strategies, labour has figured at best as a peripheral actor in contemporary global politics. Working-class interests have sooner been pursued by new transnational social movements (e.g., concerning human rights, environment, etc.) than by global union networks.[67]

On the other hand, supraterritorial bonds have deepened since mid-century in business and governing circles. Susan Strange speaks in this respect of 'a transnational managerial class... in which the life-styles of each [national fraction] resemble each other more than they do those of state officials or corporate managers who function only in a national milieu'.[68] Certain circles in other professions as well (e.g., doctors, lawyers, engineers, academics and journalists) have developed transnational affiliations of unprecedented intensity in the context of globalisation. These supraterritorial nomads – comparatively small in number but very large in influence – find their common home in airport lounges, mobile telephones, laptop computers, associations like the World Economic Forum and official global regulatory agencies.[69] They include the more than 100000 members of the 'Six Continents Club' of Inter-Continental Hotels.[70] Perhaps something like the alliance of global capitalists described (prematurely) eighty years ago in Karl Kautsky's speculations on 'ultra-imperialism' is now taking shape.[71]

Racial Solidarities

Next to religion and class, race has been another important nonterritorial touchstone for the construction of collective identities in the contemporary, increasingly globalised world system. On these occasions lines between self and other have been drawn in relation to shared inherited bodily features, especially skin pigmentation, with only secondary regard to place of residence.

People from Africa, Asia and Europe have had long-distance encounters and mutual effects from time to time for over two millennia;[72] however, racial consciousness – in particular 'Black'/'White' and 'Yellow'/ 'White' dualisms – emerged as a significant social construct only a few centuries ago and did not become pervasive throughout the world until after 1850, largely in the context of heightened internationalisation. Major intercontinental migrations and colonial expansionism in the late nineteenth century were accompanied by a spread of legal and informal racial discrimination and segregation. Projects were also launched to foster worldwide Anglo-Saxon unity and, from the turn of the century, Zionist, Pan-African and Pan-Asian resistances to racial subordination. Fifty years ago the Second World War was fought between races as well as between nations.[73]

Contemporary globalisation has reinforced and added to perceptions of racial identities and above all of distinctively black experiences (especially of exclusion) that transcend the variability of place-specific black lives. Aided by global communications and the support of numerous global governance agencies and global social movements, extensive so-called 'Third World' solidarity on more or less racial lines has developed since the mid-1950s. Although often rather shallow, this supraterritorial bonding has had considerable effect in the anti-apartheid and other civil rights campaigns. Policy consultations between leading Africans and prominent African-Americans have increased in recent times, and in the early 1990s the Congressional Black Caucus was a major voice calling for US military intervention first in Somalia and then in Haiti. Meanwhile mass media technologies have played an important part in forging notions of a global black culture. In the context of global consumerism, many marketers have consciously promoted *Black* music, *Black* writers, *Black* sitcoms and *Black* superstars. As with nationality or class, considerable ambiguity attends the definition of collective identities in terms of race, and the alleged communities in practice show substantial diversity and internal division. Nevertheless, racial self-consciousness has become if anything more acute with increased inter-racial encounters in supraterritorial flows.

Global Gender Identities

Meanwhile some of the most pronounced deterritorialisation of collective identities has occurred since the 1960s in respect of gender, that is, social constructions of self-other distinctions along female–male lines. Consciousness of supraterritorial sameness and solidarity in terms of gender has developed mainly amongst women, although recent years have also seen the emergence, mainly reactive and on a much smaller scale, of a men's movement.

World-scale womanhood is not completely new to the late twentieth century, of course. A hundred years ago campaigners for female suffrage exploited time–space compression of that day to develop effective transnational mutual support.[74] International Women's Day was first proclaimed in 1910, a number of international women's conferences were convened in the early twentieth century, and a Status of Women Committee was eventually established within the League of Nations in 1937.[75] At this time, too, as states moved towards another world war, Virginia Woolf made her renowned declaration that: 'As a woman I want no country. As a woman my country is the whole world'.[76]

However, Woolf's words did not gain slogan status until the large-scale expansion of women's movements during the past several decades. This period has seen an unprecedented proliferation and growth of permanent institutions – local and transnational, popular and governmental – devoted specifically to the status of women. Four global women's conferences with attendances running into the thousands have taken place since 1975, and women's groups have figured prominently in the NGO Forums that are now held almost annually.[77] Gender-focused identity politics have turned matters such as physical abuses of women, reproduction strategies, equality of the sexes, and women's labour into 'global gender issues'.[78] A large majority of the 111 heads of state and government attending the March 1995 World Summit for Social Development referred to women's poverty and marginalisation in their addresses, something which was inconceivable thirty years ago. Like indigenous peoples, women's groups have on various occasions found support from global governance agencies that was lacking from a patriarchal nation-state.[79] The position of women was the foremost concern of the United Nations Decade for Women (1976–85) and also figured prominently in New International Economic Order campaigns of the 1970s more generally.

Like other nonterritorial communities, the global women's movement has not been singular either in organisation or outlook. Gender politics have spawned multiple feminisms (liberal, socialist, black, pacifist, radical, ecological) as well as women's associations that have rejected the 'feminist' label. The dissolution of distance through globalisation has not erased differences amongst women along lines of religion, class, race, sexual preference, nationality, region and so on. Postmodernists in particular have assailed that brand of 'global sisterhood' which, in a form of cultural imperialism complete with missionary zeal, has constructed a single category of woman and uncritically univeralised a liberal-individualist model of women's emancipation. Yet these critics, too, have recognised a certain universality of women's oppression and have advocated the development of transnational feminist alliances, albeit out of differences and so-called 'politics of location'. With this orientation, says Chilla Bulbeck, 'The world's women's movement . . . can be many, modelled on the female symbols of the web or the patchwork quilt'.[80]

Global Youth Culture

A further nonterritorial construction of collective identity that has developed in the course of globalisation revolves around youth. Nominally this category relates to a particular age group, though more fundamentally it touches more on a lifestyle and phase of psychological development defined as 'young'.[81] Youth culture, too, predates the contemporary rise of supraterritoriality, and several international associations of students and other young people were active in the first half of the twentieth century. However, globalisation has given this form of group affiliation new manifestations, much larger (if generally more informal) world-scale networks, and unprecedented prominence. A prime target – if not creation – of global consumerism, late twentieth century youth culture includes a host of placeless customs and artefacts: promotional T-shirts, student travel, computer games, the 'world beat' of pop music, a succession of cult films and videos, transnational argot, graffiti, illicit use of global drugs and so on. Through audio-visual media, many of today's youth are arguably more familiar with the streets of America than with many parts of their 'home' countries. By 1991, ten years after its launch, Music Television (MTV) was available to 201 million households across 77 countries in five continents.[82]

With its strong tendencies towards individualism and hedonism, this supraterritorial identity form has, in contrast to the others discussed here, stimulated relatively little construction of lasting solidarities focused on mutual care. Such an inclination receded with the decline of global student activism of the 1960s. For instance, youth (and more particularly student) involvement in the various NGO Forums of the 1990s has been surprisingly small. This development is worrying insofar as young persons have borne much of the brunt of unemployment, marginalisation and authoritarian moral chastisement in the globalising political economy. An entertainment strategy seems unlikely to take youth beyond escape to emancipation.

The Lesbian and Gay Revolution

Still another construction of nonterritorial collective identity – one that is quite new to recent history – relates to sexual preference, in particular homosexuality and, on a smaller scale, bisexuality. True, same-sex desires are age-old, with some evidence suggesting that such orientations may have distinct genetic as well as social bases. However, apart from some shortlived gay activism in the early twentieth century, it is only recently that lesbians and gay men have identified themselves as 'peoples' – a 'Queer Nation' in one case – turning their sexual dispositions into a touchstone of identity, solidarity and strivings for self-determination.[83] Declarations that 'my sexuality is me' and 'I am out, therefore I am' were rare if not wholly absent before 1970.[84] Like nationalism and other identity movements, gayness and lesbianism have stimulated cultural innovation (in festivals, theatre, literature, film, fashion, bars, etc.), rewritings of history, and political organisation.

The historical concurrence of this identity revolution with the growth of supraterritorial space does seem significant. As with the other cases already discussed, globalisation has made room for lesbian and gay movements by loosening the hold of territorial identities. In addition, much 'coming out' has occurred at supraterritorial locations: on television and in film; through telephone switchboards; in global sports and music; with gay tourism and migration; by lobbying of suprastate institutions; and, unhappily, in response to the global AIDS epidemic and its attendant homophobic backlash. Global relations have afforded more possibilities for collective self-identification amongst lesbians and gay men than have been available in territorial places, where homosexuals have generally been isolated and often hidden from one another. In the global arena the movement can veritably claim, 'we are everywhere'.[85] An International Gay and Lesbian Association was founded in 1978 and fifteen years later comprised over 300 member organisations in 56 countries across all inhabited continents.[86] By the early 1990s the IGLA had been joined by a World Congress of Gay and Lesbian Jewish Organizations, an International Lesbian and Gay Youth Organization, a Gay Asian Pacific Alliance, and an International Lesbian and Gay People of Colour Conference. As this list suggests, lesbianism and gayness, like the other nonterritorial collective identities already described, have been marked by considerable diversity and various internecine disputes, showing again that to share an identity is not to remove difference and discord.

Supraterritorial Nationalism

Finally, globalisation has also shifted constructions of collective identities away from a focus on place by loosening certain ties between nationhood and (territorial) statehood. Once more the trend is not completely new. In earlier times a clear delinkage of nation and state prevailed in the former Soviet Union, for example. In addition, many members of immigrant communities across the world (overseas Chinese, for example) have long distinguished between their nationality and their place of residence and citizenship. However, global communications have made it that much easier for a people to sustain its sense of national solidarity while being dispersed across the planet, with a result that immigrants who can afford it now frequently re-emigrate back to their 'home country' as pensioners. In response to the global mobility of significant sectors of their populations, various states have in recent years increased the scope for dual nationality, either *de jure* in the case of Turkey or *de facto* in the case of officials who turn a blind eye to statutory offences of holding more than one passport. At a regional level, the Maastricht

Treaty of 1992 in a little-noted innovation subtly decoupled nationality and citizenship with its assertion, in Article 8, that 'every person holding the nationality of a Member State shall be a citizen of the [European] Union'.[87] Meanwhile a number of contemporary nationalist campaigns – including those of the African National Congress, Irish Republicans and the Palestine Liberation Organisation – have conducted global campaigns to good advantage, although their goal has still been to retrieve a territorial homeland.[88]

Across a wide range of collective solidarities, then, globalisation has encouraged an expansion of the nonterritorial dimensions of identity politics. All of the placeless groupings described above have antecedents that pre-date the contemporary period of accelerated globalisation, but each has generally increased in size, substance and prominence as a result of the disruption of the link between space and place in social relations. Care must of course be taken not to exaggerate the extent and depth of supraterritorial identities, or to underestimate the difficulties facing their various political projects. Identities based in place remain very important in the present time of globalisation, and much of the promise of deterritorialised human solidarities lies in potentialities rather than actualities. Yet it would be equally wrong to reiterate today Heidegger's conclusion, spoken forty years ago on the eve of contemporary heightened globalisation, that 'the frantic abolition of all distances brings no nearness'.[89]

RE-NATIONALISATION

From the discussion so far it is apparent that globalisation has in a number of respects unsettled and indeed challenged the position of nationality as the core framework of collective identity in the modern world system. On the one hand, the spread of supraterritoriality has aided the growth of aboriginal, racial and other alternative group affiliations noted above. In addition, it has also disrupted several structural aspects of social relations that have in the past promoted the rise of nationhood.[90] For example, whereas nationalism thrived in the context of territory-bound mercantile and industrial capitalism, globalised accumulation occurs largely through commodities such as money, information, images and communications, all of which are much less tied to place. Likewise, to the extent that national collectivities have been a product of the modern territorial state, their strength has been weakened as globalisation has undermined the state's capacities to maintain boundaries and exercise sovereignty. In addition, insofar as nationalism and militarism have historically been mutually reinforcing social structures, increased disincentives to interstate war in circumstances of globalisation have weakened another major underpinning of the nation. Feminism, religious fundamentalism and lesbian and gay liberation – each of them, as seen above, blossoming in the space of flows – have challenged the nation insofar as this construction of collective identity has been structurally bound up with patriarchy, rationalism and heterosexism.[91]

At the level of day-to-day events, too, globalisation has made the nationality principle even more problematic than it has always been. By greatly intensifying the interpenetration of languages, customs, artefacts, beliefs, races, sensibilities, heritages and other purported hallmarks of national distinctiveness, global relations have made it more difficult than ever clearly to distinguish national characters from one another. Given this greater ambiguity of nationality, as well as the greater plurality of identities (in terms of religion, class, etc.) circulating in supraterritorial settings, appeals to the national interest generally fall on less solid ground than they did a generation ago. Contemporary globalisation has also brought a marked decrease in capacities of effective territorial control, thus narrowing the scope for national self-determination through the state and reducing possibilities to exclude the 'foreigner' through official channels. Moreover, the material and moral costs of such exclusions are far less bearable in global social relations, when the consequences are immediately apparent in currency values and on the television screen.

However, it would be mistaken to conclude from these trends that globalisation heralds 'the end of the national project'.[92] For one thing, as stressed earlier, many social relations are still of the long-distance territorial kind that were crucial to the rise of the nationality principle in earlier times. Furthermore, in spite of four decades of GATT rounds and regional integration programmes, much of present-day capitalism is still bound up with national firms, national currencies, national markets and so on. Although (national) governments may have lost sovereignty, on the whole the state apparatus is larger and in various respects more interventionist than ever, including in the more globalised parts of the world. Other structural underpinnings of the nationality principle as well – militarism, patriarchy, indeed, the overall complex of modernity in which nationhood has figured so centrally – have hardly disappeared from the face of the earth with the recent expansion of the supraterritorial realm.

On the contrary, the nationality principle is often reproduced in global space. This point has already been indicated in previous remarks concerning deterritorialised nationalisms. At the level of daily life, too, telephone charge structures often reinforce the primacy of the national collectivity by making cross-border calls cost several times as much as domestic calls over a similar distance. Although several transnational conglomerates figure prominently in the mass media, most broadcast companies have operated chiefly in national fields. Many, such as the Globo network in Brazil, have helped considerably to secure national identity via television. The governments of India and Indonesia have used satellite broadcasting to the same end.[93] Global spectacles like the Olympic Games and World Cups thrive on nationalist fervour. Global governance institutions are still built around national memberships: the United *Nations*, the *International* Monetary Fund, etc. Likewise, global companies and global social movements generally organise their branch networks on national lines. Many a religious revivalist, global manager, supraterritorial women's organiser and media superstar retains at least a secondary national self-definition.

Indeed, closer contact with the 'foreigner' through global relations has on many occasions not reduced but in fact heightened awareness of, dedication to, and determination to preserve national distinctiveness. The previously described inter-national dynamic – where national identities are constructed through contact with, defence against and exclusion of the outsider – has operated in global as well as territorial space. Encounters in hyperspace can sharpen perceptions of national difference as well as consciousness of cross-national sameness. Moreover, with their removal of the protection of distance, global capital, global governance, global ecology and global communications have often provoked a greater sense of threat to national identity, prompting increased efforts to remove the alien. Thus, for example, recent years have seen considerable tightening of immigration controls and a resurgence of trade protectionism. The 1970s drive for a New International Economic Order centred largely on demands by Third World states for national sovereignty in the face of global capital. Some 150 nationalisations of enterprises took place in these countries in 1974–75.[94] Likewise, the campaign for a New World Information and Communications Order aimed to enhance national control over mass communications and to give a greater national character of the communicated material. In a similar spirit, authorities in China, Malaysia, Saudi Arabia and elsewhere have recently outlawed foreign satellite broadcasts in their respective countries, while other national governments have adopted different technical standards in an effort to repel this invasion.[95] Across the world there have been calls for revitalisation of national languages and native accents against the advance of global English: *inter alia* in the Philippines, India and France. Many parts of Europe have recently experienced a revival of xenophobic nationalism, in the shape of the *Front National* in France, the *Centrum Partij* in the Netherlands, the *Republikaner* in Germany, Zhirinovsky in Russia, Karadecj in Bosnia, and so on.[96] Amongst a wider public, too, steps in the 1990s towards a European Union have often reinvigorated national consciousness. In Denmark, for instance, an electorate fearful of compromising its national identity initially rejected the Maastricht Treaty in spite of urgings to vote *'ja'* from both government and opposition parties, trade unions, and almost the whole of the print and electronic media.

In many quarters, then, there has been a determination to hold onto national identities in spite of – and partly in reaction against – the rise of supraterritoriality and the various alternative constructions of collective affiliations that this reconfiguration of social space has encouraged. Insofar as globalisation has called into question the deeply entrenched nationality concept, it has threatened to deprive most of today's world population of their principal, if often fragile and largely illusory, sense of distinctiveness, group solidarity and self-determination. Not surprisingly, this challenge has met with resistance. Indeed, the more distance has disintegrated, the more some people have tried to make national identity matter. Lost in a world of ambiguous ethnicities, genders, classes and sexualities, many have clung ever more tightly to the apparent certainties of nationhood.

Moreover, a number of the supposedly new collective identities are sooner reconstructions of the nationality principle than a radical departure from it. For example, many ethnic revivals and indigenous peoples' movements have tended to reproduce the inter-national dynamics of nationhood in relation to a smaller territory and population. They might in this light be called 'mininationalisms'.[97] Likewise, regional identities of the kind promoted by European and Pan-African integration projects have had their own – in this case 'macronationalist' – bases of territoriality, inside-outside differentiation, collective self-protection and exclusion of the foreigner. Some contemporary religious resurgence, too, has shown nationalist attributes, witnessed for example in the Sikhist pursuit of Khalistan, the exaggerated American patriotism of the Moral Majority, the Zionism of the Kach Party, the Moro *National* Liberation Front in Mindanao, the Hindu-Indian nationalism of the BJP, and so on. In all such cases, challenges to the content of particular national constructs should not be confused with a departure from the underlying structure of nationhood itself.

In various ways, then, and contrary to the hopeful expectations of cosmopolitans, globalisation has gone hand in hand with various processes of renationalisation. Although globality and nationality have been contradictory in some ways, they have been complementary in others; globalisation has both weakened and reproduced national identities. In this respect Ben Anderson rightly asserts that 'the end of the era of nationalism . . . is not remotely in sight',[98] and it would be mistaken given present circumstances and trends to assume a twenty-first century without nations.[99] Thusfar nationhood has proved to be a (although I do say 'a' rather than 'the' advisedly) central pillar of global as well as territorial constructions of collective identity. On this evidence, a structure of identity can be as resilient as a mode of production. The significance of globalisation therefore lies not in eliminating nationhood, but in complicating the construction of collective identities.

FRAGMENTATION

Taken together, the various trends of homogenisation and heterogenisation, localisation and nationalisation, deterritorialisation and reterritorialisation suggest a further outstanding feature of contemporary constructions of identities that has been encouraged by globalisation, namely, fragmentation. In other words, links might be drawn between the expansion of distanceless social space and growing experiences of a divided or scattered self. In a global human circumstance, where every place can converge on the same place, there is a corresponding increased tendency for multiple identities to converge on the same individual, so that the other may be discovered within the self as well as – perhaps even as much as – outside it.

Such fragmentation is not entirely new to the present moment of globalisation, of course. In earlier times of internationalisation constructions of collective identities were, in practice, often not centred on single nations as completely and unreservedly as the previously cited quotations from Emerson and Niebuhr maintained. For example, intimate contacts between colonisers and colonised induced many experiences of plural and in some ways contradictory identities on both sides of those encounters. Immigrants, too, were frequently torn between original and adopted territorial homelands well before air travel and telephone calls allowed them to 'stay' in their place of birth from a distance.

However, the immediacy of the whole world in contemporary conditions of globalisation has greatly multiplied and intensified experiences of being several selves at once. A normal evening news programme can, in a matter of minutes, emphasise constructions of 'us' as Londoner,

English, British, Anglo-Saxon and European, while the following feature shows may play on religious, sexual and class identities, perhaps all at the same time. A Japanese family in Peru deposits its wealth in US dollars at a Saudi-owned bank located in Switzerland: who are they? A South African citizen of Indian descent works in Hong Kong for a British law firm: who is she? What do we make of prostitutes from Africa lining Tverskaya Street, Moscow, dressed in traditional local costume that hardly any ethnic Russian would today wear? In countless such situations, globalisation has produced hybridisation, thoroughly mixed-up differences, a bundle of sometimes complementary but often also incommensurate collective identities in the same person.

In contemporary global space, then, the self tends to be multidimensional and decentred. Fredric Jameson speaks in this respect of a 'postmodern' condition where 'everyone "represents" several groups all at once'.[100] Inderpal Grewel similarly describes 'scattered hegemonies' amongst multiple subjectivities, while Anthony Smith depicts a global culture 'tied to no place or period... a true melange of disparate components drawn from everywhere and nowhere'.[101] In a word, it often seems unclear what collective identities globalisation is perpetuating or creating.

Instead, the rise of supraterritoriality has on the whole given a more fluid character to constructions of self/other. Amongst those whose lives contain a particularly pronounced global dimension, identity can land in considerable disarray. James Rosenau has spoken in this light of a 'turbulence' of multidirectional shifts in identity and legitimacy sentiments and asserts with DiMuccio that 'instances of supranationalism and subgroupism are outgrowths of the same global dynamics'.[102] Whereas life in territorial arenas has traditionally yielded a more fixed sense of self, globalisation has encouraged 'identity surfing', sliding from identity to identity in borderless realms of unconnectedness.[103] In this sense people often drift in global space even if they remain in the same place. The ultimate fragmentation occurs when, in the vocabulary of some postmodernist analysis, 'location' becomes no more than a moment of social experience, a unique context isolated in time and space, yielding nothing in the way of durable collective solidarity.

Although such postmodernist characterisations appear exaggerated, considerable bewilderment has attended contemporary constructions of identity, in good part owing to globalisation. Supraterritoriality has brought an overall increase of fluidity and perplexity to conceptions of self and collectivity. Multiple identity categories simultaneously impinge on consciousness – race, class, gender, religion, age, family, sexuality, ethnicity, nationality, humanity – each of them increasingly ambiguous both in itself and in its relationships to the others. What is it to be 'Black', 'woman', 'Arab', 'heterosexual', 'Western', etc.? Many can be tempted to reject collective identity labels altogether. Identity is less easily taken for granted, and instead has become a subject of much personal anxiety and public debate. An acute sense pervades of the contingency of identities – of their historical rather than natural character – and of conflicts within, and overlaps and alliances across, identity categories. Identity is much more up for grabs and contested: in speech, dress codes, rituals, artefacts. No longer 'self'-confident, people are on the whole quite lost in the globalising world of the late twentieth century.

RECONSTRUCTING HOME

From the above it is clear that a great deal of interest, discussion, debate and perhaps most of all confusion surrounds constructions of collective identity in the present time of accelerated globalisation. True, challenges to the nationality principle and experiences of multidimensional, ambiguous, fluid, fragmented identities are by no means completely new to the late twentieth century. Nor can these developments be attributed solely to the rise of supraterritoriality and associated changes in the organisation of production, governance, ecology and knowledge. Indeed, the identity problematique arguably has its structurally deepest and historically longest roots in forces of individualism within the overall social complex of modernity. Nevertheless, contemporary globalisation – as a core feature of advanced (some more apocalyptically say 'late') modernity – has had important effects of highlighting, sharpening and complicating questions of self and group solidarity. Since its initial appearances in the middle of the nineteenth century, but most especially during its unprecedented expansion of recent decades, the 'space of flows' has compounded the fragility of nationhood and stimulated the growth of a host of alternative constructions of collective identity. Territorial identities have by no means disappeared in the process, but equally they are no longer obviously supreme, and many have been refashioned.

This situation presents major ethical and political problems for the attainment of community. Together with – and in various ways inseparable from – issues of distributive justice, democracy, biospheric health and security of knowledge, community is one of the sine qua nons of the good society. Yet the achievement of human solidarity – already frequently elusive in the internationalised world – is if anything being further complicated by globalisation.[104] The advent of 'the world as a single place' has not fulfilled, and for the moment offers little prospect of realising, cosmopolitan dreams of a universal human community. The challenge is rather to nurture, amidst intensified diversity, politics of identity which avoid the emphases on opposition, exclusion, hierarchy and violence that have pervaded inter-national relations of the past. In this respect the increased problematisation, through globalisation, of nationhood and identity more generally offers opportunities for new initiatives in community building.

Regrettably, recent history shows myriad failures to deal imaginatively and peacefully with issues of collective identity and solidarity under conditions of globalisation. To date questions concerning a global neighbourhood have received decidedly secondary attention next to those of a global market, global governance and even global ecology. The loss of the apparent simplicities and certainties of territorial place has provoked many a violent encounter, particularly when turbulence in the construction of collective identities has been coupled with pains of global political and economic restructuring (e.g. in the former Soviet bloc). Many have sought to retrieve an (artificial) security of monodimensional, fixed identities in religious cults, tribalism and various essentialist constructions of gender, nation and race. More often than not these shelters have had foundation stones of hate, tightly closed window blinds and firmly sealed doors. Meanwhile others have abandoned notions of collective solidarity altogether, looking only solipsistically inwards in hedonistic consumption and burgeoning 'therapy' industries. In all of these cases the other is denied, cut off and removed.

Such strategies can only come to grief in a global world, where full disconnection from the outsider (however defined) is not in fact an available option. Fortunately, however, others have responded to the global-human circumstance more creatively, for instance, in politics of multiculturality.[105] These initiatives remain in many respects inchoate, problematic and controversial. They can, if conducted uncritically, readily produce abuses of power. Hence the following remarks are informed by acute awareness of the dangers of idealised pluralism. That said, multiculturality offers far more hopeful prospects than xenophobia, racism and gay-bashing. Possible ground rules of multiculturality might be encapsulated in seven R's, namely, of relaxation, recognition, respect, reciprocity, responsibility, restraint and resistance.[106]

In advising *relaxation*, the present outline prescription for multicultural community holds that inhabitants of a globalising world should accept that their collective identities are multifaceted, fluid and liable to radical transformation. The 'space of flows' – in mass media, telecommunications, computer connections and the like – is a realm where religions, nations, classes, genders, races, sexualities, generations and so on continuously overlap and interrelate to produce complex and shifting identities and affiliations. No constructive purpose is served by denying the resulting ambiguity of selfhood and possible transience of collective attachments. 'Multiple identity syndrome' ought not to be treated as a pathology. On the contrary, in social relations with a pronounced supraterritorial aspect efforts to bind collective identities to a fixed place readily breed frustration, desperation and violence. It is therefore better to exchange primordial, biological and otherwise rigid constructions of the self for the maxim that 'identity should always be a process, never an artefact'.[107] Identity is always *en route* rather than *rooted*, and it 'must be continually assumed and immediately called into question'.[108]

A relaxed appreciation of the complex and fluid character of collective identities strengthens a second pillar of multiculturality, namely, *recognition*. This rule entails listening to others and acknowledging their 'otherness' as something more than the not-self. Ignorance and denial of difference have been regrettable and dangerous enough in territorial social relations, but they become all the more deplorably dehumanising with the removal of physical distance between peoples. Global identity politics need to be so conducted that alternative modes of being are not immediately dismissed and/or defined as a threat. In this regard postmodernist calls for a celebration of difference have been long overdue. In the present-day globalising world system, democracy and citizenship should be grounded *inter alia* in rights and duties of recognition.[109] In this spirit, a vocabulary of 'world system' should replace the discourse of 'international relations' in order, amongst other things, to promote an appreciation that self-definition and self-determination can take other-than-national forms.

Recognition is readily linked to a further principle of *respect*. Constructions of collective identity in the modern world system have too often rested on assertions of superiority, where the sense of self-worth has depended on the humiliation of the other, for example, through jingoism, racism, sexism and the like. Multiculturality requires that people have a fundamental right to give their own account of themselves and have room to construct identities and communities without unwanted interventions. The desire to be different is honoured. The strangeness of the other does not *ipso facto* occasion animosity but, certainly as a starting point, generates interest and positive welcome. The foundations of community building in a globalising world are shifted from exclusionary sameness to inclusionary diversity. This is not to endorse politics of 'anything goes', but indicates considerably more readiness to tolerate diversity than has marked prevailing practices of ethnocentrism.

Constructions of collective identity and community undertaken in a spirit of relaxation, recognition and respect will be ripe for a fourth guiding principle, that of *reciprocity*. Cultures have developed by mutual borrowing throughout recorded history, of course.[110] By removing barriers of three-dimensional distance, contemporary global relations have created a greater density of cross-cultural interchange than ever before. This circumstance should be regarded as an opportunity and not solely as a threat. Indeed, if rules of recognition and respect are honoured the element of menace should considerably recede. In a globalised social condition people ought perhaps deliberately to relocate the focus of identity construction from differentiation to meeting point. In this sense Mlinar has spoken of 'the transition from *identity as an island* to *identity as a cross-road*.'[111] Community then arises not from a dual process of homogenisation (often coercive) of the inside and exclusion (often enforced) of the outside, but in a communion of sameness and difference that are in constructive tension with one another. In these post-exclusionary identity politics, where who one is does not depend on erasures of what one isn't, the self is partly discovered in those who were previously described as 'the other'. We cannot have – and should not want – a world without difference, but we can aim for a world without estrangement.

Reduction of alienation can be much advanced by honouring a fifth rule of global community, namely, to extend a sense of *responsibility* to the other. This is not to resurrect hierarchical and paternalistic notions of responsibility of the kind that have underlain liberal imperialism, and parties in need must always retain the right to refuse 'help'. Still, constructive multiculturality rests on an ethic of care, a will on all parts of a world community to advance one another's welfare.

Of course this politics of multiculturality, which has already been actively pursued in some quarters, has not been and will in all likelihood never be free of conflict. Even if all parties in a globalising world were to give full effort to achieving the five R's so far described, difficulties of communication and diverging material interests would remain. At such moments the priority should go to a sixth R of *restraint*, namely, all possible avoidance of violence. Otherwise the phrase 'force is the only language *they* understand'could become the epitaph of a globalised world.[112]

This is not to say that working multiculturality is achieved through the avoidance of confrontation. On the contrary, the achievement of community in a globalising world will at times require *resistance*, in particular opposition to any actions and situations that violate the principles of relaxation, recognition, respect, reciprocity, responsibility and restraint. The challenge in this respect is to conduct resistance in ways that involve the least possible transgression of those other six rules.[113]

Without a doubt the politics of multiculturality just outlined face many difficulties, including in particular the following four. First, the seven principles must be honoured by all if they are to operate effectively. Hence resistance should be directed first of all at cultural imperialists who seek a homogeneous world in their image, at fundamentalists who will hear only one truth, at separatists who pursue the mirage of absolute disengagement, and at nihilists who will follow no rules. Second, the programme offers only the most general guidelines for arbitrating between differences. In specific contexts the parties will need to employ much energy and imagination to create and reinvigorate mutually enriching encounters. Third, participants in multicultural politics must remain constantly alert to power, remembering that identity is always produced in and through power relations. It is far easier to exercise (apparent) 'relaxation', 'recognition', 'respect', 'reciprocity', 'responsibility' and 'restraint' when one occupies a position of strength. There are in this respect dangers that multiculturality becomes a hegemonic ideology, although self-critical reflection (including a readiness to be persuaded by other ethical frameworks) and open discussions about power should reduce these threats. Finally, it cannot be forgotten that the quest for multiculturality takes place in a contemporary world system suffused with capitalist expropriation, democratic deficits, environmental degradation and dogmatic belief – all of which work against its realisation. Hence the project of multicultural community cannot be pursued successfully on its own; emancipation in the realm of identity has to parallel, and be part of, concurrent emancipation in the areas of production, governance, ecology and knowledge.

Notes

1. This chapter derives from parts of the argument elaborated in my *Globalisation: A Critical Introduction* (London, Macmillan, forthcoming). I am grateful for feedback on earlier drafts from Jef Huysmans, Steve Smith, the editors of the present volume and audiences at Case Western Reserve University, Sussex University, the 1994 Annual Conference of the British Inter-

Globalisation and Collective Identities

national Studies Association and the 1995 Annual Convention of the International Studies Association.

2. R. Emerson, *From Empire to Nation: The Rise to Self-Assertion of Asian and African Peoples* (Cambridge, MA, Harvard University Press, 1962 [1960]), pp. 95–6.

3. In case the point needs to be emphasised more explicitly, the present analysis draws a sharp distinction between nationhood (a form of collective identity) and statehood (a form of governance). These two social structures often appear concurrently and have historically exerted many important influences on one another; however, they are not the same thing and should not – as so often happens – be conflated. See further W. Connor, 'Terminological Chaos: A Nation Is a Nation, Is a State, Is an Ethnic Group, Is a . . .', in *Ethnonationalism: The Quest for Understanding* (Princeton, Princeton University Press, 1994), pp. 89–117.

4. J.P. Arnason, 'Nationalism, Globalization and Modernity', in M. Featherstone (ed.), *Global Culture: Nationalism, Globalization and Modernity* (London, Sage, 1990), p. 220.

5. R. Niebuhr, *Moral Man and Immoral Society: A Study in Ethics and Politics* (New York, Scribner, 1932), p. 83.

6. Cf. A.E. Zimmern, *Nationality and Government, With Other War-Time Essays* (London, Chatto and Windus, 1919); A. Cobban, *National Self-Determination* (London, Oxford University Press, 1945); and K.W. Deutsch, *Nationalism and Social Communication: An Inquiry into the Foundations of Nationality* (New York, Wiley, 1953).

7. E.g., W.E.B. DuBois, *Color and Democracy: Colonies and Peace* (New York, Harcourt Brace, 1945).

8. Cf. J.A. Armstrong, *Nations before Nationalism* (Chapel Hill, University of North Carolina Press, 1982); and A.D. Smith, *The Ethnic Origins of Nations* (Oxford, Blackwell, 1986).

9. E.J. Weber, *Peasants into Frenchmen: The Modernization of Rural France 1870–1914* (London, Chatto & Windus, 1977).

10. E.g., C.J.H. Hayes, *The Historical Evolution of Modern Nationalism* (London, Macmillan, 1931); J. Breuilly, *Nationalism and the State* (Manchester, Manchester University Press, 1982); E. Gellner, *Nations and Nationalism* (Oxford, Blackwell, 1983); G.L. Mosse, *Nationalism and Sexuality: Middle-Class Morality and Sexual Norms in Modern Europe* (Madison, University of Wisconsin Press, 1985); B. Anderson, *Imagined Communities: Reflections on the Origin and Spread of Nationalism* (London, Verso, 1991 rev'd edn); and I. Grewel, and C. Kaplan (eds), *Scattered Hegemonies: Postmodernity and Transnational Feminist Practices* (Minneapolis, University of Minnesota Press, 1994).

11. I have developed the following theoretical points in empirical studies of Dutch and Indonesian nationhood: in 'Nederland als object van een globale sociale geschiedschrijving', in D.A. Hellema *et al.* (eds), *Buitenlandse Zaken: Jaarboek voor de geschiedenis van de Nederlandse buitenlandse politiek 1994* (The Hague, SDU Uitgeverij, 1994), pp. 97–110; and 'The International Construction of Indonesian Nationhood, 1930–1950', in H. Antlöv and S. Tönnesson (eds), *Imperial Policy and Southeast Asian Nationalism 1930–1957* (London, Curzon, 1995), pp. 191–226.

12. J.E.E.D. Acton, 'Nationality' [1862], in *Essays on Freedom and Power* (London, Thames & Hudson, 1956), p. 156.
13. R. Jones, 'Earl, Logan and "Indonesia"', *Archipel*, no. 6 (1973), pp. 93–118.
14. M. Howard, 'War and the Nation-State', *Daedalus* (Fall 1979), p. 102 (his emphasis).
15. S. Brucan, *The Dialectic of World Politics* (New York, Free Press, 1978), p. 20.
16. Cited in *The Guardian 2*, 28 July 1993, p. 3.
17. J. Der Derian, *Antidiplomacy: Spies, Terror, Speed, and War* (Oxford, Blackwell, 1992), p. 94.
18. The following section cannot adequately address the many debates surrounding the highly problematic concept of globalisation. I have treated these issues at greater length in 'Beyond the Buzzword: Towards a Critical Theory of Globalisation', in E. Kofman and G. Youngs (eds), *Globalization: Theory and Practice* (London, Pinter, 1996); 'The Future of the States-System: The Globalisation of World Politics?' in J. Baylis and S. Smith, (eds), *The Globalisation of World Politics* (Oxford, Oxford University Press, forthcoming); and *Globalisation: A Critical Introduction*, ch. 1.
19. This felicitous phrase is taken from Roland Robertson. See his *Globalization: Social Theory and Global Culture* (London, Sage, 1992).
20. Ignoring questions of time-space, many in IR have equated 'globalisation' with 'internationalisation'.
21. R.E. Carpente and M. McLuhan (eds), *Explorations in Communication* (Boston, MA, Beacon, 1960), p. xi; and M. McLuhan, and Q. Fiore, *The Medium is the Massage* (London, Allen Lane, 1967), p. 63.
22. M. Castells, *The Informational City: Information Technology, Economic Restructuring, and the Urban-Regional Process* (Oxford, Blackwell, 1989), p. 348; J. Meyrowitz, *No Sense of Place: The Impact of Electronic Media on Social Behavior* (New York, Oxford University Press, 1985), p. ix.
23. M. Benedikt (ed.), *Cyberspace: First Steps* (Cambridge, MA, MIT Press, 1991), p. 1.
24. F. Jameson, 'Postmodernism, Or the Culture of Late Capitalism', *New Left Review*, No. 146 (July/August 1984), p. 83; A. Giddens, *The Consequences of Modernity* (Stanford, Stanford University Press, 1990), p. 64; Der Derian, p. 130; and J.G. Ruggie, 'Territoriality and Beyond: Problematizing Modernity in International Relations', *International Organization*, 47 (Winter 1993), p. 172.
25. K. Marx, *Grundrisse: Foundations of the Critique of Political Economy* (Harmondsworth, Penguin, 1973 [1857–8]), pp. 524, 539.
26. *The Oxford English Dictionary* (Oxford, Clarendon, 1989 2nd edn), vol. VI, p. 582; and O.L. Reiser and B. Davies, *Planetary Democracy: An Introduction to Scientific Humanism and Applied Semantics* (New York, Creative Age Press, 1944), pp. 212, 219.
27. M. Heidegger, 'The Thing' [1950], in *Poetry, Language, Thought* (New York, Harper and Row, 1971), pp. 165–6.
28. W.L. Willkie, *One World* (London, Cassell, 1943).
29. I have elaborated the following qualifications – which I cannot stress too much – in *International Relations of Social Change* (Buckingham, Open University Press, 1993), pp. 32–40; and *Globalisation: A Critical Introduction*, ch. 1.
30. D. Massey, 'A Global Sense of Place', *Marxism Today*, 35 (June 1991), p. 24.

31. E. Mlinar, 'Introduction', in Mlinar (ed.), *Globalization and Territorial Identities* (Aldershot, Avebury, 1992), p. 1 (his emphases).
32. E.g., Featherstone, *Global Culture*; A.D. King (ed.), *Culture, Globalization and the World-System: Contemporary Conditions for the Representation of Identity* (Basingstoke, Macmillan 1991); Mlinar, *Globalization and Territorial Identities*; M. Keith and S. Pile (eds), *Place and the Politics of Identity* (London, Routledge, 1993); and J. Friedman, *Cultural Identity and Global Process* (London, Sage, 1994).
33. M. Zalewski and C. Enloe, 'Questions about Identity', in K. Booth and S. Smith (eds), *International Relations Theory Today* (Cambridge, Polity, 1995), pp. 279–305.
34. H.J. Morgenthau, *Politics among Nations: The Struggle for Power and Peace* (New York, Knopf, 1948). The title ought to read 'politics among *states*'.
35. E.g., R.O. Keohane and J.S. Nye (eds), *Transnational Relations and World Politics* (Cambridge, MA, Harvard University Press, 1972).
36. Reiser and Davies, pp. 39, 201, 205, 219, 225.
37. Cf. W.E. Moore, 'Global Sociology: The World as a Singular System', *American Journal of Sociology*, 71 (March 1966), pp. 475–82; and F. Fukuyama, *The End of History and the Last Man* (London, Hamish Hamilton, 1992).
38. I owe the latter observation, made in a seminar at Cornell University in 1993, to Ben Anderson.
39. Cf. A. Pennycook, *The Cultural Politics of English as an International Language* (Harlow, Longman, 1994).
40. C. Rubenstein, 'The Flying Silver Message Stick: Update 1985–86 on Long Songs Collected 1971–74', *Sarawak Museum Journal*, 42, No. 63 (new series) (1991), pp. 61–157.
41. R.W. Cox, 'Multilateralism and the Democratization of World Order'. Paper for the International Symposium on Sources of Innovation in Multilateralism, Lausanne, 26–28 May 1994, p. 15.
42. Cf. A. Appadurai, 'Disjuncture and Difference in the Global Cultural Economy', *Public Culture*, 2 (Spring 1990), pp. 1–24; and U. Hannerz, *Cultural Complexity: Studies in the Social Organization of Meaning* (New York, Columbia University Press, 1992), ch. 7.
43. Cited in P. Beyer, *Religion and Globalization* (London, Sage, 1994), p. 28 (Robertson's emphasis).
44. Cf. J. Tomlinson, *Cultural Imperialism: A Critical Introduction* (London, Pinter, 1991).
45. D. Webster, 'Coca-Colonization and National Cultures', *Overhere*, 9, no. 2 (1989), p. 73; and 'Nike Inc.: A Global Company' (Beaverton, Nike, 1993), p. 13.
46. L. Abu-Lughod, 'Bedouins, Cassettes and Technologies of Public Culture', *Middle East Report*, No. 159 (July–August 1989), pp. 7–11; T. Dowmunt, 'Introduction', in Dowmunt (ed.), *Channels of Resistance: Global Television and Local Empowerment* (London, BFI/Channel 4, 1993), pp. 8–9; P. Batty, 'Singing the Electric: Aboriginal Television in Australia', in Dowmunt, pp. 106–25; and D.T. Fox, 'Honouring the Treaty: Indigenous Television in Aotearoa', in Dowmunt, pp. 126–37.
47. See *inter alia* F. Wilmer, *The Indigenous Voice in World Politics: Since Time Immemorial* (London, Sage, 1993).

48. I elaborate this point in 'The Future of the States-System', and *Globalisation: A Critical Introduction*, ch. 3.
49. UNPO, *The First Three Years 1991–1994* (The Hague, Unrepresented Nations and Peoples Organization, 1995).
50. R. Boele, *Ogoni: Report of the UNPO Mission to Investigate the Situation of the Ogoni of Nigeria February 17–26, 1995* (The Hague, Unrepresented Nations and Peoples Organization, 1 May 1995); and T. Swithinbank, 'Tribal Leader Faces the Death Penalty in Nigeria', *The Big Issue*, No. 130 (15–21 May 1995), pp. 8, 10.
51. See *inter alia* A. D. Smith, *The Ethnic Revival* (Cambridge, Cambridge University Press, 1981); M. Watson (ed.), *Contemporary Minority Nationalism* (London, Routledge, 1990); and M. H. Halperin and D. J. Scheffer, *Self-Determination in the New World Order* (Washington, DC, Carnegie Endowment for International Peace, 1992).
52. B. Nietschmann, 'The Fourth World: Nations versus States', in G.J. Demko and W.B. Wood (eds), *Reordering the World: Geopolitical Perspectives on the Twenty-First Century* (Boulder, Westview, 1994), pp. 227, 234; and J. Saurin, 'The End of International Relations? The State and International Theory in the Age of Globalisation', in J. MacMillan and A. Linklater (eds), *Boundaries in Question: New Directions in International Relations* (London, Pinter, 1995), p. 247.
53. T.R. Gurr, 'Peoples against States: Ethnopolitical Conflict and the Changing World System', *International Studies Quarterly*, 38 (September 1994), p. 350.
54. R. Strassoldo, 'Globalism and Localism: Theoretical Reflections and Some Evidence', in Mlinar, *Globalization and Territorial Identities*, p. 46.
55. See J.A. Agnew, *Place and Politics: The Geographical Mediation of State and Society* (Boston, MA, Allen and Unwin, 1987); and E.A. Swyngedouw, 'The Heart of the Place: The Resurrection of Locality in an Age of Hyperspace', *Geografiska Annaler*, 71B (1989), pp. 31–42.
56. D. Harvey, 'From Space to Place and Back Again: Reflections on the Condition of Postmodernity', in J. Bird *et al.* (eds), *Mapping the Futures: Local Cultures, Global Change* (London, Routledge, 1993), p. 4.
57. S.G. Jones (ed.), *CyberSociety: Computer-Mediated Communication and Community* (London, Sage, 1994).
58. M.E. Marty and R.S. Appleby (eds), *Fundamentalisms Observed* (Chicago, University of Chicago Press, 1991); and R. Robertson and W.R. Garrett (eds), Religion and Global Order (New York, Paragon House, 1991).
59. B.B. Lawrence, *Defenders of God: The Fundamentalist Revolt against the Modern Age* (New York, Harper & Row, 1989).
60. J. Simpson, *Behind Iranian Lines* (London, Fontana, 1989 [1988]), pp. 29–30; and M.J. Landau, *The Politics of Pan-Islam: Ideology and Organization* (Oxford, Clarendon, 1990), pp. 259–60.
61. J. Esposito (ed.), *The Iranian Revolution: Its Global Impact* (Miami, Florida International University Press, 1990).
62. Beyer, *Religion and Globalization*.
63. M. Juergensmeyer, *The New Cold War? Religious Nationalism Confronts the Secular State* (Berkeley, University of California Press, 1993), p. 5.
64. S.P. Huntington, 'The Clash of Civilizations?' *Foreign Affairs*, 72 (Summer 1993), pp. 22–49.

76 *Globalisation and Collective Identities*

65. L.L. Lorwin, *The International Labor Movement: History, Policies, Outlook* (New York, Harper and Brothers, 1953); and E.H. Carr, *The Bolshevik Revolution 1917–1923, Volume 3* (London, Macmillan, 1953).
66. J. Brecher, and T. Costello, *Global Village or Global Pillage: Economic Reconstruction from the Bottom Up* (Boston, MA: South End, 1994), chs 5–8.
67. S. Strange, *States and Markets* (London, Pinter, 1994 2nd edn), p. 138.
68. Cf. K. van der Pijl, 'The International Level', in T. B. Bottomore (ed.), *The Capitalist Class: An International Study* (New York, Harvester Wheatsheaf, 1989), pp. 237–66; and S. Gill, 'Structural Changes in Multilateralism: The G7 Nexus and the Global Crisis'. Paper for the International Symposium on Sources of Innovation in Multilateralism, Lausanne, 26–28 May 1994.
69. D. Churchill, 'Better Business Options', *Business Life* (March 1995), p. 28.
70. K. Kautsky, 'Ultra-Imperialism' [1914], *New Left Review*, no. 59 (January–February 1970), pp. 45–6.
71. Cf. W.H. McNeill, *The Rise of the West: A History of the Human Community* (Chicago, Chicago University Press, 1963); and M. Bernal, *Black Athena: The Afroasiatic Roots of Classical Civilization* (London, Free Association Books, 1987).
75. Cf. J.W. Dower, *War without Mercy: Race and Power in the Pacific War* (New York, Pantheon, 1986).
73. A. Whittick, *Woman into Citizen: The World Movement Towards the Emancipation of Women in the Twentieth Century* (London, Athenaeum, 1979), ch. 2.
74. C. Bulbeck, *One World Women's Movement* (London, Pluto, 1988), p. 119.
75. V. Woolf, *Three Guineas* (London, Hogarth, 1938), p. 197.
76. H. Pietilä and J. Vickers, *Making Women Matter: The Role of the United Nations* (London, Zed, 1994 rev'd edn).
77. V.S. Peterson and A.S. Runyan, *Global Gender Issues* (Boulder, Westview, 1993).
78. D. Stienstra, *Women's Movements and International Organizations* (Basingstoke, Macmillan, 1994).
79. Bulbeck, p. 153.
80. J. Fornäs, and G. Bolin (eds), *Youth Culture in Late Modernity* (London, Sage, 1995).
81. C. Sturmer, 'MTV's Europe', in Dowmunt, *Channels of Resistance*, pp. 51–2.
82. J. Gough and M. Macnair, *Gay Liberation in the Eighties* (London, Pluto, 1985); B.D. Adam, *The Rise of a Gay and Lesbian Movement* (Boston, MA: Twayne, 1987); M. Cruickshank, *The Gay and Lesbian Liberation Movement* (London: Routledge, 1992); and M. Warner (ed.), *Fear of a Queer Planet: Queer Politics and Social Theory* (Minneapolis, University of Minnesota Press, 1993).
83. P. Flowers, 'My Sexuality Is Me', in E. Healey and A. Mason (eds), *Stonewall 25: The Making of the Lesbian and Gay Community in Britain* (London, Virago, 1994), p. 26; and K. King, 'Local and Global: AIDS Activism and Feminist Theory, *Camera Obscura*, 28 (January 1992), p. 85.
84. Healey and Mason, *Stonewall 25*, p. 10.
85. P. Tatchell, *Europe in the Pink: Lesbian & Gay Equality in the New Europe* (London, GMP, 1992), p. 70; and *Yearbook of International Organizations 1993/1994 Volume I* (Munich, Saur, 1993), p. 1008.

86. J.H.H. Weiler, 'European Union: Democracy without a Demos?' (Brighton, Sussex Papers in International Relations, 1995).
87. Cf. B. Anderson, *Long-Distance Nationalism: World Capitalism and the Rise of Identity Politics* (Amsterdam, Centre for Asian Studies Amsterdam, 1992).
88. Heidegger, p. 165.
89. I treat the assertions in this paragraph at greater length in *Globalisation: A Critical Introduction*, chs 3, 4 and 7.
90. Recall sources cited in note 10.
91. R. Brown, 'Globalization and the End of the National Project', in J. Mac-Millan and A. Linklater (eds), *Boundaries in Question: New Directions in International Relations* (London, Pinter, 1995), pp. 54–68.
92. E.W. Ploman, *Space, Earth and Communication* (Westport, CT, Quorum, 1984), pp. 102–3, 121.
93. R. Jenkins, *Transnational Corporations and Underdevelopment: The Internationalization of Capital and the Third World* (London, Methuen, 1987), pp. 178–80.
94. *Guardian*, 12 March 1994, p. 13; *NRC Handelsblad*, 19 May 1994, p. 4; T. Walker, 'World in a Box', *Financial Times*, 22 December 1994, p. 12; and D. Webster, 'Direct Broadcast Satellites: Proximity, Sovereignty and National Identity', *Foreign Affairs*, 62 (Summer 1984), p. 1172.
95. Cf. G. Ford, *Fascist Europe: The Rise of Racism and Xenophobia* (London, Pluto, 1992).
96. L.L. Snyder, *Global Mininationalisms: Autonomy or Independence* (Westport, CT, Greenwood, 1982).
97. Anderson, *Imagined Communities*, p. 3.
98. Cf. J. Kristeva, 'Open Letter to Harlem Désir' [1990], in *Nations without Nationalism* (New York, Columbia University Press, 1993), p. 50.
99. F. Jameson, *Postmodernism, Or, the Culture of Late Capitalism* (London, Verso, 1991), p. 322.
100. Grewel, 'Introduction', in Grewel and Kaplan, p. 7; and A.D. Smith, 'Towards a Global Culture?' in Featherstone, *Global Culture*, p. 177.
101. J.N. Rosenau, *Turbulence in World Politics: A Theory of Change and Continuity* (Princeton, Princeton University Press, 1990); and R.B.A. DiMuccio and J.N. Rosenau, 'Turbulence and Sovereignty in World Politics: Explaining the Relocation of Legitimacy in the 1990s and Beyond', in Mlinar, *Globalization and Territorial Identities*, pp. 60–76.
102. L. Brock, 'Im Umbruch der Weltpolitik', *Leviathan*, 21, no. 2 (1993), p. 170.
103. Some of the most thoughtful explorations of this problem have been undertaken by Andrew Linklater, e.g., in 'Community, Citizenship and Global Politics', *Oxford International Review*, 4 (Winter 1993), pp. 4–7.
104. Cf. C. Taylor, *et al.*, *Multiculturalism: Examining the Politics of Recognition* (Princeton, Princeton University Press, 1994 rev'd edn).
105. This characterisation takes inspiration from and expands on David Slater's 'three R's' of recognition, respect and reciprocity, described in 'Other Domains of the Global: The Geopolitics of Theory and North/South Relations'. Paper for the conference 'Global Politics: Setting Agendas for the Year 2000', Nottingham Trent University, 25–27 July 1994. I thank Lucy Ford for pressing me to include responsibility in the package.

106. Keith and Pile, p. 30.
107. M. Dillon, 'Asylum-Seeker and Stranger'. Paper delivered at the Annual Convention of the International Studies Association, Chicago, 21–25 February 1995; and J. Gallop, *Feminism and Psychoanalysis: The Daughter's Seduction* (London, Macmillan, 1982), p. xii.
108. Cf A. Touraine, 'Democracy: From a Politics of Citizenship to a Politics of Recognition', in L. Lmaheu (ed.), *Social Movements and Social Classes: New Actors and New Agendas* (London, Sage, 1995).
109. Cf. F. Braudel, *A History of Civilizations* (London, Penguin, 1994 [1963]); and McNeill, *The Rise of the West.*
110. Mlinar, 'Introduction', p. 2 (his emphasis).
111. Cf. R.W. Cox, 'Civilizations: Encounters and Transformations', typescript of a lecture at York University, Toronto, 10 November 1994, p. 32 (his emphasis).
112. I specifically invoke a principle of 'resistance' rather than 'revolution' insofar as the latter has historically so often involved intolerance, unilateralism, imposition and unwarranted violence.

4 Ethnicity: Inside Out or Outside In?

Richard Davies

This chapter argues that the explanatory power of theories of International Relations would benefit not only from a deeper and critical engagement with general issues of collective identification, but particularly from a better understanding of specific concepts like ethnic identity, or ethnicity, which problematise its traditional focus on the state. These identities are not reducible to mere dimensions of domestic politics as they exist within, between, across and even regardless of states, whose activities they both help or hinder. Ethnic identities often generate much greater loyalty than any national identification to which an individual should nominally subscribe.

The need for a greater understanding of ethnicity has been emphasised by numerous events in the post-Cold War period. A brisk survey of the post-Cold War global landscape illustrates the limited number of issues and events which have dominated this period: the break-up of the USSR, civil war in former Yugoslavia, the Gulf War, the carnage of Rwanda and Burundi, regional inter-state integration, fears about international migration, the failure of UN interventions and increasing concern about global environmental degradation. It is instructive that collective identity, and particularly the related phenomena of ethnicity, ethnic nationalism, and ethnic conflict, are central to most of these events, constituting 'the most ubiquitous, explosive, and intractable problem at the end of the twentieth century, and the greatest challenge to the framing of an international order based on justice and parity.' Some observers argue that there has been a worldwide eruption of inter-ethnic conflicts, caused by an 'ethnic revival', as witnessed in Chiapas in Mexico, Sri Lanka, Kurdistan, Quebec, the Spanish Basque Country, and the various conflicts in the former Soviet Union. More tellingly, for each of these high profile struggles there are other long-term conflicts which have continued virtually unnoticed by western analysts, for example in Kashmir, East Timor, and Sudan.

The causes of ethnic conflagrations are diverse and multiple, and often the only factor which these disputes have in common is an apparent ethnic component. Thus, in discussing issues under the rubric of ethnicity, we should be aware that these may specifically relate to cultural difference, inequality of status, self-determination, religion, secession, territorial disputes, minority politics, and even genocide. What is clear, however, is that a mere focus on the state does not provide an adequate framework for the comprehension of issues with an ethnic dimension as the dynamics involved may operate simultaneously both above, below and at the level of the state. This implies that in certain circumstances the state may in fact be much less significant than other actors, if not peripheral. Consequently, there is a need for students of the global to expand the debate and adopt new conceptual tools to understand these developments. Yet while IR has moved towards a pluralist view of the world, little has been written within the discipline on the role and importance of collective identity in global politics.[2] Moreover, in spite of an ever-expanding body of literature on ethnicity within other disciplines, IR works which tackles this area are even rarer.[3]

This chapter then seeks to remedy this apparent deficiency on an introductory basis. The first section begins by discussing a few selected theoretical views on the sources of ethnicity and what constitutes an ethnic group in order to highlight the problem of definition. This is followed by an examination of the distinctions between ethnic groups and nations, and the character of ethnicity. The second section considers a number of roles and functions of ethnic identity, and its relationship with the 'nation-state'. Thereafter the chapter discusses the ways in which ethnicity arises at other levels – the subnational, transnational and global – and provides examples of some of its numerous guises. This provides an opportunity to identify the actors who participate in ethnic politics on the global stage and the implications arising from their participation.

THE CONCEPT OF ETHNICITY

Sources of Ethnicity

It is now widely accepted that human beings have multiple identities which are informed by both their genetic inheritance (sex, appearance and race) and their experience of the social world (language, religion, class, sexuality), although theorists are often at odds over the significance which one should ascribe to each and indeed over the source from which identity is derived. Ethnicity is the condition of belonging to an ethnic group, the sense of ethnic identity felt by the members of an ethnic community It is one of the many aspects of human diversity, and one which 'significantly affects international, intergroup, and interpersonal relations'.[5] The term derives from the Greek ethnos meaning a group or people characterised by common descent and therefore a basic human category in itself as opposed to a subgroup of a larger unit.[6] Therefore, designating ethnic groups as minorities in a given society contradicts this meaning, for if common descent is the defining criterion then an ethnic group may be the dominant element in a state, and indeed transgress state boundaries.

As the chapter by Farrands earlier in this volume has shown, some theorists contend that a hierarchy operates within these multiple identities and that culturally and politically national identification transcends other loyalties. Yet this is to privilege the status of the nation, or more particularly the nation-state, without foundation. Ethnic groups have repeatedly been taken to mean specific minorities or marginal groups in a society, often immigrants with limited political power and suffering socio-economic inequalities, and who are expected to assimilate or continue as 'exotic or troublesome survivals'.[7] Whilst this may sometimes be the case, this presents a partial view of ethnicity. The world system is mainly composed of multi-ethnic societies known as 'nation-states', and ethnicity should be seen as a structural feature of societies affecting all their inhabitants. Structural ethnicity does not imply that it is static in nature because ethnicity is transformed over time by processes of immigration, social reproduction and change, nation-building and national integration. Nevertheless, for those ethnic groups which face institutional discrimination, inequality or separation from group members by externally-imposed territorial borders, ethnicity and ethnic identity may be of greater subjective importance than any sense of 'national' identity. Ethnicity may in fact act as an alternative source of identification in the face of a dominant identity regarded as illegitimate.

Let us consider a selection of views of ethnicity put forward by some of the most distinguished names in this field. Broadly speaking two major sets of approaches have developed which seek to explain the sources, persistence or resurgence of ethnicity. Although these two views may appear mutually exclusive, reflecting wider 'nature versus nurture' debates, one could argue that they are indeed complementary.[9] The first approach is generally referred to as the primordial, which considers ethnicity as stemming from a given division of human beings into ethnic groups in nature and therefore beyond human control: the identity comprising what a person is born with. According to writers such as Isaacs, this 'basic group identity' is a 'ready-made set of endowments and identifications which every individual shares with others from the moment of birth by the chance of the family into which he is born at that given time in that given place'.

This view of ethnicity is often identified with the work of the anthropologist Clifford Geertz, who provided a detailed definition of this approach:

> By a primordial attachment is meant one that stems from the 'givens' or... the assumed 'givens' of social existence: immediate contiguity and kin connection mainly, but beyond them the givenness that stems from being born into a particular religious community, speaking a particular language,... and following particular social practices. These congruities of blood, speech, custom, and so on, are seen to have an ineffable,... overpowering coerciveness in and of themselves. One is bound to one's kinsman, one's neighbor, one's fellow believer, ipso facto, as the result not merely of personal affection, practical necessity, common interest..., but... by virtue of some unaccountable absolute import attributed to the very tie itself.[10]

Such a view disregards factors like the individual's social, economic and political circumstances and suggests an identity not based on a sense of rational interest, but a sense of self based on emotional ties and emanating from natural affinities of kinship and language. The individual is born into an existing extended community and this ascribes the individual with an identity which remains with them and cannot be lost, unlike a class identity. However, it is clear that many groups which have been involved in so called 'primordial' conflicts are not rooted deeply in history, but rather are known to be recent historical creations.[11]

The second group of approaches are variously known as the contextual, circumstantial, or situational. In contrast to primordial approaches, ethnicity is seen as a product of particular economic, political and social conditions. In this view, ethnicity is an adaptive identity which is determined by, or may vary with, the context in which an individual finds himself or herself and thus the attitudes which one has towards a particular set of circumstances. Ethnic identity in this case is voluntaristic rather than an enforced identity.

The situational approach is frequently associated with the anthropologist Fredrik Barth.[12] Barth was aware that boundaries between ethnic groups persisted and that discrete ethnic identities were maintained in spite of groups overlapping and cohabiting with one another, and people moving between groups.[13] He thus rejected the idea that ethnic groups have a permanent and fixed cultural and biological character, and argued that ethnicity is a dynamic form of social organisation. The central factor in this scheme is the maintenance and demarcation of social boundaries across which inter-ethnic relations are conducted and which define a group in relation to other groups. A boundary is taken to mean a vessel which may encompass varying real or symbolic elements at different times – language, history, territoriality, economic factors. The criteria which are used in any reformulation will be dependent upon continually changing objectives and situations faced by the group. The process of maintaining boundaries is not one-sided. Boundaries are constructed through a constant interaction and contrast between 'us' and 'them'. Furthermore, ethnic identity is not only decided by group members themselves, but ascribed by 'outsiders'.

In other situational approaches ethnic groups are considered as alternative forms of social formations to social class, and ethnicity, or ethnic consciousness, is perceived as variable and contingent so that it may, or may not, be articulated in a specific context.[14] In his theory of elite competition, Brass maintains that ethnic communities are created and transformed by particular elites in societies undergoing modernisation, or dramatic social change, through processes often involving competing rival elite groups who represent various religions, native or alien aristocracies, or colonial or imperial groups. Such elites may compete for status and power. These groups adopt distinctive symbols, practices and dialects from a variety of possibilities. Ethnicity is therefore an instrument for mobilising individuals in pursuit of power for the benefit of individual or collective interests. This idea of leaders evoking a sense of ethnicity for their own ends by selectively drawing on a putative ethnic heritage has been explored by other writers.[15]

A.D. Smith views the polarity of the primordial/situational debates as presenting extremes and instead stresses the historical and symbolic-cultural attributes of ethnic identity: An ethnic group is a type of cultural collectivity; one that emphasizes the role of myths of descent and historical memories, and that is recognised by one or more cultural differences like religion, customs or language.[16]

Such a group is historical in that it is a product of historical forces and also because these historical memories are necessary to its continued existence. Smith draws a useful distinction between two forms of ethnic group, ethnic categories and ethnic communities (or ethnie), similar to a classification made by Brass.[17] An ethnic category is a group considered by non-group members, or outsiders, to constitute an objectively distinct cultural-historical grouping, but one which has marginal self-awareness. For example, in the nineteenth century the Slovaks of Carpathia had a common religion and dialect, but had few shared historical memories and no myth of common descent.[18] Conversely, an ethnie is a group distinguishable through objective criteria but is also subjectively conscious of its distinctiveness or is regarded as distinctive by at least some of the group. According to Brass, an ethnie demands recognition as an equal to other such groups. Smith identified six main attributes to distinguish an ethnie: a collective proper name; a myth of common ancestry; shared historical memories; differentiating elements of common culture; an association with a specific 'homeland' and a sense of solidarity within significant sectors of the population.[19] Here, the subjective content is clearly central to the notion of an ethnic group. It is less important that there is any real evidence of shared descent, because 'it is fictive descent and putative ancestry that matters for the sense of ethnic identification'.[20] This approach also indicates two main ways in which ethnies are formed: the amalgamation of separate entities and subdivision into smaller units. To sum up, whilst this approach rejects the primordialists' argument that ethnicity is a 'given', it recognises the need for individuals to know 'who they are' even if this only takes the form of a myth of descent.

Distinguishing Nations and Ethnic Groups

The concepts of ethnic group and nation have been subject to many (mis)interpretations. There are many real and apparent similarities and overlaps between the two concepts. However, given the potential scope for misunderstanding, there is a need for clarification.

In his work on ethnicity and nationality formation, Brass suggested a scale along which levels of social and political consciousness might be measured. He identified three critical points on this scale; ethnic category; ethnic community; and nationality.[21] As we have seen, an *ethnic category* may be distinguished objectively by reference to specific elements. However, the individuals comprising it do not value the group's distinctiveness or pursue political objectives on this basis. If ethnic categories become self-conscious of their distinctiveness and adopt particular symbols to reflect this and distinguish them from others, in order to create internal solidarity, and also demand recognition and equal treatment, they then become *ethnic communities*. If an ethnic community's demands exceed demands for equality of treatment and goes on to demand corporate recognition of the group and self-government, and is successful in attaining these objectives within an existing or new state, then they become a nationality. Brass argues that this process of transformation requires ethnic groups to increasingly infuse objective differences with symbolic and subjective meanings, and for elites to expand the number of attributes which are shared and which distinguish them from others.

Although Smith explicitly rejects primordialism as the basis of ethnicity, he believes that most nations have ethnic cores around which they are formed.[22] Whilst most nations are polyethnic, they are initially constructed around a dominant ethnie which attracts or annexes other groups, and whose myths, memories and territory are adopted. Smith acknowledges the overlap between ethnie and nation, but he is clear that we are dealing with two different historical constructions. A nation is 'a named human population sharing an historic territory, common myths and historical memories, a mass, public culture, a common economy and common legal rights and duties for all members'.[23] The overlaps between Smith's view of ethnie and the nation are immediately apparent, so where do the distinctions lie in this scheme? Ethnies lack several facets of a nation: ethnies do not have be resident in a homeland, whilst a nation's association with a territory must be one of physical possession rather than symbolic or historical; ethnies may not have a common or public culture; ethnies do not need economic unity, a common division of labour, or a common legal code. In spite of the emphasis on ethnic cores, Smith noted that many modern nations have been formed in ex-colonial states without immediate antecedent ethnies. Nevertheless, the centrality of ethnic origins to the nation remains pertinent because it has provided a popular model for nation formation elsewhere. Thus, even where there is no such ethnic core, elites have attempted to create a community of history and culture along similar lines to maintain 'national' survival; that is of the survival of nation-state.

The two views discussed above appear to resolve some problems and yet create others. For example, in his definition Smith includes political, legal and economic dimensions which seem to more aptly describe a nation-state, which is essentially a political community. Yet the idea of nation is 'fundamentally cultural and social...[which] defines and legitimates politics in cultural terms, because the nation is a political community only in so far as it embodies a common culture and a common social will'. We should also be clear that a nation may exist without a state, as in Scotland, and a state may exist without a unified nation, as is the case with the Russian Federation. The Scottish nation also provides a useful example of a nation rooted in diverse ethnic origins, combining Pictish, Celtic, Norse and Anglo-Saxon peoples, yet possessing a strong national identity. It would seem that there is much disagreement on what constitutes a nation , but a tentative distinction may be drawn on the basis of two main models of the nation developed by Kohn. Kohn described these as the Western and the Eastern model.[24]

The Western model of the nation suggests that it is a rationally based entity which has developed from, and upon the basis of, pre-existing absolutist states. For example, France, the United Kingdom (UK) and the United States of America (US). In this conception the nation is an association of people inhabiting a shared historic national territory under common laws and institutions, under which there is legal equality of citizens in a political community and a common mass civic culture. By contrast, the Eastern model views the nation as organic and concerns itself more with a common ethnicity and native folk culture of language, customs and religion. Notable examples argued to conform with this model are found in Germany and across eastern Europe, although it should be stressed that examples approximating both models occur across the globe and no nation will exactly conform to these.

The main differences between these two ideal types is that the former is perceived as voluntaristic with individuals freely committing themselves to the nation, while in the latter the individual has little choice regarding his or her nationality as this is acquired at birth by virtue of a 'community of descent'. It is instructive that in the exemplars of the Western model, the nation was forged through long-term convergence regardless of ethnicity within the framework of the state. This process involved utilising unifying instruments in the shape of a common territory, language, political beliefs, legal and administrative systems, and a central government, so that today nation and state are virtually synonymous. Within the Eastern model the determining criteria of one's nation are to be found in such 'objective' factors as common language, heritage, religion, customs, history and territory, all of which are seen to be quite independent of any state structure. The nations conforming to this type are considered to have developed within the old dynastic empires – Austro-Hungary, Ottoman, and Russian – and the elites purporting to represent them asserted their so-called right to national self-determination during their decline. Thus, these nations are seen to have preceded the state. The political nation-state was built upon this foundation. Clearly the two models are not mutually exclusive; rationalistic 'Western' nations have resorted to adopting similar symbols used by ethnically defined nations in order to develop a sense of belonging. The functional needs of the state also make the adoption of shared languages and religions useful.[25]

The Character of Ethnicity

The character and attributes of ethnicity are aspects which are not often clearly articulated. Like all forms of groups solidarity, ethnicity is neither soley benign nor soley malign, but may combine both elements. The malign aspects of ethnicity are often all too obvious. This chapter has already noted an apparent increase in the number and intensity of ethnic conflicts globally. It is clear from recent events in the former Yugoslavia and elsewhere that one's membership of a particular ethnic group may provide grounds for exploitation, discrimination, oppression or even genocide. The effects of negative stereotyping and oppression against particular groups, or asymmetries in inter-ethnic relationships, may have long term effects on the economic, cultural and psychological welfare of social groups across several generations, creating a permanent underclass and preventing equality of opportunity. The effects of this can be seen from the experiences of those groups who have been affected by irredentism, imperialism, colonialism and slavery, or who have not been able to modernise at the same pace as neighbouring ethnic groups.

Yet out of this same sense of group belonging can come many benign effects. As with other forms of identity, ethnicity provides a sense of belonging and a way of knowing 'who we are'. This enables identification with other individuals of a similar background, something which it can be argued is essential to the security of the individual. This sense of community may be of increasing importance in an age of growing bureaucratisation and impersonal mass societies, and a world of political alienation and isolation.[26] From an ethical perspective, this sense of ethnic identity might only be considered to be benign when it does not impinge on the well-being of others. However, an oppressed group may use its sense of ethnic identity as the basis for political mobilisation against the forces of discrimination in order to agitate for social and political change.

THE ROLES AND IMPLICATIONS OF ETHNIC IDENTITY

Whatever its source, ethnic identities are able to mobilise large numbers of people, evoking high degrees of allegiance and playing important roles at sub-national, national, transnational and global levels. In its many forms ethnicity is utilised as a justification for, or as grounds for opposing various political projects: forced assimilation, genocide, ethnic cleansing, self-determination, secession, irredentism, nation-building, and demands for autonomy and equality. This chapter will now consider a limited number of the guises in which ethnicity appears, identify some of the key actors at the different levels and indicate some of the implications arising from ethnic identification.

The Politics of Recognition

The notion of recognition figures highly in the politics of identity. Ethnic groups often want to be acknowledged as legitimate actors in national and international politics. Such demands for recognition can be articulated in diverse ways and certainly do not have to result in calls for secession from an existing state to create new ethnically-based states, as was the case in the former Yugoslavia. This 'right' of self-determination, according to the 'principle of nationality', reached its peak in the peace settlements post-World War One. Through this process, US President Wilson aimed 'to create a continent neatly divided into coherent territorial states each inhabited by a separate ethnically and linguistically homogeneous population'.[27] The result was a multiplicity of smaller and less viable states, which remained as multi-national as the empires from whence they had arisen. This flawed scheme, and the ensuing pursuit of homogeneity at the expense of minorities, sowed the seeds for future ethnic conflict, expulsions and genocide, and its deadly consequences continue to plague us today. However, we should be clear that the attainment of the goal of self-determination is not necessarily pursued. Many ethnic groups either fail to become nations or make no attempt to become nations. Indeed, given that there are some 5000 distinct ethnic groups worldwide, the idea of each obtaining its own nation-state is highly impractical.[28]

Recognition can take many other important forms. These frequently take the form of calls for limited autonomy and regional self-government, control of education, and power-sharing in federal structures. However, these claims may not be acceptable to dominant groups within a nation-state. In Turkey there is an apparent unwillingness to accept Kurdish claims to autonomy and the right to use their language in public life, even though most Kurds apparently acknowledge the improbability of creating their own state. The failure to provide even limited recognition to groups which perceive this as important to their collective consciousness may lead to open conflict within and across borders, and all its attendant costs and problems.

Interest Group Politics

In states characterised by ethnic heterogeneity, ethnicity often constitutes a major dimension of societal structure which some believe to have greater powers of explanation and mobilisation than other social cleavages such as class. These two dimensions are not in fact mutually exclusive and have been argued to be interrelated.[29] Economic, social and political inequalities persist within and between many states and ethnic groups, causing asymmetries in inter-ethnic power relations and the distribution of privileges, leading to a situation which has been termed as 'internal colonialism'.[30] The position of England relative to the 'Celtic Fringe' of Scotland, Wales and Ireland is an example of this.

Such asymmetries may give rise to violent or non-violent conflict over scarce resources or the perpetuation of a given culturally-based division of labour, access to education or other opportunities, and equal rights. The principal arena for these confrontations tends to be in the institutions of power and governance, and in schools and colleges, as these provide instruments of control as well as high status employment opportunities.[31] In the absence of strong class solidarities, or where ethnicity and class are effectively synonymous, ethnicity may form the basis for mobilisation in the struggle over socio-economic and political objectives. Where inequalities result from ethnic discrimination and also affect material interest, ethnicity provides a cohesive basis for mobilisation because of the power of its subjective attachments.

Provision of Stable Identity in Uncertain Times

In modern psychological thought security, including security of self and collective identity, is understood to be one of a human being's most fundamental needs. In times of major social change or upheaval these identities may be called into question. Geertz drew attention to problems of post-colonial states, which embarked on processes of nation building to create a sense of solidarity and belonging within the confines of a heterogeneous former colonial territory. The populations of these states are faced with a variety of competing loyalties, many of which relate to long standing cultural identities. Thus, where there is disaffection with the construction of new national identities, ethnic or 'tribal' bonds provide a ready made alternative focus which can be made tangible in terms of calls for partition, the annexation of neighbouring territory (irredentism), or merger with kinship groups across the national boundaries. This highlights the potential 'nightmare scenario' of redrawing the sovereign boundaries of states leading to a domino-effect style unravelling of the whole post-colonial structure. The potential for catastrophe has been largely acknowledged and few elites are prepared to take such risks. Nevertheless, ethnicity retains its potency as a focus of identification in the absence of strong and legitimate alternative identities.

This phenomenon is not restricted to the developing world. For immigrants across developed countries adapting to a new way of life can be problematic. Assimilation into the dominant ethnic group in a 'host' country may not be possible due to xenophobia or hostility. This kind of climate may in fact lead to dis-assimilation by groups supposedly once assimilated, but who have become disaffected with the larger group. It has been suggested that this is the case with Mexican-Americans in the US.[32] Identification with ethnic groups stemming from one's own country or region provides a degree of security for those not able, or willing, to assimilate.

Continuing or resurgent ethnic identification may be equally important to indigenous groups as a consequence of social change. A community of language and culture may be perceived as providing certainty, especially to non-dominant groups, when the decline of old regimes gives rise to growing insecurity. Following the fall of communism in Eastern Europe, modern forces of societal integration proved weaker than older, persisting ethnic solidarities in the face of the collapse of economic and political systems in countries throughout the region. Recent bouts of extended recession, fears regarding immigration, and other patterns of social change have given a fillip to the strength of ethnicity as a source of identity in Western Europe too, in a period which has been characterised by a 'snapping of connecting threads'.[33]

In contrast, Rex argues that these developments are part of a wider set of changes:

> The bounding of social life by... nation-states has been superseded by a state of affairs, in which the social relations... tend to have a global, rather than national character. This process is incomplete, and forms of identity appropriate to an earlier stage linger on in conflict with the overall trend, and, moreover, are sometimes reasserted as a form of resistance. The revival of ethnicity... has to be understood in these terms.[34]

However, in spite of such processes of globalisation which are argued to be 'opening up spaces' for individuals to reassess their identities, the nation-state clearly retains certain powers over the politics of identity as this next section illustrates.

The Formation of 'In' and 'Out' Groups

Ethnic groups exist in a spatially divided world whether they constitute a majority or minority. Within the territorial confines of the nation-state, the issue of ethnicity is not merely a matter of self-definition, but something regulated in law through constitutions, and nationality, citizenship and ethnic/race relations laws. The status accorded to individual ethnic groups, or ethnicity as a legitimate form of social organisation, will determine the rights which these groups can claim, the level of opportunities open to them and the resources available to these. Groups may be accorded equal status under the law, but they may also find themselves suffering from institutionalised discrimination.

Some of the differences of interpretation regarding issues of ethnicity and nationality can be illustrated by a simple comparison of two apparently similar developed West European states, the Federal Republic of Germany (FRG) and the UK. In the FRG both German nationality and citizenship are based on ethnicity, or the law of 'blood right' (*ius sanguinis*). By contrast, until the introduction of the British Nationality Act of 1981, British nationality was based primarily on territory (*ius soli*), deriving from birth within the frontiers of the state, adoption, and naturalisation regardless of ethnicity, or through a parent or grandparent born in the UK. However, since the act came into effect in 1983, individuals born to non-British nationals no longer automatically obtain British nationality or citizenship, thereby heralding the limited introduction of ius sanguinis into British law.[35]

The use of nationality laws, and the use of exclusive ethnic criteria particularly, define who can be a member of 'our' nation(-state) and who can be excluded as an 'outsider'. The end of the British Empire has led to substantial changes in the definition of 'British territory' and notions of British nationality, which has become more exclusive and ethnically-defined. Thus, many people who were brought up in the British Empire, and who considered themselves 'British', found themselves labelled with a different political identity in the post-colonial era, making migration to the 'mother country' a difficult prospect. In the FRG, the emphasis on ethnic criteria as the basis of nationality has meant that the supposed descendants of Germans who migrated to eastern Europe several generations ago could claim German nationality on the basis of ancestry, in spite of not speaking German or ever having seen Germany. At the same time, Turkish Gastarbeiter long-resident in the FRG who have contributed to the German economy are as unable as their German-born children to obtain nationality due to these ethnic criteria. Clearly, one ethnic group within the territorial state predominates and is able to define the parameters of national membership. The dominant group has the power to define ethnic groups and dictate their status in the 'national' political, cultural and economic life.

The Multi-level Implications of Ethnicity

In a world divided into a system of nation-states, there are a number of implications arising from the character of ethnicity and the treatment of ethnic group. These can be seen in political relations both within and between states, and at sub-national, national, transnational and global levels. At the subnational and national levels, processes aimed at creating broader regional and national identities from existing ethnic groups tend to stress particular attributes and symbols of identification, which may or may not be common to the individuals perceived to be members of the identity group. The more exclusive these factors become, the greater the likelihood that these attributes and symbols will be the subject of contestation between elites or subgroups, leading to a number of potential scenarios. Firstly, one set of attributes may be accepted as the group norm, and groups deviating from this are assimilated and differences levelled. Secondly, differences which are seen as minor and do not threaten new group norms, such as regional dialects and accents, may be tolerated as residual vestiges of a divergent past. Thirdly, groups which perceive the formation of broader identities as excluding attributes of their own identification may assert themselves and demand recognition, either through local autonomy or calls for separation. Finally, the dominant group may find the existence of anomalies intolerable and embark on a programme of genocide or expulsion ('ethnic cleansing').

Where the process is located within the boundaries of a single state, such problems may be resolved by creating a new administrative structure, or through a process of secession leading to the creation of a new political structure. On the other hand, many groups have failed to identify with newly formed collectivities in nation-building projects, particularly in the post-colonial era, leading to circumstances such as: a long-term disruption of normal life where order is maintained only through a military presence, as in Northern Ireland and Kashmir; a de facto division of the state, as in Sri Lanka, Sudan, and Georgia; a complete break-down of order with a variety of groups in control, as in Somalia, Sierra Leone, and Liberia; popular uprisings, as in Chiapas in Mexico. The potential scenarios are endless and are not restricted to any particular region of the globe. The actual form, severity, and durability of conflicts will depend to a large degree on the underlying reasons for differences, the attitude of significant 'others', and the ability of groups to negotiate and recognise each others'concerns.

However, in many instances where ethnic identity arises as a cause of difference and conflict, it cannot be dismissed as a mere internal issue:

> Significant expressions of ethnic politics are not...confined to domestic affairs.The demands of ethnic groups may spill over state borders; external actors may attempt to intrude into domestic ethnic conflicts; and some ethnic networks may operate as transnational actors within several states, often with scant regard to their governments.[36]

The fact that ethnic groups are not neatly grouped within state territories, but find themselves in majorities and minorities, straddling the boundaries of two or more states, or even in several non-contiguous states, stems largely from the manner in which modern territorial states developed as well as from waves of migration. This has a number of potential transnational and global ramifications. It also implies that we must consider many more actors than the state, and elites when addressing ethnic politics. Esman usefully identifies five 'transnational expressions' of ethnic politics, which will be utilised to illustrate the impact of ethnicity beyond the boundaries of the state. These are irredenta, diaspora, strategic interventions, international organisations and transnational networks.[37] Let us consider how the transnational dimension may arise by building a set of hypothetical scenarios, based on a situation where one particular ethnic group – the 'Yola' – inhabits the territory of two adjoining sovereign states, 'Yolaland' and 'Geatland', along with other ethnic groups. In Yolaland, the Yolas constitute the dominant majority group, whilst in Geatland they are in a minority.

In the first instance, the minority Yolas of Geatland finds themselves politically and culturally oppressed by the majority Geats. The Yola majority leaders in neighbouring Yolaland make common cause and promise to defend the rights of their kin, because of popular agitation for intervention by the Yolaland state. If demands exceed mere moral support and become calls for the incorporation of group members and the territory which they inhabit in Geatland – necessitating a change in state borders – this is termed irredentism (rather than secession which entails part of one state breaking away to form another). Irredentist claims may dissipate, as currently appears to be the case with Russian claims to the Crimea in the Ukraine, but they may also lead to action, such as Hitler's annexation of the Sudetenland from Czechoslovakia, or the Armenian seizure of Nagorno-Karabakh from Azerbaijan. The global potential for irredentist conflicts is immense, given the post-imperial legacy of arbitrarily-drawn state borders which cut across traditional ethnic or tribal homelands in Africa, Asia, and the former Soviet Union, a potential mitigated only by the success of nation-building projects.

An alternative strategy open to the neighbouring Yola majority is to undertake a more measured diplomatic approach and call for restraint and equal treatment of the Yola minority in order to avoid a rapid escalation to conflict. The Hungarian government has recently found itself pressurised by public opinion to support the interests of ethnic Hungarians in neighbouring Slovakia, Romania and Serbia, who have faced curbs to their freedom of expression. However, whilst tensions have been present in inter-state relations, disagreements have been resolved without escalation. As part of a diplomatic effort, the Yola majority could attempt to raise the problems in the neighbouring state with regional or international institutions like the United Nations (UN). Whilst such organisations eschew involvement in the 'internal affairs' of member states, they may be forced to become involved to prevent regional destabilisation, the spreading of conflict or preventing genocide, or in defence of human rights. The UN has been involved in ethnic conflicts in Rwanda, Bosnia, Cyprus, and Palestine, but it has had limited success. However, where particular dominant ethnic groups have used ethnicity as the basis for institutional discrimination, international organisations have been utilised to exclude such states from international activities and make them pariahs. Many observers believe that the international trade and arms embargoes, and bans on sporting and cultural links, helped to bring about an early end to South Africa's system of apartheid. The Russian government has recently made veiled threats regarding the treatment of ethnic Russians in the newly-independent Baltic states, while the European Union (EU) has exerted pressure via the 'carrot and stick' of trade relations, in order to induce them to improve the status of these groups.

The Yolas of Geatland might also be able to draw support from a further significant and organised actor in ethnic politics, the diasporic community. Diaspora are communities composed of individuals of immigrant origin permanently living in a host country, although not fully assimilated through design or exclusion, and who maintain links with their countries of origin. Diaspora tend to organise for cultural or political reasons within the host country, but they are also often able to exercise profound influence in the affairs of the mother country through direct remittances, financial and military support for opposition groups, and propaganda. Certain diaspora – the Chinese in South-East Asia, and Jewish, Irish, and Cuban Americans – are particularly well-established and organised, and have become significant players through their ability to influence the foreign policy of the host country. The Sinn Fein political party in Northern Ireland obtains considerable financial and political support from the powerful Irish-American lobby, and in the post-Communist period several east European diasporic communities have played an important role in transforming their 'homelands'. Many diaspora can be considered truly transnational actors, operating in numerous countries, coordinating their approach towards the country of origin, as well as the activities of multi-national corporations and international institutions. Business, political or criminal networks and organisations which are united by a sense of collective identity and common interest might operate across state borders. Notable examples are the Mafia, the Kurdish Workers' Party, and the various Palestinian groups.

Finally, the Yola might also draw support from 'strategic interventions'. These interventions manifest themselves in two main ways. Firstly, an ethnic group may take advantage of a particularly opportune moment in the global or international situation to follow its own ends, particularly if such an opportunity is unlikely to present itself again. Regional minority ethnic groups have utilised European integration in this fashion, and now have a forum in the shape of the EU's Committee of the Regions. Secondly, some states take advantage of ethnic problems in other states to further or protect their interests, for example by providing assistance to protagonists in conflicts in an attempt to enfeeble or influence other competing states. The long-running rivalry of India and Pakistan provides a good example of such opportunism, as illustrated by previous conflicts in the Punjab, Kashmir, or former East Pakistan (Bangladesh). However, there is potential for disaster in such interventions.

CONCLUSION

This chapter began by suggesting that the explanatory power of theories of International Relations would benefit from an engagement with issues of collective identity, and in particular with the concept of ethnic identity. It argued that this identity was not reducible to domestic politics because its dynamics were played out both above and below, as well as at the level of the state, thereby problematising IR's traditional focus on the state. With an increasing number of actors intruding onto the stage in an increasingly complicated world, this seems an appropriate response. However, the need to adopt this concept is particularly pressing given the apparent proliferation of ethnic conflicts witnessed since the end of the Cold War and the continuing power of ethnicity to mobilise individuals.

In the light of the above, this chapter aimed to provide a limited introduction to an area of study which is highly developed in other social sciences, and which provides a potential source for International Relations researchers to mine towards explicit theorisation. The author is keenly aware that a number of problem areas, such as the sometime conflation of race with ethnicity, have not been raised here due to limits on space. Nevertheless, it is hoped that this exposition has posed many questions and perhaps this will provide a spur for further research. Aside from these limitations, this chapter aspired to show a number of things. Firstly, that ethnicity is highly contested, both as a cross-disciplinary conceptual tool applied to divergent ends, and in terms of its source, notably between 'primordialists' and 'situationists'. Secondly, that there are difficulties involved in drawing a distinction between a nation and ethnic group, a process which by itself has been the subject of detailed discussion.[38] Thirdly, that the character of ethnicity and ethnic identity is not, in spite of the apparent media focus on negative aspects, one sided and indeed that it offers many positive facets to individuals who identify with the ethnic group. Fourthly, that ethnicity appears in many guises and that its implications are not restricted to the domestic realm. Rather, these are located at the subnational, national, transnational and global levels. Moreover, given its presence on the global stage, issues of ethnicity do not only engage the masses and elites of particular states, but also diaspora communities, international institutions, and even – somewhat ironically – other state governments pursuing national interest politics *àla* realism.

Ethnicity and ethnic identity are multi-dimensional and complex notions, but ones which are assuming a renewed importance in an international system characterised by uncertainty, improved communications facilitating continued contacts between diaspora and 'homelands', demands for equal treatment and respect for human rights, increasing awareness of the multi-cultural and multi-ethnic nature of nation-states. Ethnic groups continue to come into contact with one another across the world in numerous important ways. This illustrates the increasing importance of ethnicity as a source of identification. These contacts may result on the one hand in peaceful co-existence in a multi-cultural society, assimilation and integration, the development of dual identities, calls for secession or autonomy, or on the other hand perhaps genocide, domination, or repression. All of these factors have implications for IR, and the more we are able to understand identity and difference, the sooner IR will obtain a greater purchase on the nature and reasons for ethnic conflict. But if this is still seen as insufficient evidence of the legitimacy of ethnicity's claim for consideration, then sceptics should note this comment by Calhoun:

> The discourse of nationalism is inherently international. Claims to nationhood are not just internal claims to social solidarity, common descent... [t]hey are also claims to distinctiveness vis-à-vis other nations, claims to at least some level of autonomy and self-sufficiency, and claims to certain rights within a world system of states... In other words, they share a common external frame of reference.[39]

These sentiments apply equally to ethnic groups. Ethnicity and ethnic identity are not concepts which should be left to political scientists and anthropologists to analyse on a case-by-case basis. The failure of IR to address this area leaves a large hole in its theoretical armoury and, given that future historians may regard it as the badge of the third millennium, IR ignores this most potent of social and political forces at its peril.

Notes

1. A.D. Smith and J. Hutchinson (eds), *Nationalism* (Oxford University Press, 1994) p. 11.
2. O. Waever *et al.,Identity, Migration and the New Security Agenda in Europe* (Pinter, London, 1993).
3. B. Seechtermann, and M. Slann, *The Ethnic Dimension in International Relations* (Praeger, London, 1993).
4. Brass, 'Ethnicity and Nationality Formation', *Ethnicity*, No. 3, 1976, pp. 225–241.
5. A. Bacal, *Ethnicity in the Social Sciences: A View and a Review of the Literature on Ethnicity,* Reprint Paper in Ethnic Relations No. 3, University of Warwick Centre for Research in Ethnic Relations, 1991.
6. W. Connor, *A Nation is a Nation, Is a State, Is an Ethnic Group, Is a ...,* in Smith and Hutchinson (eds), *op. cit.,* pp. 36–46.
7. N. Glazer and D.P. Moynihan (eds), *Ethnicity: Theory and Practice* (Harvard University Press, Cambridge, Mass., 1975) p. 5.
8. *Ibid.,* p.34.
9. A. Bacal, *op. cit.,* pp. 21 – 22.
10. C. Gertz, *Old Societies and New States: The Quest for Modernity in Asia and Africa* (Free Press, New York, 1963) p. 109.

11.   Glazer and Moynihan, *op. cit.*, p. 19.
12.   F. Barth, *Ethnic Groups and Boundaries* (Allen & Unwin, London, 1969).
13.   J. Rex, *Race and Ethnicity* (Open University Press, Milton Keynes, 1986).
14.   P.R. Brass, *op. cit.*, p. 226.
15.   E. Roosens, *Creating Ethnicity*, Sage (London, 1989).
16.   A.D. Smith, *National Identity* (Penguin, Harmondsworth, 1991) p. 120
17.   A.D. Smith, in P.R. Brass, *op. cit.*, pp. 226–7.
18.   A.D. Smith, National Identity, *op. cit.*, p. 21.
19.   A.D. Smith, *loc. cit.*
20.   A.D. Smith, National Identity, *op. cit.*, p. 22.
21.   P.R. Brass, *op. cit.*, pp. 226–227.
22.   P.R. Smith, National Identity, *op. cit.*, p.40.
23.   *Ibid.*, pp. 61–62.
24.   H. Kohn, *The Idea of Nationalism* (Macmillan, London, 1967).
25.   J. Rex, 'Ethnic Identity and the Nation-State: The Political Sociology of Multi-cultural Societies', *Social Identities*, Vol. 1, No. 1, 1995, p. 27.
26.   A. Bacal, *op. cit.*, p. 18.
27.   E. Hobsbawm, *Nations and Nationalism Since 1780: Programme, Myth, Reality* (Canto, Cambridge, 1992) p. 133.
28.   A., *op. cit.*, pp. 33–34.
29.   E. Wallerstein, *The Modern World System* (Academic Press, New York, 1974).
30.   M. Hechter, *Internal Colonialism: The Celtic Fringe in British National Development* (Routledge & Kegan Paul, London, 1975).
31.   P.R. Brass, *op. cit.*, p. 234.
32.   A. Bacal, *op. cit.*, p. 48.
33.   E. Hobsbawm, 'Nationalism and Ethnicity', *Intermedia*, Vol. 20, No. 4–5, 1992, p. 15.
34.   J. Rex, *op. cit.*, 1995, pp. 21–2.
35.   R. Cohen, *Frontiers of Identity: The British and the Others* (Longman, London, 1994) pp. 18–19.
36.   M. Esman, 'Ethnic Actors in International Politics', *Nationalism and Ethnic Politics*, Vol. 1, No. 1, 1995, p. 112.
37.   M. Esman, *op. cit.*
38.   Connor, *op. cit.*
39.   C. Calhoun, 'Nationalism and Ethnicity', *Annual Review of Sociology*, Vol. 19, 1993, pp. 211–39.

5 Gendered Identities in International Relations
Jill Krause

INTRODUCTION

This chapter explores issues of gender and identity in the context of current debates in International Relations. The chapter is divided into three main sections. The first section, state, nation and the logic of identity, sets the discussion of gender and identity in the context of recent critical 'interventions' in International Relations that have come from feminists, critical theorists, postmodern and poststructuralist thinkers. By setting the discussion of gender and identity in this context, it is hoped that the student will see how these issues relate to current theoretical debates in the discipline and so continue a theme found in some of the other contributions to this collection (see, for example, Youngs). To this end, it seeks to challenge the 'orthodoxy' within the discipline, that the nation-state is the only significant source of political identification and allegiance in the world. By focusing on issues of gender and identity, feminist critique reveals the problems of ideological exclusivity in International Relations theory and the processes of exclusion and marginalisation that are involved in the construction of a 'historically specific account of political identity in a spatially bounded community'.[1]

The second section focuses on issues of gender and identity in both national and global contexts. It explores the complex ways in which gender identities are central to the construction of political identities. It begins by suggesting that although gender is a central facet of human identity, it is not an 'essential' or 'natural' characteristic and must be understood both as an aspect of personal identity and in social and political terms. To illustrate how and why, this section draws upon feminist scholarship from other fields of study to show how gender identity shapes and is shaped by nationalist struggles and is central to the construction of the nation as an entity with a distinctive identity.[2] The example of nationalism and the nation is not chosen because this form of collective identity has been privileged in International Relations.

Nor is it to paradoxically reaffirm the centrality of the nation-state in international relations. Rather, the aim is to provide the student with a concrete, familiar and seemingly 'unproblematic' example of collective identity in order to raise a series of questions about the importance of social relations and inequalities of power in the construction of collective identities. However, focusing on issues of gender and identity in this context, also serves a useful purpose in covering what have been traditionally regarded as the central concerns of International Relations, but encourages the student to think about them in a radically different way. It suggests that the student of International Relations also needs to be aware of how gender is central to the construction of the 'inclusive' and 'exclusive' categories which establish rights of citizenship. Having illustrated the complexity of issues of gender, identity and power in the construction of 'the nation', this section then seeks to draw out the implications of the highly problematic nature of identity in the contemporary world. Increasingly, our sense of both personal and collective identity is influenced by a whole range of factors specific to the immediate social and cultural context in which we carry out our day to day activities. However, it is also influenced by the social changes impelled by global economic activity, by transnational ideologies and the powerful ideas and images disseminated by the global media. Issues of gender are important in understanding some of the complex and dynamic linkages between the 'global' and the 'local' and competing claims of collective identities.

The chapter concludes by returning to the theme of the theoretical challenges to International Relations that arise when issues of identity are problematised. It also suggests that International Relations needs to develop new approaches to conceptualise and theorise social relations and power relations in a global age. Focusing on gender and identity leads us to ask rather different questions about the social processes involved in the construction of those 'bounded communities' called nation-states which have so occupied International Relations scholars. However, highlighting gender as a factor in understanding both personal and collective identity further illustrates why the assumption of stable and homogeneous identities which underlies the use of the nation-state as the basis for political identity in International Relations is highly problematic. It suggests that taking the nation-state to be the single irreducible component of identity, disguises the increasingly complex ways in which identities are formed and transformed. The chapter concludes by suggesting that feminist perspectives which are attempting to negotiate the complexities of gender and identity in global perspective are making an important contribution to new ways of understanding the world beyond the territorial and conceptual boundaries of the state and nation.

STATE, NATION AND THE LOGIC OF IDENTITY

Why has International Relations come to see human beings as constituted in 'imagined communities' of nation states? What have been the consequences of taking the nation-state to be the single irreducible component of identity and privileging this particular form of human attachment? Why is the 'international' reduced to relations between sovereign states? How does this process of mapping the discipline 'include' and 'exclude' other expressions of identity? It is because International Relations has been largely concerned with studying aspects of relations between sovereign 'nation-states', that neither issues of identity nor gender have explicitly engaged the attentions of scholars until relatively recently. However, while not explicitly addressed, both have been deeply embedded in both the subject matter and theoretical approaches of the discipline.

Issues of identity, for example, are deeply embedded in a great deal of work on security in International Relations which has been concerned with protecting the distinctive identity of 'human collectivities'.[3] Deeply ingrained in this type of analysis are ideas about the moral worth and distinctive identity of human collectivities called nation-states. The idea of a 'national interest' – a central organising concept in International Relations – relies upon the assumption that our identification with 'the nation' overrides all other dimensions of social and political identification. The 'national interest' is in essence about the preservation of the political expression of the nation – the sovereign state – and defence of the nation from 'foreigners' who threaten its political and territorial integrity and its distinctive identity.

The state-centrism of International Relations is usually attributed to its historical origins. The academic study of International Relations grew out of the experience of war. From the perspective of European elites, the problem of war seemed to be inextricably linked to the existence of nation-states and the unrestrained pursuit of 'national interest'. Early International Relations scholars did not regard the conflation of the 'nation' with the 'state' as problematic because nationalism had been a central force in shaping the European 'state system'. However this practice only served to reinforce the idea that the state was in some way founded on the consent of the governed or the will of the people and therefore invested with a certain moral authority. Since the existence of political communities called nation-states were held to be central to the problem, it seemed that the starting place for the study of international relations was the nature of the state and sovereignty, and its purpose to find ways of accommodating states with competing interests and claims in the 'international realm'. The normative purpose of International Relations came to be seen as encouraging respect for the principles of self-determination, and recognition of the sovereignty of nation-states. Realism – a school of thought that has been so overwhelmingly dominant that it may with justification be described as the orthodoxy – maintains that power is central to relations between states. Realist thought combines many of the themes and insights found in the work of early modern political theorists such as Machiavelli and Hobbes.[4] The state is seen to be essential to political order and stability and also embodies the collective identity of the nation. However, beyond the boundaries of the nation-states lies the 'anarchy' and disorder characteristic of human life in the absence of government, and where the rule of law gives way to the dictum that 'might makes right'.

The first stage in 'mapping' the discipline of International Relations thus resulted in the reduction of human identities to identification with the nation-state. The assumption that the state in some senses embodies the collective identity and will of 'the people' reduces all aspects of social relations which play a role in shaping identities – including violence and conflict, for example – to relations between sovereign-states. However, when attempts are made to theorise relations between states, an additional problem occurs; that of reification. That is, taking the abstract idea of the 'state' and giving it a concrete existence by investing it with an identity. In this way, the state can be conceived of as a *purposive individual*. This idea of state autonomy and 'state as actor' has influenced International Relations more than any other device. It relies wholly upon the assumption that the nation-state can be viewed as the irreducible component of identity. By investing the state with an identity it is possible to suggest that our identities are stable and homogeneous, that we identify first and foremost with the nation-state and that our relations with 'others' are mediated through the state. The notion of the autonomous, sovereign state expresses the need for singular identity as a first stage in theorising relations between states. Employing the device of 'state as actor' thus allows International Relations to draw distinctions between international and national politics. This device reinforces the idea that there are clearly demarcated boundaries between what is 'inside' and what is 'outside' the state. This in

Jill Krause 103

turn allows International Relations to impose a logic of identity on world politics.

International Relations as a Gendered Discourse

Within International Relations, feminism has served as mode of intervention. That is by foregrounding questions of gender and identity, feminist critique has exposed the ideological exclusivity of International Relations theory and highlighted what has been lost, marginalised or excluded in the construction of the 'state as actor'. Feminists are sceptical about the possibility of speaking on behalf of the nation-state because, 'feminism has revealed how few women in any country actually get to make these policies so glibly labelled "national" policies'.[5] However, the problem goes beyond the issue of the degree to which elites are directly representative. Feminists are also concerned about the wider issue of the way in which the imagined community of the nation-state is conceptualised. In this respect feminist theorists echo the criticisms made by postmodern writers and poststructuralist theorists. That is the concept of 'sovereign man' which underpins the idea of an autonomous state is inherently problematic. Feminist readings of International Relations texts have shown how the 'state as actor' has a particularly masculinised identity and draws upon male identified roles as the basis for political identity. This process involves the denial and displacement of the feminised 'other'. The conception of state as actor makes necessary the exclusion of women and female identified values and roles.[6] Feminists critique has also revealed the use of gendered imagery and symbolism in realist theory. The whole conception of the state, autonomy and indeed sovereignty in so far as it supposedly expresses the will of the collectivity contains a specific gender bias.[7]

The origins of this particular masculinist bias are found in the gendered discourse of political theory from which International Relations has borrowed key concepts. It has been argued that the nationalist appeals in Machiavelli's work tapped into particular kind of homo-social bonding and collective masculine identification.[8] Machiavelli's advice to The Prince without traditional authority was to found his rule on the masses; allowing them to bask in the reflected glory of identification with great men. The idea that the individual seeks strength through combination with others and that the state serves as a kind of symbolic substitute for the self has deeply influenced realist thought. However, women were held to be a threat to the political order because the were invested with a sense of other men's honour and so excluded from the political community.[9] Similarly, Hobbes conception of 'sovereign man' depended upon an image of human relationships in an imaginary 'state of nature' that was structurally sexist, denying the historic roles of women as child rearers and bearers.[10] This idea of a 'state of nature' is frequently used in International Relations to describe the condition of human life in the absence of government. However, the state of nature is built upon a conception of 'human nature' that involves a high degree of abstraction. Human beings are abstracted from all social relationships and the state of nature becomes 'a strange world where individuals are grown up before they are born and where wives, sisters and daughters do not exist'.[11] Feminist critiques have been concerned to show how in drawing upon Hobbes for key concepts and ideas, International Relations has become a wholly gendered discourse.[12] However, feminist critiques of Hobbes also have important implications, not only in understanding the ideological exclusivity of International Relations theory, but also in raising important questions about how knowledge of the world is constructed.

Related to the problems of reductionism, reification and gender bias are concerns about the nature of the knowledge claims made about the world. The critique of the conception of 'sovereign man', which is central to feminist and all 'critical' approaches extends to the claims made about the nature of these bounded communities called nation-states and the relationship between those 'inside' to excluded 'others'. For the purposes of theorising, International Relations invests the state as 'purposive individual' with particular characteristics – sovereign man is a rational, choice-making individual who is able to legitimise violence.[13] Sovereign man is in some senses held to embody the 'truth' about International Relations. Discussions about the nature of the state are framed in terms of ideas about power, rationality and the calculation and pursuit of instrumental interests. That is relations between nation-states are couched in the language of modernity, the profoundly gendered language of secular political thought and modern science. In order to understand the world, the idea of sovereign man is placed firmly at the centre of the conceptual universe. In this way sovereign man becomes subject. International relations are understood as relations between him (the state) as the central actor and a series of marginal and displaced 'others'. This raises questions about what other kinds of knowledge and experiences are excluded and marginalised in the process of constructing this particular 'truth'?

Much International Relations theory starts out from the position that the theorist, the subject of knowledge, stands apart from the world, the object of his or her contemplation. The constant separation of the subject and object of knowledge characteristic of positivism is rooted in the scientific rationalism of the seventeenth century. Modern science radically transformed ideas about what constituted knowledge of the world and heralded a new relationship between the 'knower' – the subject and the 'known' – the object – of knowledge. In early modern science knowledge of the world came to be associated with the control of nature. Attempts by theorists to impose categories on the world involved a process whereby the powers of 'reason' were to control and dominate 'nature'. Just as the subject stands apart from the object of knowledge, 'nature' was conceived as that which was 'outside' and separate from the self.[14] Feminists have argued that the powers of reason were held to be essentially 'masculine' characteristics while nature was in turn identified metaphysically with the 'feminine' realm; the tumultuous world of passion and emotion. The construction of knowledge thus involved a process whereby the 'feminine' realm of nature was subjugated by the power of 'masculinised' reason.

International Relations theory that has drawn upon this particular discourse employs masculinist means of 'knowing the world'. The conception of order and anarchy in realist thought is profoundly gendered. The image of the sovereign state-as-subject is juxtapositioned against images of a disorderly and threatening 'state of nature'. identified with the feminised 'other' It has been built upon a model of 'abstract masculinity' characterised by need for singular identity, separation and denial of relatedness. Nancy Hartsock has argued that the construction of the self in opposition to the feminised other who threatens its very existence reverberates throughout the construction of the masculinist world-view and gives rise to a 'barracks community' where masculinity and virility is associated with power, domination and subordination.[15] These gendered connections have profound consequences in terms of how relations with others are conceived. The experience of this mind/body duality which underlies the rationality/irrationality dichotomy lays a series of dualisms characterised by rigid dichotomies; self/other, culture/nature, male/female, national/ international. Like gender, 'nation' is a relational term whose identity derives from its inheritance in a system of differences. The nation is defined in terms of what it opposes.

GENDER AND IDENTITY

However, theories about international relations do not just reflect gender bias. It could be argued that all attempts to construct knowledge of the world inevitably reflect particular standpoints that are marked with respect to gender or class or culture and involve the denial or displacement of other kinds of experience. It could be argued that all attempts to theorise give rise to exclusionary perspectives that assert sovereign claims to shape human identities, construct linear histories and impose social and political boundaries.The model of 'abstract masculinity' which underpins the model of the autonomous state in realism does not in any sense reflect the essential characteristic of all men, but is heavily influenced by other factors like social class and dominant cultural conceptions of masculinity. Furthermore these same conceptions of masculinity only make sense in particular historical contexts. However, opening up the issue of gender, power and knowledge claims is important, because it leads us to ask further questions about why some conceptions of the world are accepted and other rejected and why some knowledge claims are taken seriously while others are dismissed. It also encourages us to take seriously the consequences of inequalities of power relations; not just in the practice of international relations, but also in terms of how that practice is represented. However, once the partial and particular nature of knowledge claims is acknowledged and the patriarchal nature of the state power and the masculinised identity of the state as actor is recognised what more do feminist perspectives contribute to our understanding of issues of identity and power? Feminism can move beyond critique and help us understand the complex ways in which gender identities are central to the construction of political identities.

Gender is one of the most obvious facets of our personal identity. It is clear that in an important sense our view of ourselves, how we relate to others and how we understand our world and our place in it are all coloured by our perception of ourselves and others as gendered individuals. The ways in which we experience gender and the ways in which we come to understand ourselves as gendered is undoubtedly influenced by other factors such as social class or ethnicity which cut across gender historically. While we might identify with a particular ethnic group, or our experience of gender might be influenced by the cultural context in which 'masculinity' and 'femininity' if defined, at the same time, our identification with a particular culture, or our sense of ethnic or national identity is profoundly influenced by gender.

However, gender as a central facet of human identity has to be understood not only in terms of personal identity but also in social and political terms. Ideas about gender have been used historically to justify different and usually unequal treatment between men and women. Thus gender does not just describe the supposedly 'natural' characteristics and social roles appropriate to men and women, but as Catherine MacKinnon has argued, gender is a 'lowering' that is imposed. Our sense of ourselves as gendered individuals is political because it not only gives us a sense of who we are and where we are located within a complex social order, but also our sense of worth and value within that order in relation to others. Feminists have been concerned to show how gender is constituted by the structure of various social institutions, which tie gender into intricate patterns of domination. Gender, therefore, has to be viewed not only in terms of personal identity, but also in terms of power and social relations of inequality. Although gender is socially constructed, ideas about gender are so pervasive and powerful that they come to be seen as 'natural'. Gender identity becomes politically significant when orthodox ideas about gender are challenged by those who have an interest in breaking down the existing gender order.

Taking the example of nationalism and the 'nation' as an expression of collective identity, it is possible to explore the ways in which gender, social relations and power are central to understanding how collective identity is constructed. This is not to suggest that the exploration of gender and identity in the context of International Relations must necessarily be confined to the example of nationalism. However, focusing on gender in this context serves a useful purpose in highlighting the ideological nature of central organising concepts in International Relations theory; most notably the 'national interest'. It also illustrates the ways in which power relations operate in the context of political struggles and influence the ascription of identity. Adopting a feminist perspective both illustrates in concrete ways why the assumption of homogeneous and stable identities is problematic and also opens up questions about the complex influences on the formation of identities.

Gender, Nationalism and Identity

In addressing issues of identity in an 'international' context, Zalewski and Enloe make the observation that identity is not just a question of self-identification. Identities are constructed by others who have a stake in making up certain social categories and in trying to make people conform to them. Therefore, we need to be sensitive to the operation of power in the ascription of identities. The example of the construction of the nation in nationalist ideology, illustrates in concrete terms why power relations are important in the construction of collective identities. Nationalism is based upon the idea that the community of the nation is 'natural', because irrespective of difference, there is a natural bond between members of the national group. However, the 'nation' is not a natural entity but is also constructed. Nationalist consciousness is created by appeals to symbols and imagery. Essential in the process of inculcating a nationalist consciousness is the telling of a particular story about the nation and its history. Feminist scholarship has shown the relevance of gender relations in our understanding of the construction of the nation and shown the significance of women, sexuality and family as symbols in the reproduction of the nation and its boundaries. They have also explored the significance of gendered symbolism and imagery in the story of the nation.

Benedict Anderson's account of nationalism emphasises the importance of kinship.[17] The nation is held to be something to which one is naturally tied. The power of nationalism lies in its appeals to a sense of belonging-of being at 'home'. The association of women with the private domain of the home and family, reinforces the powerful imagery involved in merging the idea of national community with that of the selfless/devoted mother. This automatically triggers the response that one should ultimately be prepared to come to her defence or die for her. The sense of belonging and attachment is actually centred on male bonding As such, it has special affinities for male society and this special affinity for male society legitimises male domination over women.[18] The rhetoric of nationalism is heavily sexualised and gendered. Not only is nationalism couched in terms of 'love of country', but within this image of the nation, women serve as the repository of group identity. National identity is equated with ideas about gender, parentage and skin colour. Women not only bear the burden of being the mothers of the nation, but their bodies may also be used to reproduce the boundaries of the national group, transmit its culture and become; 'the privileged signifiers of national difference'.[19] It is because women embody the symbolic values of chastity and motherhood, that rape in warfare must be seen as a political act through which the aggressor attacks the honour of other men and through this breaks the continuity of the social order which it is women's responsibility to uphold. Women might even constitute the symbolic configuration of the nation. It is not uncommon to find that the nation is depicted as a woman. This deeply ingrained image of the homeland as a female body whose violation by foreigners requires citizens to rush to her defence is a powerful image in nationalist ideology. Its success depends upon the portrayal of women as chaste and dutiful.

Kandiyoti has noted a 'janus faced' quality in nationalist discourse.[20] On the one hand it presents itself as a modern project which challenges traditional cultural and political values and in so doing opens up a degree of fluidity in social relations and transform political identities. By opening up a degree of fluidity in social relations nationalist struggles often create the conditions that allow women to challenge traditional gender roles and create spaces for women to create new identities and imagine new possibilities for themselves. (See Pettiford in his collection.) In so doing, the participation of women is often a direct challenge to the privileged position of men within the social order. On the other hand, nationalism draws upon cultural values drawn from some imagined past. The search for national identity may involve harking back to a national culture destroyed or suppressed by the experience of 'foreign' domination. Thus while nationalism may reconstitute the political order on a radically different basis, women cannot be the total negation of tradition. It falls to women to become the guardians of national culture, indigenous religion and family traditions. These same traditions and values are used to justify imposing particular constraints on women's activities, keeping women within boundaries prescribed by male elites. Kandiyoti claims that 'the vagaries of nationalist discourse are reflected in changing portrayals of women as victims of social backwardness, icons of modernity or the privileged bearers of cultural authenticity'.[21]

The contradictions in nationalist projects might work effectively to limit women's claims to enfranchised citizenship. Historically the integration of women into the modern state has often followed a different trajectory to that of men.[22] Kandiyoti has similarly argued that because national identity is articulated as forms of control over women, to a great extent this can infringe upon their lives as enfranchised citizens. Where women's rights are achieved during struggle, they can always be 'sacrificed on the alter of identity politics' in another time.[23] Women are controlled in different ways in the interests of demarcating identities. Regulations concerning who one can marry and legal status of off-spring are frequently used to reproduce the boundaries of the national community. No nation-state in the world has granted women and men the same privileged access to the resources of the nation-state and claims to nationality frequently depend upon marriage to a male citizen.[24]

Power and the Ascription of Identity

Women as a group are not excluded from the nation in the way that other groups defined by their skin colour or ethnic origin might be. Furthermore, it is clear that women, like men, frequently have a very strong sense of identification with the nation and often actively support nationalist causes. However, feminist scholarship has shown that despite the emphasis on the 'naturalness' and organic unity of the 'national family', groups participate in nationalist struggles for very different reasons. Different social groups participate in national struggles for different reasons; according to their class, gender or even age.[25] Participation may be motivated by a desire to gain access to education, or employment or mobility.[26] Women might participate because they want to promote what Maxine Molyneux has called their practical gender interests. In participating in struggle, women not only desire emancipation from foreign domination, but often implicitly or perhaps explicitly challenge many of those same 'authentic' cultural traditions which have historically legitimised patriarchal relations and the subordination of women.

Thus the experience of struggle often challenges and transforms the very authentic identities it seeks to preserve. The experience of struggle opens up new arrivals, transforms identities and legitimises new roles and new identities.[27] At times of conflict it is not unusual to find that, 'tensions open up between women who find spaces to create new identities and new opportunities for themselves and also some degree of fluidity in social relations unless steps are taken to prevent this'.[28] We need to understand, therefore, the way power relations operate in times of struggle and in consolidating the social and political orders. Political conflicts are often about redefining social reality. At times of great change and transformation whose definition prevails? Existing power relations undoubtedly affect this process. Chatterjee has argued that the relationship between the 'women's question' and nationalism is inherently problematic. Problem arises when one politics is taken over and spoken for by another.[29] When the imagined community of the nation is authorised as the most authentic unit of collective identity, men are often in positions of power and so able to define its meaning. This may even extend to the ways in which women's contribution to nationalist struggle is recorded. As one scholars notes:

> if a man carries food to armed fighters over long distances he is acknowledged as a fighter, while if a woman does it she is 'helping' the man in her natural way of nurturing... even in the hardest times of struggle, women are confined to the kinds of tasks which will not disturb the future social order.[30]

Indeed this might even extend to how the struggle to redefine 'woman's place' is interpreted. It is not unusual to find that women who actively campaign for women's rights are stigmatised and accused of 'betraying the nation'.[31] Gender may be important in shaping the goals of women activists in nationalist struggles but at the same time existing gender relations constrain the possibilities of realising far-reaching changes in the social position of women as a group. Gender relations are deeply embedded in wider power relations. Women's sense of identity and allegiance is also strongly influenced by class and ethnic differences. Furthermore, women's protest must be seen in the context of pre-existing political organisations and socio-economic structures It is precisely because the 'women's question' is kept from achieving its own politicisation that it is easily spoken for by the discourse of nationalism.[32]

Gender and Identity in Global Perspective

The work of feminist scholar in other fields of study provides many insights which are useful to the student of International Relations. The centrality of ideas about gender in the construction of the identity of the national group and the use of women's bodies to demarcate the boundaries between 'insiders' and 'outsiders' is perhaps a starting point for thinking about the powerful social and psycho-sexual processes central to the construction of identities. However, the sources of political mobilisation, do not necessarily coincide with state boundaries (see Davies in this collection). Furthermore, increasingly we are influenced by events happening well away from the immediate context of our day to day lives. At the same time transnational movements and ideologies play a role in shaping social and political identities. In a global age social and political relations are shaped, formed and transformed by global processes. Increasingly, our sense of ourselves as gendered and the social meaning attached to gender is influenced not only by factors specific to our immediate locality, or indigenous culture, but also by global influences.

These same processes are shaping and reshaping identities, changing the nature of global politics and creating the conditions for different forms of political identification and action. The global dimension of gender relations, the ways in which global process influence gender and the significance of gender and identity in understanding the global is now coming to engage the interests of feminist scholars working in international political economy.[33] The expansion of capitalism as an economic and social system to global proportions has transformed social orders and created the conditions for different forms of alliances. This is changing the nature of feminist politics. For example the feminisation of poverty is a global phenomenon and is intimately connected to the wider processes of global economic restructuring. The same processes are producing many and varied sites of resistance. At the same time feminists movements have increasingly recognised the need to view the problems of women in particular localities in global context. Processes of structural adjustment, the reform of GATT and privatisation have all become global gender issues and are being addressed in international forums.[34]

The impact of global forces, transnational movements and ideologies need to be explored in relation to how individuals develop a sense of who they are, their sense of belonging and political allegiance. The impact of global processes, technologies and ideas is, of course, specific. However, while recognising the importance of specificity and difference, feminist theorists interested in addressing global gender issues also wish to explore the degree to which the position of women as social economic and political subjects is transformed by global processes and the ways in which this creates the conditions for feminist politics that addresses global concerns. In the context of globalised inequalities and globalised power relations, questions of gender have assumed a significance in understanding the dynamic between the global, the state and the local and competing claims of collective identification. Rather than taking identification with the nation-state as a given, then, there is a need for International Relations to understand the way identities are formed and mapped into wider symbolic and political identifications and the way 'global processes' – for example, transnational ideologies, global economic restructuring, and the global media and communication industries – influence this process.

CRITICAL THEORIES AND INTERNATIONAL RELATIONS

So where does this take the student of International Relations? Critiques of International Relations do rather raise questions about the 're-constructive' project. That is, if the notion of 'the state as actor' and the nation-state as the irreducible component of identity which underpin 'orthodox' International Relations theory is so inherently problematic, how can we develop ways of understanding the world that avoid the biases and distortions of this 'orthodoxy'? How do we capture the complexities of the world we are trying to understand? Furthermore, what does feminism contribute to the re-constructive project? Our answers to these questions will depend upon our assumptions about the nature of the world we are studying – our ontology – and upon our epistemology; that is our underlying assumptions about the nature and purposes of knowledge.

International Relations scholars who adopt what might broadly be described as 'critical' approaches and perspectives have begun to challenge both the state centric and positivist assumptions of the discipline. In many respects, these 'critical interventions' serve to highlight the problematic character of identity in the contemporary world. Feminists, postmodern and poststructuralist thinkers and critical theorists each in their own distinctive way open up questions of identity in a global context. They are also particularly sensitive of the degree to which new social movements have not only raised new issues, but have also demanded that particular identities, be they youth, feminist, gay, or ethnic be recognised. Feminist theory, critical theory, post structuralist and postmodern thought also have profound implications for how we conceptualise social, economic and power relations in a global context, and for our understanding of forms of identification, attachment and allegiance in the world.

The postmodern thinker argues that we are living in 'postmodern' world and this is challenging and changing many previously taken-for-granted assumptions and 'certainties'. We can no longer safely foreground identity within any particular category be it gender, class, ethnicity, culture, sexual orientation or nationality. Postmodernity is characterised by multiple and changing forms of identification. Many of us experience a great deal of conflict and uncertainty about where our allegiances lie and with who or what we identify. It is then more appropriate to thinks of ourselves as having multiple or hyphenated identities.[35] Identities are not homogeneous, but rather inter-relationships of difference marked by translation and negotiation.[36] Identities can be more usefully understood as inter-relationships of difference that are formed and transformed by both local and global processes, rather than stable and homogeneous. It is for this reason that Walker objects the way International Relations constructs and simultaneously limits and affirms a historically specific account of political identity within a spatially bounded community when truth and meaning are in doubt and forms of identity in question.[37] The postmodern thinkers regards all attempts to theorise and gain knowledge of the world as inevitably giving rise to exclusionary perspectives and argue that the 're-constructive' projects in should be abandoned in favour of a more ambivalent conception of politics that allows more room for the inclusion of people and activities usually excluded.[38]

Feminist are attempting to develop approaches to theorise gender in an inter-national or global context at a time when feminist theory has become particularly sensitive to the degree to which reductionist approaches to theory marginalise or render invisible other experiences. The challenges to feminist theory which have emerged in recent years have centred on the importance of articulating the different experiences of women. The impact of 'globalisation' is uneven and we cannot assume that in any straightforward sense, globalisation is giving birth to a 'global sisterhood'. Recognition of the cross cutting of other divisions, such as social class, race or ethnicity, suggests that feminist theory cannot be built upon simple binary oppositions of 'male' and 'female', but must be sensitive to the complex linkages between different forms of inequality. In the context of feminist theory, this means that analysis must recognise the complex ways in which gender cuts across class and race. Some feminist scholars go so far as to argue that power relations in the contemporary world are so multifaceted and nuanced that they defy simplistic or reductionist forms of analysis and explanation and that 'gender' as a category can be separated from other facets of identity. Furthermore, postmodern, poststructuralist and some feminists warn that power is always implicated in claims to know. Feminist theories do not simply describe reality, but they construct their own 'reality'. The world is seen from a particular point of view which is coloured by the gender of the theorist, but also other factors like class and the cultural context in which it is constructed. This is not to say that these various schools of thought discount or disregard the significance of unequal power relations or the need to develop strategies of resistance, but are equally suspicious of feminist meta-narratives of 'oppression' and 'women's liberation'.

However, other feminist scholars while alive to the complexities of identity and sensitive of the problems of exclusion, are concerned that postmodernism gives few guidelines or signposts to those who are concerned not only to understand the world but to move beyond this initial stage of understanding to suggest ways it can be changed.[39] While not denying that issues of where identity is 'centred' are highly complex, many feminist theorists believe that one should be careful not to prioritise difference over identity, arguing that postmodern thinkers overstate the degree of fluidity in social relations and disregard the degree to which we are involved in forms of social relationship which are inherently unequal and in which some groups of people are consistently privileged at the expense of others. Furthermore, postmodernism and feminist thought influenced by postmodernism cannot provided guidance to how we address some of the most pressing problems facing humankind (see Smith in this collection). The postmodern thinker may recognise that there are multiple readings of the 'text' of international relations, but if these are by implication equally valid do we have any grounds for challenging the status quo and changing aspects of our world that we find unacceptable? This is a particularly important consideration for feminists because historically feminist theory has defined its purpose not only in terms of making women's lives visible and allowing their voices to be heard, but also in suggesting ways in which oppressive relations based upon the social significance assigned to gender can be transformed. Critical theory and many schools of feminisms share the desire to reconstruct International Relations theory in the spirit of its original emancipatory project. In this respect both are closer to the Marxist understanding of the purpose of theory; that is that the point in trying to understand the world is to change it. Some schools of feminist theory and critical theory reaffirm the normative concerns of international theory in that they raise questions about justice, inequality and power. At the same time they are alive to the problems of gender, class and cultural bias.

It is undoubtedly the case that 'identity construction can be contradictory and these contradictions can be hard to live with'.[40] At the same time because gender is central in shaping our understanding of the world and our relationship to others, the validity of specifically feminist theory cannot be denied. Therefore, feminists have been attracted to some schools of thought that ground the hitherto rather abstract activety of theorising in the concrete experiences of everyday life. So called 'standpoint' theories are often held to be an attempt to reaffirm some kind of 'essential' or 'authentic' experience to serve as the grounds of knowledge claims. However, it is possible to recognise that thought is conditioned by experiences specific to a particular historical and social location, but nevertheless maintain that knowledge can be constructed from this same historical and social location. In this way a standpoint is not so much an attempt to reaffirm a kind of essential identity, but rather a point of departure. Feminist standpoints can then be used strategically to address directly questions of exclusion and used to intervene and subvert dominant conceptions of 'reality' in much the same way that this chapter has used gender as a specific example in order to challenge the biases and distortion of orthodox International Relations theory. However, a standpoint can also form the basis from which to begin the search for common ground. This requires reflexive theories that help us make sense of ourselves and the complex ways in which our identities are formed and mapped. Such an approach opens up the possibilities of conversation. We can only know from our own standpoint, but 'this involves us thinking about who we are not, about our identity and difference'.[41] Such an approach recognises the multiplicity of experiences, but is distinct from a postmodern relativism. The commitment to conversation is based on a radically different understanding of the purpose of human knowledge and understanding. It reaffirms the normative nature of theory and echoes the central insight of post-Marxist critical theory that the purpose of knowledge is to serve a human interest in emancipation. Undoubtedly, the quest for more theoretical inclusivity opens up many more difficult questions and issues. However, at the same time the study of the complex systems of 'inclusion' and 'exclusion' that have in a sense always been the central concern of the student of International Relations remain as relevant and important as ever.[42]

Notes

1. R.J.B. Walker, 'Gender and Critique in the Theory of International Relations' in V.S. Peterson and A.S. Runyan, *Gendered States; Feminist (Re) Visions of International Theory* (Boulder Colorado: Lynne Rienner Publications, 1992 p. 180).
2. There are obvious dangers in attempting to draw general conclusions from such a diverse range of sources and empirical studies. However, feminist scholarship in these areas is useful in highlighting the more general issues about power relations and the ascription of identity relevant here.
3. B. Buzan, *People, States and Fear, An Agenda for International Security Studies in the Post-Cold War Era* (Hemel Hempstead: Harvester Wheatsheaf, 1991).
4. See for example, A.J.R. Groom and W. Olson, *International Relations Then and Now; Origins and Trends in Interpretation* (London: HarperCollins, 1991).
5. C. Enloe and M. Zalewski, 'Questions of Identity' in K. Booth and S. Smith, *International Relations Theory Today* (Cambridge: Polity Press, 1995, p. 281).
6. R. Grant, in R. Grant and K. Newland, *Gender and International Relations* (Milton Keynes: Open University Press, 1990).
7. J. Krause, 'Power, Autonomy and Gender in Realist Thought' in F. Pfetsch, *International Relations and Pan-Europe* (Hamburg: Lit Verlag, 1993).
8. H.F. Pitkin, *Fortune is a Woman: Gender and Politics in the Thought of Niccolo Machiavelli* (Berkeley: Berkeley University Press, 1986).
9. *Ibid.*
10. N. Hirschmann, *Rethinking Obligation; A Feminist Method for Political Theory* (London: Cornell University Press, 1992).
11. S. Benhabib, 'The Generalised and Concrete Other; The Kohlberg-Gilligan Controversy and Feminist Theory', in S. Benhabib and D. Cornell, *Feminism as Critique* (Oxford: Polity Press, 1986):
12. See A.S. Runyan, 'The 'State' of Nature: A Garden Unit for Women and Other Living Things', in V.S. Peterson and A.S. Runyan, *op. cit.* for a fuller discussion.
13. R. Ashley, 'Living on Borderlines; Man, Poststructuralism and War', in J. Der Derian and M. Shapiro, *International /Intertextual Relations; Postmodern Readings of World Politics* (Lexington, MA: Lexington Books, 1989).

14. C. Navari, 'Knowledge, The State and the State of Nature' in M. Donelan, *The Reason of States* (London: Allen & Unwin, 1978).
15. N. Hartsock, 'The Barracks Community in Western Political Thought', *The Women Studies International Forum*, Vol 5. No. 3/4 1982.
16. C. Enloe and M. Zalewski, *op. cit.*, p. 288.
17. B. Anderson, *Imagined Communities* (London: Verso Books, 1983).
18. A. Parker *et al.*, *Nationalisms and Sexulaities* (London: Routledge, 1992).
19. Kandiyoti, D., 'Identity and its Discontents; Women and the Nation', *The Millennium Journal of International Studies*, 20.3. 1992. p. 429.
20. *Ibid.*
21. *Ibid.*, p. 429.
22. *Ibid.*, p. 435.
24. See discussion in Parker *et al.*, *op. cit.* p. 6.
25. N.J. Kriger, *Zimbabwe's Guerilla War; Peasant Voices* (Cambridge: Cambridge University Press, 1992).
26. *Ibid.*
27. R. Ridd and H. Callaway, *Caught Up in Conflict* (New York: New York University Press, 1987).
28. *Ibid.*, p. 45.
29. P. Chatterjee, 'Whose Imagined Communities?', *The Millennium Journal of International Studies*, Vol. 20, No. 3, 1991.
30. M.A. Helie-Lucas, in E. Isaakson, *Women in the Military System* (Brighton: Harvester Wheatsheaf, 1988).
31. *Ibid.*, p. 127
32. Chatterjee, *op. cit.*
33. Krause, J. 'The International Diensions of Gender Inequality and Feminist Politics; A "New Direction" for International Political Economy?', in A. Linklater and J. Macmillan (eds), *Boundaries in Question: New Directions in International Relations* (London: Pinter, 1995).
34. J. Krause, 'Gender in Global Perpective' in E. Kofman and G. Youngs (eds), *Globalisation; Theory and Practice* (London: Pinter, 1996).
35. See C. Sylvester, *International Relations and Feminist Theory in a Postmodern Age* (Cambridge: Cambridge University Press, 1993).
36. J. Rutherford, *Identity, Community, Culture and Difference* (London: Lawrence & Wishart, 1990).
37. R.J.B. Walker, *Inside/Outside; International Relations as Political Theory,* (Cambridge: Cambride University Press, 1993).
38. *Ibid.*
39. I would view my own work in this vein. See also Sandra Whitworth, *Feminist Theory and International Relations* (Basingstoke: Macmillan, 1995).
40. Zalewski and Enloe, *op. cit.*, p. 288.
41. K. Hutchins, 'The Personal is International; Feminist Epistemology and the Case of International Relations', conference paper, *The British International Studies Association* (University of Warwick, 1991).
42. The argument that the central concern of International Relations is essentially systems of 'inclusion' and 'exclusion' is made by Andrew Linklater in 'The Question of the Next Stage in IR Theory; A Critical Theoretical Point of View', *The Millennium Journal of International Studies*, Vol. 21., No. 1, 1992.

6 Nationalism and Middle Eastern Identities
Margaret Law

INTRODUCTION

This chapter reflects the overall intellectual direction of the book, illustrating its main arguments. It shows how identities in the Middle East have evolved in their *specific* historical context. It shows how globalisation structures and the concomitant increase in communications and other external processes have affected identity formation, reproduction and transformation. Circumstances which are to a certain extent unique in the area, or are at least found in a uniquely intense form there, have created a situation where identities are less homogenous, more 'overlapping', more psychologically conflictual and more fluid than almost anywhere else in the world. The chapter will look at the complex nature of identity formation in the region, a process which Simon Bromley[1] has said has led to a social structure in the area that takes the form of a 'mosaic'. The foci of primary loyalties in the area bring into question the fundamental assumptions of traditional international relations surrounding the centrality of the state and the relationship between state society and 'the international'.

IDENTITIES IN TRADITIONAL ARAB SOCIETY

In traditional Arab society, the most important loyalty belonged to the group or tribe. At the same time, for the majority of inhabitants (those who held Islamic beliefs) there was also an understanding of living together in a community of believers (the Umma) under God to whom they owed ultimate loyalty.[2] These identities historically complemented rather than contradicted each other. The central tenets of Islamic belief such as the brotherhood of believers and the importance of love and of charity were reinforced at local level by tribal associations and practices. At the same time there were outward manifestations of the recognition of the all-embracing nature of God's community. Secular concepts such as nations and nationalism familiar in the West, were

118

terms which were strange to Arabic society prior to European colonialism. The Western ideology of nationalism, at least in its modern form, is divisive not only in the sense that its emphasis is on separation and difference from those who are not considered to be part of the nation, but also in the sense of the separation between the realms of the secular and the religious. Islam on the other hand, emphasises the sense of community, both in the sense of the uniting of peoples and in its pervasiveness into every aspect of life.

Some would go further than this to assert the difference between Western and Islamic societies' conception of social structure, and would argue that Islam is incompatible with secular nationalism and with representative government.[3] Others such as Esposito[4] have shown that there is in fact no such homogeneity and in practice there is a diversity among Islamic groups regarding their political goals. There has in the main been at least a degree of accommodation to the notion of the nation state. At this stage it is necessary merely to note that the Western notion of the state is one which was new to the Islamic experience, although there is a rich and distinctive Islamic political tradition.

THE COLONIAL EXPERIENCE

Through the process of colonisation and decolonisation, Europeans divided their empires into states.[5] Europeans not only imposed their rule territorially, but also in terms of their organisation of society, superimposing Western political forms on societies which as stated earlier, had different primary foci of loyalty. Therefore Middle Eastern states *as states* were largely foreign constructions based on the identity of the metropole and forged by administrative convenience. They rarely respected natural territorial boundaries (in terms of, for example, ethnicity) which were often broader or more locally confined than the imposed borders. They were also administered largely by foreign officials.

For the inhabitants, therefore, there was a change in the way in which society was organised, and in terms of its focus. In the process, there were gradual semantic changes, so that the meaning of the word 'Umma' for example, (traditionally the entire religious community), gradually changed to mean the nation state.[6] These changes can be seen as a deliberate attempt by the imperial powers not only to control large parts of the area directly but also as a means of imposing Western ideas.

Modern Middle Eastern states rapidly came to seem like modern European states, in that they had distinctively modern ways of organising

the societies they controlled in terms of political and economic structures. In order to participate in an international system organised by
the West, they had to adopt Western political forms. Most did not do
this until the 1930s. The exception was the Ottoman Empire in the 17th
and 18th centuries, which despite its distinctively Turkish diplomatic system, participated in the European international system. Following military defeats,[7] Turkey lost its significance in international diplomacy and
also ceased to be a convincing role model for other states in the region.
But if states had the seeming appearance of the western model, they
retained important aspects of their traditional society, and developed
the characteristics of a 'post-colonial' or 'subaltern' culture, half dependent on the original colonial power, and half struggling for an independence which they were unable to create free from their heritage of
western dominance.

The pattern of intense state building in the area during the colonial
period can be illustrated by the case of Iran. Whilst during the First
World War, Iran had virtually disintegrated as a political entity, the Anglo
American Treaty of 1919 gave Britain virtual control over Iranian military
and financial resources. It also led to the establishment of a strong central government with a relatively effective set of institutions. Unfortunately for the imperial powers it also provided the platform for Iranian
nationalism directed against them.[8]

NATIONALISM AT THE END OF THE COLONIAL PERIOD

Whilst nationalism is perceived to be a European ideology, mobilised by
Europeans or European educated elites as a form of modernised politics,
it became of course the channel through which political protests against
imperial power could be articulated. In other words, embryonic nationalist movements had to work within the framework of ideas, discursive
practice and institutions which were available to them. Political protest
was thus articulated in a specifically 'Western' way, existing units of association adapting to be better placed to exert influence on the Western
style government structures in place, or new organisations forming as
pressure groups and protest movements from scratch.[9]

Importantly, Middle Eastern states were not only modernising in
terms of political form, but also as a result of the colonial experience,
through accelerated interactions with the global economy. In the First
World War, external economic pressures accelerated the emergence of
an urbanised middle class and a concentration of wealth in ways which

fed new divisions in society. New technologies and new trade patterns fostered by colonial powers between the wars promoted new industries and a further intrusion on the established merchant classes of industrial capitalism. These trends in economic structure and social organisation were intensified during the second world war. For example, between 1942 and 1946 the Middle East was treated as a single economic unit by the British, American and French military systems. This had contradictory implications for identity formation at the time and in later years. On the one hand, the region became increasingly linked to global, interdependent patterns of culture and ideas, including education and consumerism, which evoked reactions and support in equal measure across the region. On the other hand, inequalities of economic position and access to knowledge and social power increased. Resentment against the colonial powers and against those who associated with them increased with those increased inequalities, while social power was redistributed as the class system evolved. As the social conflicts in Algeria have suggested, a nationalist middle class which emerged on independence after 1945 has, a generation after it won power, found itself imagined and defined as a cultural colonial force in the face of the disadvantaged and the excluded, who have developed political and social protest movements based on Islam and the popular economic nationalism of the Islamic Salvation Front (FIS).

POST-COLONIAL STATE BUILDING

After independence, rulers aimed at and achieved much the same effect of directing allegiance and loyalty towards the centralised state. In other words, the territorial state which was inherited from the colonial powers provided the context in which attempts to administer the population and nation-building projects were undertaken. This determination to build a strong centralised state was partly because of the perceived equation of Westernisation and modernity, partly because of the need to maintain external security, and partly as a means of consolidating domestic societal control and to resist coup attempts. The dividing effect of the securing of external borders had the effect of redirecting loyalty towards the centre.[10] This was enhanced by rulers through the creation of authoritarian systems which gave individual rulers enormous domestic power, for example, Assad in Syria and Nasser in Egypt.

It was also perceived however, that in order to maintain the support of domestic populations, rulers must legitimate their regimes by being seen to extend social and economic provision for the people, especially as the private sector was perceived by many to be inadequately providing for societal needs in the early days of independence. Nationalist parties had often fiercely criticised the economic policies of the colonial powers for their failure either to develop the economy, or to provide social welfare programmes. Domestic economic and social needs were sometimes provided for, without necessarily extending political rights, as for example in Saudi Arabia.[11] The failure of post-independence regimes to meet the material needs of their peoples rapidly enough simply repeated the perceived failures of the former colonial rulers and led to domestic instability and sometimes to a loss of power. Coups were successful in Syria in 1949 and Egypt in 1952.

There was, therefore, the desire to use the extensive state apparatus to promote programmes of social welfare and economic development. As Dawisha argues, it 'placed in the hands of the rulers, methods of social and coercive suppression that made earlier means of... control pale into insignificance... A two-pronged maxim was followed: put fear in peoples' hearts, but also try to win their support no matter how grudgingly given.'[12] It is a paradox that sometimes the impetus for Arab unity, to be discussed later in the chapter, itself accelerated the state building process, as during the union of Syria and Egypt 1958–61. Nasser the leading partner in the union, desired that Syria build up its state apparatus.

For ordinary Middle East citizens this meant that they met with the state machinery in many aspects of daily life. For example, in many Middle Eastern states there was a huge expansion of state controlled police and security networks and educational programmes. In Egypt, the number of young people in all types of education rose from 1 900 000 in 1953/4 to 4 500 000 in 1965/6.[13]

As stated earlier, this state-building process occurred in the region at a time of rapid change, especially in terms of the transformation of the economy which itself provided an impetus for the development of the state machinery. Middle Eastern leaders saw the creation of an industrial base and the expansion of international trade as essential to the process of modernisation. Although they promulgated anti-imperialist rhetoric against the West, regimes seemed to emulate their declared enemies in terms of how they perceived the scope for the realisation of economic modernisation.

These processes were intensified in some states, notably in Egypt under Nasser from 1952 onwards. Nasser initiated extensive programmes of economic development (for example the decision to build the Aswan High Dam), and of social welfare. The labour intensity of such projects under state control served both to extend the state machinery itself and to increase the number of people working within it. This was also as a result of a revolution in agriculture which reduced the number of people working on the land. These factors led to the detachment of large numbers of the population from old communities and the psychological attachments to that community. It also led to their participation in new types of both urban economic and urban political activity. It succeeded in fostering a new kind of loyalty to the state. This group formed a new middle class elite especially in Nasserite Egypt. Along with new associations and new foci of loyalty there developed a new recognition of concepts such as the rights of citizenship and political representation, although they were much less often realised in practice.

New regimes consolidated control in a number of ways. For example, in rural areas in Egypt the state instituted new organisations at local level in which government officials instructed local farmers about methods in agriculture and marketing. This experience in Egypt was similar to that of Turkey earlier in the century, where local groups in the fields of business, commerce and labour were segregated from each other and closely supervised by the state, ensuring the state's key function as a social and political focal point through which social exchanges had to operate. It thereby maintained its visibility and power.[14]

Furthermore what could be seen as the attempt to re-create more assertive local associations can also be seen as acceptance that attempts to change perceived wrongs in society would now only be successful through the newly created channels of centralised power within the framework of the state. Thus in Egypt professional associations were brought under state control in such a way that the definition of the part they were to play in the modernisation process was in the hands of the regime.[15] In this way the state asserted control both from above and below.

Although this new state-focused politics had secular origins, in religious matters rulers generally held to Islam, and saw it as a support for the legitimacy of the regime. In Jordan, King Hussein has continued to use his descent from the prophet Mohammed to legitimate his personal power. All however, either explicitly or implicitly asserted the primacy of the realm of the political over that of the religious.[16] For example, the clergy were paid official salaries and so were brought under state influence: secular educational and legal systems were promoted, challenging the previous religious monopoly of those systems. Some regimes went further and made the membership of independent religious parties and movements such as the Muslim Brotherhood illegal.[17] Islam therefore did not provide a significant obstacle to the consolidation of the rule of the state, although in other examples, especially Saudi Arabia and the Gulf states, it provided a valuable instrument for state building and social control.

POST-COLONIAL IDENTITIES

However, whilst forces of modernity and the type of intense state building which was typical of the Middle East would seem to be instrumental in the focusing of loyalty towards the state, making the state the primary focus of identity, the structures which we usually associated with modernity were themselves developed in the context of economic, cultural and social globalisation. This allowed for the development of economic interdependence, the spread of printing and newspapers, broadcasting stations, films and foreign travel. New patterns of work and leisure affected, albeit in different ways, all classes and groups in society. These processes set the framework for a reinforcement of a common Arab identity, Arabism, which had the capacity to transcend the new political boundaries. This was aided by the growth in literacy during this century, and by the adoption of a simple grammatical Arabic which became uniform in all Arab countries.[18] Modernisation, globalisation and economic interdependence led to an increase in interaction between states, but also to an increase in the interaction of populations across state boundaries. This made possible the recognition and assertion of different levels of identity and ultimately to the possibility of conflict between them.

State formation was thus taking place in a period when people were being invited to imagine themselves as members of different communities. Some of these were based on culture or language such as one of the pan-Arabic movements. Some were based on religion, for example the wider Umma or a localised religious group. Middle Eastern Islam provides examples of a wide diversity of religious and spiritual practice beyond the conventional distinction of Sunni and Shia, which shape affiliations and social groupings as well as levels of personal and group commitment. Yet others were still based around the clan or family, which remains a compelling structure of socio-economic and cultural organisation, and a key basis for political action, as the clan bases of civil war in Lebanon and Mauretania demonstrate.

Currently the most common reason given for the failure of development of a territorially defined national consciousness in the region is Islam. Some argue that it has been the attempted relegation of Islam to the sidelines in some states accompanied by lack of material progress which has led to popular disaffection with the state and to the Islamic revival from the 1970s to the present day.[19] This issue is beyond the intended scope of this chapter. In the 1950s and 1960s the reason for this lack of 'national' feeling in the Western sense was ascribed to Arab Nationalism,[20] but in the light of experience since then we can conclude the process is considerably more complex and its causes more multi-layered.

SPECIFIC FORMS OF PAN-ARAB NATIONALISM

Historically and contemporarily, there are various types of pan- Arabism. These range from those who share a sense of common history and therefore a degree of fraternity leading to a desire to co-operate in various ways to those who believe that only the uniting of all Arabs under a single Government will bring the necessary political strength to establish the Arab world in their rightful global position. Whilst Islamic and Arabic societies were weaker and poorer than those in the West, some exponents of political pan-Arabism considered and consider themselves to be in some way superior to Western societies by virtue of the fact that the Prophet was an Arab, came from an Arabic environment and that the revelation was in the Arabic language.[21] Political unity has been seen by some such pan-Arabic movements as the necessary precursor to the full assertion of that superiority.

Aspirations for pan-Arabic unity in the political sense began to be articulated in the 1920s and 1930s and were therefore historically located and developed in a period of enormous social and economic change. The drive for unity was expressed in terms of common historical experiences, common culture and common language. Opportunities for the expression of such aspirations were intensified not only by the process of increased globalisation referred to earlier but also more generally by the religious practices of the majority of Arabs who share the same Islamic faith and are brought physically together on a regular basis by pilgrimage.

In some states in this period, the idea of Arab unity was inculcated in schools, clubs and colleges at the behest of the state.[22] This tended to be in states led by rulers at least partly motivated by personal or dynastic ambition such as King Faisal rather than for more ideological reasons.[23] The older religious practices referred to earlier, and the more general improvements in communications re-vitalised or at least kept a sense of Arabism alive, by linking Arab speaking peoples together. This led to an increased awareness of the artificiality of foreign-imposed borders. These new groups uphold what Benedict Anderson[24] calls an 'imagined community' – a primary loyalty which is socially constructed, based on culture, and conceived in secular terms. This community, constructed on social myths and rituals and practices, sustains a sense of shared history and ideal loyalty, a focus for common identity. The appeal is to a shared and glorious past and future.

During the 1930s and 1940s some Arab regimes encouraged greater co-operation on a state-to-state basis because of a basic Arabism or a sense of fraternity among Arab speaking peoples. This was reflected in the creation in 1945 of the League of Arab States between Syria, Iraq, Saudi Arabia, Egypt and The Lebanon. The impetus for greater unity was provided by the Arab-Israeli conflict and the beginnings of the Cold War. The defeat of the Arab armies in Palestine in 1948/9 and the perception that the Middle East could be a theatre of competition between East and West seemed to stress the advantages of political unity. As Dekmajian has said in reference to the popular appeal of pan-Arabism under the leadership of Nasser in the 1950s 'in early 1958 all indications were that Abd al-Nasser was at the zenith of his popularity among Arabs'.[25]

This veneer of unity however masked deep divisions. Even in the 1940s the inherent weaknesses of Arab unity could be observed. The Arab invasion of Palestine to aid the Palestinians in 1948 can be seen as a manifestation of unity of action, but even this masked considerable divisions and disputes.[26] The Arab League volunteer and regular armed forces fought under state commanders involved in personal rivalries and ambitions. Subsequent defeats against the Israeli army only served to strain Arab relationships further. It should also be noted that the Arab League itself is based upon the principles of state independence and sovereignty rather than pan-Arab unification.[27]

THE DURABLE WEAKNESSES OF PAN-ARAB UNITY

The reasons for the fragility of aspirations to Arab unity are numerous and have been widely discussed. The defeat of the Arab armies in 1948/9 seemed to encourage Arab unity, notably because of its provision of a common enemy. The expulsion of the British/French armies at Suez and the resultant stressing of 'Arab' rather than 'Egyptian' victory by Nasser served to mobilise Pan-Arabic sentiment among Arab masses as noted above. However, whilst Nasser could see the advantages of Arab unity for Egypt, other Arab leaders were worried about a super state which would place their own state in a subservient position to Egypt. There was also the ever-present fear that unrestrained support for the goals of Arab nationalism could involve them in future dangerous wars with Israel.[28] This reflects the importance to Arab leaders of the preservation of *state*-power and security.

A successful Pan-Arabism seemed to promise an undermining of a part of the claims of individual regimes to legitimacy as leaders of their own nation states. Whilst regimes were aware of the cultural ties between inhabitants of different states and were also aware of the political benefits of anti-colonial sentiment when it was asserted in Arabic terms as well as in national consciousness terms, they were also aware of the dangers that pan-Arabic ties posed to their own authority. They therefore used Arabism to win local support and enhance their own legitimacy but were ambivalent about the possible outcome of enhanced aspirations of pan-Arabism.[29]

The increasing number of independent Arab states in the 1960s and 1970s meant that power was much more diffused in the area. Individual states had also consolidated and therefore grown in power which meant that it was much more difficult for one regime to exercise authority or power outside their own state territorial boundaries. Existing Arab states were proving by this time to be much more durable than in earlier periods. No regime was removed by force in the sense of a change in the basic way each state was run in the 1960s and 1970s. Even President Sadat's assassination in Egypt in 1981 merely led to a change in leaders rather than a basic change in type of regime.[30]

Contemporarily the Arab/Israeli conflict has continued to act as a barrier limiting Pan-Arabic tendencies, in that Middle East citizens have remained unwilling to die for the Arab cause. Whilst providing an arena to a certain extent for state to state co-operation, regional organisations have provided the excuse for interfering in each others perceived domestic affairs and has led to hostility and subsequent reinforcing of individual regimes which has weakened drives for greater unity.

The underlying reason for such weakness in the cause of Arab unity however, may not be so contemporary, but may be historically located. Whilst there are undoubtedly strong cultural links between Arab peoples, specifically in the realms of language, historical experience and religion, which have given the area a superficial appearance of unity for centuries, the area has only rarely enjoyed political unity. Therefore whilst there are undoubtedly cultural and economic links there is no precedent for union politically. The collapse of the Ottoman empire in 1918 could have led to the foundation of a large Arabic state. The long term ambition of the

Hashemites had been to bring the territorial fragments of the old Ottoman Empire of Hejaj, Syria, Palestine and Iraq together in some form of federated state.[31] As J.J. Malone[32] said 'Faisal... recognised that a greater Arab majority would reduce the Kurdish problem to manageable proportions and he knew the value of Syrian entrepreneurial skills intellectual attainment and diversified resources'. This aspiration however was thwarted by European imperialist mandatory division and control.

ARAB UNITY IN THE MIDDLE EAST TODAY

Attempts to further unify the Arab world however, are still made today, often focusing on cultural unity. The Union of Arab Historians announced in 1987 that 'With a pen, the Arabs will be united'.[33] Thus the idea was promoted that by creating a Higher Arab Board to rewrite the history of the Arab nation this would lead to the reinterpretation of Arabic history stressing *unity* rather than *division* in the Arab world. This has not appeared to date to have been successful. There are underlying reasons for this and these have been discussed above but there have also been positive actions taken by regime leaders in the past few decades to strengthen the external boundaries of the state and firmly direct loyalty towards the state rather than to a broader entity.

Regimes have tended to stress *difference from* rather than *similarity with* other states. In Syria in 1977 Assad said, 'There is a strong feeling among Arabs, a spiritual feeling that we are all a single nation of people... but it will take along time to convert that spiritual feeling into a material reality – perhaps not in my lifetime, for there are still too many differences between one Arab state and the next'.[34] This has been propagated by Arab leaders, reflected by for example, the introduction of celebrations of national anniversaries and holidays. Although Middle Eastern flags contain linked symbols and colours, each state has introduced a unique national flag.[35] Clear cut territorial elements appeared in various modern Arab states' stamps and sometimes on money notes.[36] Iraq for example, under the leadership of Saddam Hussein has developed a localised set of symbols and practices which stress national difference and superiority. These symbols and practices, for example, archaeological excavation and the establishment of archaeological museums, by asserting a past lineage, link particular Arabs historically to particular pieces of land rather than to a general Arab homeland.

This was seen as a domestic political necessity. When the Ba'ath Party seized power in Iraq in 1968, it was faced with the problem of consolidating control over a heterogeneous population: Shia Muslims, Sunni Muslims, Kurds and others. It needed to present an ideology which might minimise divisions and allow for the consolidation of Ba'ath power. Pan-Arab nationalism was not felt to be workable because of the presence of the (non-Arabic) Kurdish community. The Ba'ath Party therefore, launched a campaign aimed at the fostering of national sentiment based on loyalty to Iraqi territory. Saddam Hussein presented the notion of a distinct Iraqi people which included both Arabs and non-Arabs.[37] In order to avoid criticism from Pan Arabists this was achieved through a cultural campaign (such as the development of the archaeological excavations mentioned above) rather than via a campaign which was overtly political.[38]

In Turkey a similar campaign began much earlier. In order to avoid the perceived commitments which would have accompanied an ideological or emotional supra-nationalism,[39] Attaturk was keen to develop a distinctively *Turkish* nationalism which was both historically deeply rooted and territorially and ethnically well-defined. Similarly in Egypt after World War One, overt attempts were made to create an Egyptian nationalism based on Egyptian territory. The idea of the political elite in Egypt was to use its Pharaonic past as a source of national self-assertion and for it to be the central cultural symbol for modern Egypt.[40] There was even an effort to dissociate Egypt from its Arab past by linking it to the history and civilisation of the Mediterranean and Europe or India.[41] Even Nasser did not attempt to obliterate the notion of an Egyptian nationalism completely, despite his rhetoric surrounding the Arab nation. While he dropped the name 'Egypt' during the United Arab Republic (UAR) period, referring to it as the 'Southern region', the postage stamps issued in the Southern region depicted Pharaonic, distinctively Egyptian symbols.[42]

Many post-colonial and post-revolutionary societies re-write their people's history in the process of power consolidation and nation-building. This was first officially undertaken in the Middle East in Nasserite Egypt where historians explicitly considered Egyptian history to be their realm of interest; the writing of 'other' Arab countries histories was considered to be the domain of those 'other' countries citizens.[43] The stress is on the perceived difference between Egyptians and 'other' Arabs, and therefore on a psychological 'separateness' and not unity.

Intra-Arab co-operation today is expressed by, for example, the redistribution of wealth from rich to poor states in the interests of the economic growth of the area as a whole, but on the basis of brotherhood rather than unity. The disinclination, however, of wealthier Arab states to share their wealth tends to militate against even this type of intra-Arab co-operation.[44]

Some would argue that it is the more localised loyalty to the clan which remains of primary importance in the area even today.[45] In Jordanian elections during the early 1990s, the Islamic Action Front lost more than half their seats to the tribal leaders who hold three times as many seats as the Islamists. The Christian Science Monitor claimed that the voters in the Arab World 'appear to be swayed more by their family and tribal loyalties than by political platforms'.[46]

This was also the case in earlier decades. 138 students from the American University of Beirut were questioned in 1957 and 1969 regarding their associational choices. The choices they had were family, ethnic, national background (Arab), religion, state and political party. In both years for the aggregate group the family ranked first, followed by ethnic association, religion, state and political party.[47] Families shape the pattern of social life, marriage, business co-operation and vendettas across the region, and these could hardly be said to have declined at all throughout a century of 'modernisation' in politics and economy.

In some cases this primary affiliation to family or clan serves to legitimate the existence of the ruling state power. The Kingdom of Saudi Arabia for example, contains a collection of families and religious and ethnic groups who were united together through conquest by Abd al 'Aziz ibn Sa'ud during the first twenty five years of this century. The ruling family did not and does not try to undo *existing* identities but has tried to create an overarching loyalty based on a feeling of common community of which membership is exclusive and privileged. This perception is grounded in myths of identity surrounding the cohesiveness of the Saudi national entity at the head of which is the Saudi royal family. The royal family becomes an extension of the tribal family. Older obligations to economically weak tribal families were substituted when Ibn Sa'ud rose to power in the 1920s by alternative ones – to the ruling family. This was done by their assumption of the role of tribal leader in very material ways.[48] The ruling family for example, assumed the obligation to provide for the welfare of women who have no male relative to support them. The role of the tribal shaykh in determining marriage alliances is now carried out by representatives of the monarchy, which thus becomes the symbolic tribal leader.[49] They claim the unique qualification to defend Islam and its holy places, laws and traditions and to ensure the moral well being of the Muslim community.[50] The Saudi royal family choose a group of 'Ulama' (Islamic clerical leaders) who are more loyal to preserving the power of the ruling Saud family than to spreading the faith.

In some states, even those with very centralised systems of Government, the realities of structural power during the Cold War made it unnecessary for post-colonial states to penetrate the entire territory which they claimed to be theirs and so in, for example Egypt, there are populations who live to a certain extent remote from the control of the state. During the Cold War, external forces could under certain circumstances be relied upon to assist in the re-establishment of societal control in such cases where legitimacy of the regime was not recognised throughout the entire territory. This is no longer the case.[51]

With the ending of the Cold War regimes dependent on the reassuring presence of their external patrons have become increasingly vulnerable. Furthermore during the years of the Cold War, tribal areas of the Middle East remained largely self- sufficient whilst the urban elite were dependent on cash flows from the superpowers. This is no longer so forthcoming. It is more possible that these weakened capital cities will be under the threat of attack from social forces from the remote tribal areas.[52]

Furthermore large immigrant populations and consequent probable political fragmentation in all rich countries is likely to continue to hinder the process of state integration.[53] The speed at which economies and societies have been transformed during the second half of the twentieth century has posed such major socio-cultural problems.[54] As Avinieri argues of the Middle East as a whole 'never has there been a society. . . so divided, fragmented and polarised in reality'.[55]

CONCLUSION

Politics in the Arab world continue to be a struggle between those groups whose concerns are either greater than, equal to, or are smaller than the state. Whilst many Arabs recognise that Arab territorial states have developed from being merely artificial creations and now have a certain durable dynamic of their own, others see the continuing legitimacy of the existing order to be dependent upon the economic development of Middle Eastern states. The Arabs of the wealthy Gulf states see great advantages in the enormous economic benefits derived from citizenship of their states and this contributes to identification of the citizen with the government in power. On the other hand, the sympathy expressed by many Arabs and Palestinians across the region for Saddam Hussein during the Gulf War suggests that many Middle East citizens do not take for granted the boundaries between Arab states because they do not consider the division of the Arab world to be a permanent feature of the area.[56] The films of Syrian comedian Durayd Lahham which deal with the abuse of human rights in the Arab world and the artificial and impractical nature of borders in the area are now becoming popular in some countries.[57] This suggests a degree of popular sympathy with the notion of a certain unity within a broader entity and a lack of total identification with existing territorial states.

Furthermore, some moderate Arab states are seen as being too closely associated with the interests of Western powers and the interests of Arab ruling families and that the needs of the citizens are seen as being subservient to those interests.[58] Such popular dissatisfaction could lead to a more general perception that economic and social needs would be better provided for by alternative political structures. This would have as its consequence the de-legitimation of existing regimes.

Notes

1. S. Bromley, *Rethinking Middle East Politics* (London: Polity, 1994).
2. A.S. Ahmed and H. Donovan, *Islam, Globalization and Postmodernity* (London/NewYork: Routledge,1994).
3. P. Vatikiotis, *Islam and the State* (London: Routledge, 1987).
4. For example, J. Esposito, *Islam and Politics* (Syracuse, New York: Syracuse University Press, 1991).
5. R. Owen, *State, Power and Politics in the Making of the Modern Middle East* (London/NewYork: Routledge, 1992)
6. *Ibid.*
7. B. Tibi, *Arab Nationalism: A Critical Enquiry* (Macmillan: London, 1971).
8. M. Reza Ghods, 'Iranian Nationalism and Reza Shah', *Middle Eastern Studies*, Vol. 27, No. 1.
9. R. Owen, op. cit.
10. *Ibid.*
11. *Ibid.*
12. A. Dawisha and I.W. Zartman (eds), *Beyond Coercion: The Durability of the Arab State* (London: Croom Helm, 1988).
13. R. Owen, *op.cit.*
14. C. Dodd, 'Aspects of the Turkish State: Political Culture, Organised Interests and Village Communities', *British Journal for Middle Eastern Studies*, Vol. 15, Nos 1 and 2, 1988.
15. R. Owen, *op. cit.*
16. F. Halliday, 'The Politics of Islamic Fundamentalism in A.A. Ahmed and H. Donnan (eds), *Islam, Globalization and Postmodernity* (USA/Canada: London, Routledge, 1994).
17. R. Owen, *op. cit.*

18. F. Moussa Mahmoud, 'Literature as a Unifying Influence in Modern Arab Culture', *British Society for Middle Eastern Studies Bulletin*, Vol. 5.1, 1978.
19. F. Ahmed, 'Politics and Islam in Modern Turkey', *Middle Eastern Studies*, Vol. 27, No. 1, pp. 3–21
20. S. Bromley, *op.cit.*
21. E. Kedourie, *Politics in the Middle East* (Oxford: Oxford University Press, 1992).
22. Cleveland, *The Making of an Arab Nationalist* (Princeton Univesity Press, 1971).
23. F. Massalha, 'Faisal's Pan-Arabism 1921–32', *Middle Eastern Studies*, Vol. 27, No. 4, pp. 607–679.
24. B. Anderson, *The Imagined Community* (Ithaca: Cornell University Press, 1983).
25. H. Dekmajian, *Egypt Under Nasser: A Study in Political Dynamics* (London 1972).
26. T. Mayer, *Arab Unity and the Palestinian Question 1945–8* (University of Washington Press, 1994).
27. S. Bromley, *op. cit.*
28. R. Owen, *op. cit.*
29. *Ibid.*
30. *Ibid.*
31. F. Massalha, *op. cit.*
32. J.J. Malone, *The Arab Lands of Western Asia* (New York, 1973).
33. U. Freitag, 'Writing Arab History: the Search for the Nation', *British Journal of Middle East Studies*, Vol. 21, No. 1, 1994.
34. M. Ma'oz, *Assad-The Sphynx of Damascus*, London, 1988.
35. A. Baram, 'Territorial Nationalism in the Middle East', *Middle Eastern Studies*, Vol. 26., 4 October 1990, pp. 425–448.
36. J.J. Malone, *op.cit.*
37. U. Freitag, *op.cit.*
38. A. Baram, *op. cit.*
39. *Ibid.*
40. I. Geshoni, and J.P. Jankowski, *Egypt, Islam and the Arabs, the Search for Egyptian Nationhood 1900–1930* (Oxford University Press, 1986).
41. *Ibid.*
42. *Ibid.*
43. Alaf Lutji al-Sayyid Marson, 'Egyptian Historical Research and Writing on Egypt in the 20th Century', *MESA Bulletin*, Vol. 7, No. 2, 1973.
44. A. Baram, *op. cit.*
45. M. Fandy, 'Tribe versus Islam: The Post Colonial Arab State and the Democratic Imperative', *Middle East Policy*, Vol. 111, No. 2, 1994.
46. Christian Science Monitor, Nov. 10, 1993.
47. S. Reiser, 'Pan-Arabism Revisited', *Middle East Journal*, Spring 1983, Vol. 372.
48. C. Helms, *The Cohesion of Saudi Arabia*, (Baltimore: Johns Hopkins University Press, 1981).
49. S. Habib, *Ibn Saud's Warriors of Islam* (University of Washington Press, 1993).
50. E.A. Doumato, 'Gender, Monarchy and National Identity', *British Journal of Middle East Studies*, Vol. 19 No. 1, 1992.

51.   M. Fandy, *op. cit.*
52.   K.O. Salih, 'Kuwait: Political Consequences of Modernisation', *Middle Eastern Studies*, Vol. 27, No. 1, pp. 46–56.
53.   J.M. Landau, Man, *State and Society in the Contemporary Middle East* (London: Pall Mall) 1977).
54.   *Ibid.*
55.   S. Avinieri, 'Beyond Saddam: The Arab Trauma', *Dissent*, Vol. 38, No. 1, Spring 1991.
56.   As'ad Aubkhahil, 'A New Arab Ideology? The Rejuvenation of Arab Nationalism', *Middle East Journal*, Vol. 46, Winter 1992.
57.   *Ibid.*
58.   *Ibid.*

7 La Lucha Continua? Identity and the Nicaraguan Revolution
Lloyd Pettiford

FOREWORD

More so than ever before, I realised while writing this chapter that over
the previous fifteen or so years I had made an unconscious, but definite,
effort to make Nicaragua and its revolution into something they were
not. I wanted the revolution, at the time and in retrospect, to be a noble
and infallible success; to be truly the good example so feared by Washington. When Nicaragua had problems I attributed those problems entirely
to the enormous economic and military pressures emanating from the
USA and did not see the inadequacies of Sandinista (FSLN – Frente
Sandinista para la Liberación Nacional) rule. The truth was not always
so simple and Jenny Pearce is right to note that 'the revolution was not
the romantic affair often portrayed by many sympathetic Europeans'
such as myself.[1]

Nonetheless, I am pleased and proud to say that 19 July 1979 is still a
special day for me and that I do not underestimate the achievements of
the revolution. The following should serve to clarify any ambiguity in my
opening comments and demonstrate that if the Nicaraguan revolution
did not create the community I had imagined, it was far from the failure
I supposed it to have been in February 1990 when a coalition of 14 parties
ousted the FSLN in elections. The Nicaraguan revolution was 'not
just . . . a significant political event but the beginning of a process' and as
such it is not over.[2]

INTRODUCTION

'Concerns with individual and collective identity are ubiquitous. We
know of no people without names, no languages or cultures in which
some manner of distinctions between self and other, we and they are not

made.'³ This chapter seeks to examine this ubiquitous issue of identity in a specific context and in an accessible manner. The context is Nicaragua, a country less than two hundred years old in the formal legal sense but which has been, throughout its history, ravaged by foreign intervention and natural disasters.

The Nicaraguan revolution of 1979 represented a clear attempt to break with the past and to establish a Nicaraguan identity as a response to imperialism and its Nicaraguan instruments. In this sense Nicaragua clearly contradicts Hobsbawm's generalisation that nationalism requires 'too much belief in what is patently not so' since the domination of the country by the United States, and the negative consequences of this, is scarcely deniable.⁴

This chapter traces Nicaraguan history before, during and after the revolution in terms of the formation of a national identity. However, despite the importance of the 1979 revolution and the Sandinistas in terms of the development of a distinctively Nicaraguan national identity it should be remembered that this revolutionary organisation was none-theless patently centralist, hierarchical and patriarchal; its treatment of the Miskito Indians of the Atlantic coast and the lack of women in the party's leadership, combined with its use of the Nicaraguan's women's movement as an organisation made up of women rather than for women, demonstrate a less sensitive approach to all issues of identity.

Since their formal independence in the early nineteenth century, the states of Central America, including Nicaragua, have been profoundly influenced by their near northern neighbour, the United States. That this would, and should, be so was first made explicit in the Monroe Doctrine of 1823 and since that time the region's economies and social structures have been clearly shaped by their relationship with the regional, subse-quently global, hegemon. Whilst this is not altogether surprising, the tra-gedy of Central America has been to find itself so far from God but so near the United States.

The structures created by this markedly unequal relationship have been crucial in the context of the ongoing and recent civil conflicts in the region: The Nicaraguan Revolution of 1979 and the subsequent war against the US-funded and founded Contra rebels; the civil war in El Sal-vador, which began in 1979 and formally ended in 1992 (although severe tensions remain); and the Guatemalan civil conflict which has fluctuated in intensity since the 1960s and continues to this day. In part, at least, these conflicts can be seen as splits over what constitutes national iden-tity. For elite groups the reference point is the United States and the idea of modernity; dominant elites in the region have a view of their own indigenous cultures which is entirely Western. For the majority of the population, however, the reference points, in terms of national identity, are indigenous and focus on anti-imperialist figures such as Augusto Sandino and Farabundo Martí. This chapter will explore these and other ideas in the context of Nicaragua, perhaps the most fascinating country in the region.

Sadly, some of the fascination of Nicaragua stems from a tragic (if occasionally inspiring) history. The chapter will start by looking at pre-revolutionary Nicaraguan history, emphasising the huge influence of the United States, a crucial factor in terms of the (non)-development of a distinctly Nicaraguan identity. This section is dealt with as briefly as is possible but is absolutely essential to an understanding of what follows.

Next the revolutionary period itself will be considered and how this altered the situation. The revolution which, in the minds of many, came to an end when the Sandinistas were removed from power at the ballot box in February 1990 has had numerous labels attached to it; Socialist, Popular, Totalitarian, Marxist, Christian and Nationalist are amongst the most common. Certainly the development of an anti-imperialist, nationalist identity was important.

Finally, the post-Revolutionary period will be examined. Once again the United States has sought to exert undue influence on the country, seeking to crush even the legitimate opposition of the Sandinistas. However, despite the impossibility of continuing Sandinista rule and maintaining all the revolution's aims under pressure from the Contras and the global economy, Nicaragua and issues surrounding identity in the country have changed markedly in character.

NICARAGUAN HISTORY

The particular interest of the United States (and Britain) in Nicaragua in the 19th century lay in the possibility of using the San Juan River as the basis for the building of an inter-oceanic canal (built ultimately, of course, through Panama, a country especially created for the purpose!) For a long time, and despite the clear warning issued through the Monroe Doctrine, the United States had to vie for influence with the British. Indeed the British set up a separate (Miskito) Kingdom on the east (Atlantic) coast of Nicaragua and were only finally thrown out in 1894, allowing Nicaragua to finally become fully physically united.

The overall effect of foreign intervention in Nicaraguan affairs during the nineteenth century was to exacerbate already bloody rivalries between the local Liberal and Conservative oligarchies, with the United States siding with the Liberals based in León and Britain with the Conservatives of Granada. This effectively held back the formation of a truly unified nation with an effective national identity and stunted the development of strong, uniform state structures.

Within this feud, 1855 saw the remarkable intervention in Nicaragua of William Walker and his army of North American adventurers. Originally Walker was recruited by Nicaraguan Liberals as a mercenary to overthrow the Conservative President Fruto Chamorro. This he successfully achieved, but instead of handing over power to the Liberal Party, Walker formed his own administration, declaring himself President and decreeing English to be the country's official language. Walker's attempt to establish an unofficial quasi-US state in Nicaragua was ended in 1857 by armed intervention from all the Central American republics, backed, of course, by Britain. The whole incident severely discredited the Liberal leadership, ushered in thirty years of Conservative rule and effectively delayed the expansion of coffee production and Nicaraguan incorporation into the international economy.

By the end of the nineteenth century, the US-favoured Liberals had finally regained the presidency in the form of José Santos Zelaya and expelled the British. The new President's policy saw the expansion of coffee production and was on behalf of the new landed class thus created. However, Zelaya caused friction with US capital through his desire to control the behaviour of foreign investment and in 1909, 400 US marines landed at the Caribbean port of Bluefields in support of a Conservative uprising. Hence, Zelaya was ousted; the coup marking the beginning of over 20 years of direct United States involvement in the politics of the republic, including two lengthy periods of military occupation.

The US State Department sent Thomas Dawson to help organise a new Conservative dominated coalition, led by Adolfo Diaz. However, the coalition lacked stability and by 1912 faced a liberal uprising together with an attempted coup organised by the Conservative minister of war. A US marine force of some 2700 arrived and ensured the survival of Adolfo Diaz's government. US troops stayed for an initial period of 15 years. With the Conservative's reliance upon the US for their survival, Nicaragua became a virtual US protectorate.

A series of treaties were signed between the two governments which effectively demonstrate the unequal nature of the relationship. The Castillo-Knox treaty gave $15 million in US loans in exchange for the right of the US to intervene directly in Nicaragua in order to protect US interests. Brown Brothers Bank of New York advanced a $1.5 million loan in return for control of Nicaraguan Customs. Most controversially the Bryan-Chamorro treaty stated that 'the government of Nicaragua grants in perpetuity to the government of the United States forever free from all taxation or other public charge, the exclusive property rights necessary and convenient for construction, operation and maintenance of an interoceanic canal'. As part of the deal the US paid Nicaragua $3 million which passed straight into US banks holding the Nicaraguan debt!

The effect of US control of Nicaragua was to provide an artificial stability such that when the Americans left in 1925 the country quickly slid into civil war. In 1927, and with the Liberals armed by Mexican 'Bolsheviks', the US again sent in the marines causing a stalemate in the conflict. Agreement was brokered for elections and for the US to stay and train a police force; a non-partisan National Guard. The US thus believed it had created a constitutional and compliant elite-led system and was confident enough to leave the country again in 1933.

Three years later the leader of the National Guard, Anastasio Somoza filled an effective power vacuum and took over Nicaragua having already tricked and then ruthlessly disposed of the nationalist hero Augusto Sandino. Sandino had successfully fought US imperialism but considered the task done and relaxed his guard once its physical presence, in the form of US marines, had returned home.

The rule of the Somoza family (Anastasio and his two sons) lasted over 40 years. It did so by a combination of factors: political dominance, which included severe repression by the National Guard; economic policies which stimulated growth with inequality; and a foreign policy which demonstrated unswerving anti-communism and absolute servility to US interests. (Nicaragua offered to send the National Guard to help out in both Korea and Vietnam and was used as a base for the ill-fated 'Bay of Pigs' fiasco which was designed to topple Castro's Cuba.) Of course, despite the longevity of the family dictatorship, the legend of Sandino, as a great nationalist hero, was to outlast the family who killed him.

Nicaragua's history of US domination, both actual and by proxy, did nothing to lessen the divisions within the dominant class originally based on the cities of Granada and León. So, whilst US imperialism, and the poverty and repression which resulted, provided much of the motivation for revolution, to cut an oft-told story short, it was this divisiveness of the Nicaraguan dominant class which proved the key to revolutionary success by the Sandinistas; in neighbouring El Salvador, for instance, the cohesiveness of the oligarchy prevented a guerrilla take-over.

So, FSLN combatants marched triumphantly through the streets of Managua on 19 July 1979.[5]

THE NICARAGUAN REVOLUTION

'The Sandinista revolution was clearly under the hegemony of a Marxist vanguard party.'[6] It is not uncommon to hear this view of the Nicaraguan revolution from those of both the left and right of the political spectrum, who use it to justify outright hostility or fawning admiration of the Nicaraguan revolution. However, it can be reasonably argued that both groups (and to be fair it often seems that you must be either one or the other in Central American contexts) have been guilty of interpreting the bases of the revolution to fit their own ends.

After the Sandinistas hugely popular victory in 1979 it was not long before Nicaragua's break with the past was subject to outright hostility from the Reagan administration. Given the history of US dominance over the country this is not surprising; 'the unrelenting opposition of the US government to the Sandinistas [to any genuine expression of Nicaraguan national identity] would, most likely, have sabotaged whatever political programme [the Sandinistas] attempted to implement'.[7] Indeed, once the Sandinistas had been defeated in 1990 the new UNO government quickly had to face the reality that the US government would be hostile to any signs of Nicaraguan independence.

Ostensibly though US opposition was based on a professed perception of the Sandinistas as pro-Soviet communists who were reluctant to define democracy conventionally and consequently threatened US security. Hazel Smith describes the core of this Sandinista 'unorthodox democracy' as an insistence that it 'must mean more than the holding of free and fair elections every few years. [That] it must also mean the participation of all sectors – women, Black people and minority ethnic groups, youth, trade unions etc. in the organisation and advancement of their own sectoral interests and in day-to-day decision making.'[8] However, such a view was attributable less to (call it what you will) Communism/Marxism/Socialism in the movement than to the reality that the FSLN saw itself as the vanguard of a national liberation struggle aiming to liberate all Nicaraguans from imperialism and its Somocista instrument. Consequently, even the self-definition of Sandinismo as Marxist-Leninist may be viewed as a natural reaction to US imperialism rather than any natural affinity with the former Soviet Union.

In fact, it was not the Sandinistas but others (within the elite class) who saw the revolution in class terms since it seriously curtailed their previous dominant position in terms of labour relations. Encouraged in labelling the regime using words long since equated with Satan in Washington, these people often retired to Miami or set about varying degrees of economic sabotage. In this way, the Sandinistas, who had also received large amounts of Somoza's substantial holdings, inherited large tracts of abandoned land, in effect forcing them into some degree of state control. The extent of the Sandinistas' pre-meditated desire to establish such a position, let alone its commitment to establishing a Marxist-Leninist state, has been much over stated. Sandinista policy, such as it existed in any coherent form, could be more accurately characterised as a belief in a greater emphasis on the poor (economically marginalised) via the frequently repeated slogan 'the logic of the majority', combined with a greater voice for all those politically marginalised under Somoza, which was virtually everyone!

According to Elizabeth Dore and John Weeks, in their convincingly argued research paper entitled 'The Red and the Black', 'the insurrection led by the Sandinistas represented a struggle for national liberation in an almost pure form'.[9] The Sandinista emphasis was on nationalism; this is fundamental. The Sandinista project was not to dispossess the landed as a matter of principle; it is simply that this class, who had benefited most from the previous social order, were most likely to betray the nationalist, anti-imperialist revolution. Rather than a communist 'expropriate the expropriators' the Sandinistas were more likely to 'expropriate the traitors'.[10] Accordingly, in the Nicaraguan revolution, all patriots were welcomed within the coalition of the majority, regardless of class, whilst all traitors were excluded.

This, of course has implications in the context of subject matter of this book. In seeking to throw off the imperialist yoke the Sandinistas led a pure national revolution. Despite the Sandinistas' own rhetoric (see above) what of those whose identity was expressed, first and foremost, in other than Nicaraguan nationalist terms? Using Calhoun's observations about the United States in a Nicaraguan context, it might be argued that Sandinista in-group essentialism was linked to the suppression of other identities by a general pressure to conform to standard views of anti-imperialist Nicaraguanness and by dependence on expert authoritative (i.e. FSLN) sources as to what constituted that identity.[11] These ideas are now examined with reference to Nicaragua's Indian population and then the women's movement.

THE ATLANTIC COAST INDIANS AND THE REVOLUTION

The policy ineptitude of the revolutionary leadership of the Pacific side of the country towards the Atlantic coast population may be more clearly understood by an appreciation of 'the millennia of geographical, demographic, political and social separation of the two regions'.[12] Nonetheless, the treatment of Nicaragua's predominantly Miskito Indians of the Caribbean coast provides an excellent example of Sandinista ignorance and/or intolerance of those who did not identify with the Sandinista nationalist project and proved good ammunition for those unsympathetic to the revolution.[13]

The Miskito and other smaller Indian groups live in an area (approximately a 300 mile triangle) straddling the Nicaraguan border with Honduras which was largely ignored by Spanish invaders in the sixteenth century. Since that time the region was the object of competing colonialisms, namely: British, initially as a staging post in the seventeenth Century due to limited Spanish attention prior to that time; Spanish, as an attempted reaction to this unwelcome British incursion; and latterly that of the United States, who after 1823 sought to restrict all European involvement in 'their' hemisphere. As a result, the area was also the subject of a struggle, largely successful, by its indigenous inhabitants, to maintain their cultural and ethnic identities. Despite this, culturally and historically, the area is less a part of Spanish America and more an isolated out-post of the British Caribbean. Indeed, the historical influence of the British led to a psychological legacy in terms of an Indian tendency to regard with suspicion Spanish speakers and those from the Pacific coast. Furthermore, the Moravian Church, whose missionaries were important in the area after 1849, and who developed the written Miskito language, helped to instil in the Indians the further element of anti-Catholicism.

Many separatist Miskitos fought with Sandino in the 1920s extracting a promise of a Miskito nation in exchange for this support. However Sandino's forces attack on the Atlantic coast port of Puerto Cabezas, coinciding as it did with the Great Depression, cost the jobs of thousands of Miskitos. Sandino got the blame and many of his Miskito followers fled to settle in or near Managua on the other side of the country. Thus while the isolated Atlantic coast Indians were relatively free from the National Guard's extortion and brutality, and largely allowed to 'get on with it', the Sandinista experience of Indians was of those who had resettled, and who, along with the majority of Spanish speaking Nicaraguans, had good reason to seek the overthrow of Somoza. Resulting from this and other misunderstandings, mistrust built up.

The FSLN leadership, in common with most people on the Pacific coast, knew little and understood less about the ethnic considerations of the Atlantic coast where British colonialism had resulted in a racially based system of social stratification. The Sandinistas' Atlantic coast strategy was primarily modernisation based on an interpretation of its problems as fundamentally economic. However, the racially based social identities which had been instrumental for the survival and expansion of colonialism, which had employed divide and rule tactics, were not and are not a simple expression of economically determined class interests. Whilst the Sandinistas thought that economic development would resolve all demands, including those for autonomy, the institutionalised racism endemic in the Atlantic coast system could not be overcome by economic development which might simply reproduce existing relations.[14]

Sandinista reforms, in the areas of literacy, health and economic development sought to use young educated Miskitos and bi-lingual teachers and instructors. However, teachers were not always bi-lingual, health planning paid little heed to Miskito input whilst providing more promises than facilities and economic development programmes were often tacked onto schemes run from Managua. Sandinista involvement in Miskito affairs looked very similar to any other colonisation by foreigners. Furthermore, the use of educated Miskito teachers, together with territorial and language factors, stimulated Miskito (national) consciousness and the Indians again talked of Sandino's promise to them.

In this atmosphere, the Sandinistas were worried that the Miskitos would try to ally with the Reagan-backed Contra rebels, of which there is indeed some evidence. Accordingly the border which separated not only Contra bases in Honduras from Nicaragua but also divided the Miskito 'nation' was more effectively patrolled. The Sandinistas saw this as an essential aspect of national defence but to the Miskitos it was an unfair intrusion. Consequently, other Sandinista programmes were weakened; attempts at setting up women's and farmer's groups as part of participatory democracy were perceived by Miskitos as putting paid FSLN informants into their midst.

The exclusively nationalist and economistic focus of the revolution was arrogant and colonialist, whatever the intention, and consistently failed to accurately gauge the depth of Miskito feeling. However, it says a lot for the Sandinistas that they were more educible with regard to the Miskitos than the US ever was with regard to them. The FSLN did admit failures in its policy and sought to change and to implement a new flexible and integrated approach to the Atlantic coast. Carlos Vilas noted in the aftermath of Sandinista electoral defeat that the ethnic communities of the Atlantic coast had come an enormous way toward the establishment of autonomous government. This would seem, in fact, to understate the situation somewhat.

An autonomy commission was set up which recognised the mistakes of previous top–down strategies. In 1985 it embarked on a two-year programme of consultations, including house to house surveys and community meetings. The people were consulted on the basis of a draft document entitled 'Principles and Policies for the Exercise of the Right to Autonomy by the Indigenous Peoples and Communities of the Coast' which was published in all the main Indian languages as well as a simplified illustrated version for those lacking in literacy skills. The amended version, enshrined in the Nicaraguan (Sandinista) Constitution of 1987, gave the Indians, according to one participant in the constitutional debate, the chance for the first time to participate as 'first class human beings in the national society'.[15]

It would not seem an overstatement to suggest that in the decade of the revolution 'the government (FSLN) and the community organisations of the Atlantic coast region developed a unique and successful political project for self government'. This, despite the war, despite the economic difficulties and despite Hurricane Joan, which destroyed much of the southern part of the region around the port of Bluefields in October 1988. Indeed, the fact that there were problems in the first place can largely be attributed to the fact that, unlike under Somoza, the revolution opened a space for demands to be made rather than simply ignoring or not hearing them. Whilst the post-FSLN government 'may try to tinker with the detail of the autonomy project . . . it shows no sign of being able to dispense with it'.[16]

WOMEN AND THE REVOLUTION

Women fought with Sandino and had been involved in the anti-imperialist struggle ever since. 'The role of mother, which defined the exclusive social destiny of the overwhelming majority of women and was greatly revered in Nicaraguan society, contrasted sharply with the mothers' inability to protect their children from the brutal excesses of the dictatorship. This contradiction served to galvanise many women into participating in activities in support of the armed struggle against Somoza.'[17] The 1969 historic programme of the FSLN, ten years before the actual revolution, promised to establish economic, political and cultural equality between woman and man. It must be observed that the revolution, and its always all-male Sandinista leadership, has not always worked toward this aim, as a look at the history of the Nicaraguan women's movement will show. In 1977, the Association of Nicaraguan Women Confronting the National Problem (AMPRONAC) was set up and was greatly influenced by the Sandinista struggle of which it was a part. Accordingly, its work was largely clandestine, at least from 1978. Two weeks after the revolution, and expressly to protect it, the women's movement reappeared in the guise of AMNLAE (The Luisa Amanda Espinosa Association of Nicaraguan Women) named after the first Sandinista woman to die at the hands of Somoza's National Guard.

As the Revolution got underway, laws were enacted to 'guarantee' the equality of women and men. Unequal divorce laws were abolished. The pre-1979 situation when men had all legal rights and few legal responsibilities to their children were similarly replaced. The rural practice whereby a male head of household often received the single wage packet for all family members working within a single enterprise was scrapped in favour of a requirement for separate wage packets for all workers. It became illegal to portray women as sex objects, and, whilst it is not doubted that this law was contravened, the law was enforced even against publications loyal to the FSLN.

Women benefited, as did all Nicaraguans, from health and education programmes and from freedom from repression. Furthermore, outside the FSLN nine-man National Directorate, 31.4% of government leadership posts were held by women. The figure falls well short of half but is in excess of women's proportionate membership of the FSLN at about 25%. It might be argued that given strong historical influences such as the Catholic Church within a very 'macho' society, and the fact that it is unlikely that 'Nicaragua, being a poor country would have the material means to alleviate to any significant extent the physical burdens borne by women' the achievements of the revolution seem noteworthy.[18] Figures concerning the role of women in various areas of society related to the labour force, government, military, police and education 'all indicate that the revolution had been reasonably successful in involving women'.[19]

However, again there is conflict between being Nicaraguan and being a woman. For instance, legislation on domestic work, which argued that all family members able to contribute should do so, was fiercely contested; many felt it could lead to the polarisation of relations between the sexes thus weakening the Sandinista nationalist anti-imperialist project. Indeed, war time priorities and restrictions of rights, whilst they may be expected, led to the relative neglect of women's issues. This includes

AMNLAE itself, which Hazel Smith argues, neglected its main concern 'to bring together and represent the large numbers of women who were beginning to take the first steps toward participating in the revolution; women who were, in practice, transcending their traditional roles'.[20] 'AMNLAE's position on participation in the productive life of the country as a pre-requisite for women's liberation, a position identical to that of the FSLN, precluded an analysis of women's oppression in the reproductive sphere'.[21]

FSLN legislation and the necessity of war both led to the proletarianisation of women by 'allowing' and 'forcing' them to do what had historically been men's work. However, the perception persisted that certain work was too technical to be undertaken by women and the traditional gendered division of labour was not radically altered during the revolution. Furthermore, many women simply ended up with a double working day and whilst this was not addressed the professed goal of equality remained far off. In addition, the Sandinistas failed to seriously address domestic violence and the revolution lacked a clear policy on the mistreatment of women.

In short, despite the enactment of much crucial legislation, the revolution failed to heed the demands of women and indeed feared the consequences of such demands for its anti-imperialist aims. It may well be argued that the Sandinistas' concern with the poor automatically tended to favour women; certainly compared to the days of the dictatorship when women hardly counted in political life and survival was frequently a struggle, there were economic improvements and increased opportunities for women during the almost 11 years of the revolution. However, women wanted the double working day addressed, greater control over family size, access to child care facilities and concrete action on domestic violence.

In looking at the revolution and women the FSLN may again be criticised for insensitivity. Even so, despite disagreements on the feasibility and acceptability of various policy specifics, the need for women's emancipation received widespread support, in turn opening a political space in which women could work to achieve their own liberation in a revolutionary context. However, as Chuchryk notes, it 'is difficult to legislate changes in behaviours marred by centuries of patriarchal relations between men and women'.[22] But despite this obvious difficulty the evidence suggests that women were using 'the political space to organise' which the revolution offered them. This is backed up by the formation of the National Feminist Committee (CNF) after the Sandinista election defeat.[23] This is expanded upon in the concluding section.

POST-REVOLUTIONARY NICARAGUA AND CONCLUSIONS

The electoral defeat of the Sandinistas in February 1990 marked for some the end of the Nicaraguan revolution. This is valid in a certain sense. However, as Dore and Weeks point out, such an interpretation treats revolution as derivative from the actions of leaders and governments rather than from the often chaotic unfolding of social conflict.[24]

Thus, one description of the revolution could be as a transition period of nation-building, of which the most profound and lasting impact was not to be found in the material realm, but instead in the way the revolution brought to many Nicaraguans, including women and the people of the Atlantic coast, new opportunities to contribute to community and national life.

The nation-building face of the revolution is undeniable; it inspired people to action in 1979 and, fuelled by US intervention, nationalism often substituted for political debate throughout the 11 years of Sandinista rule. Hobsbawm's generalisation may not hold for Nicaragua in the sense that its nationalism was based on an undeniable historical experience rather than lack of truth; however, as Renan observed, part of being a nation is getting its history wrong [25] and the Sandinistas' tendency, as the revolution progressed, to characterise the legitimate demands of its own supporters for economic justice (prioritising the needy) as being treacherous agents of US imperialism certainly fits such an assessment. Indeed, in trying to promote a true sense of Nicaraguan identity the FSLN erred in placing disproportional emphasis on external factors; that is to say defining national identity in a negative rather than positive way. (The Sandinista anthem, for instance, contains the words 'Yankee – enemy of humanity.')

The Sandinistas also tended to forget the existence of multiple identities in terms of context and to forget, as the political sociologist Hannah Arendt has noted, that plurality is basic to the human condition. True, the FSLN did establish rural and urban union federations, the ATC and CTS, later merged into a National Worker's Front (FNT), as well as the Sandinista Youth organisation (JS) and the women's organisation AMN-LAE but these mass organisations came to be seen by Nicaraguans not as organs of grassroots democracy, but as party-dominated instruments to mobilise support for state policies.[26] It can be seen as a major failing that making loyalty to nation the ultimate test was a serious error.

However, the revolution had significance beyond giving expression to Nicaraguanness. In terms of identity the revolution was and is multi-faceted and the Nicaragua which emerged from Sandinista rule would never be that which fought for it. As Richard Wilson has put it, identity is best seen 'as a paradox rather than as a statement; one which blurs and dissolves as soon as it is confidently asserted'. [27]

The revolution certainly stimulated class awareness or consciousness, sparking in the working and peasant classes a sense of potential political power. Unfortunately for the Sandinistas, many, particularly rural peasants, came to question whether the Sandinistas really represented them. As mentioned above this questioning caused former supporters to be labelled as agents of imperialism and led to a decisive swing against the FSLN in the 1990 elections. The Sandinistas thought it inconceivable that they could lose these elections and indeed 'the dramatic upset was a stunning reminder of how easy it is to project onto others our own hopes and convictions'. [28] However, many Nicaraguans clearly felt betrayed and exercised their political muscle accordingly.

Women started to have a higher profile under the Sandinistas in a society profoundly dominated by men and macho values. Indeed in the 1990 election the UNO candidate who replaced Ortega was a woman, Violeta Chamorro, who allied herself in the early years of the revolution with the FSLN. The women's organisation AMNLAE was set up, one of the Sandinistas' mass national organisations. However, this is not to over-state the case. That there is a long way to go is evident. For instance, the 1990 Presidential campaign of the FSLN's Daniel Ortega characterised him as the 'knife-bearing fighting cock' and his female opponent as weak and feeble. At the 1991 FSLN party congress, amid a process of reconsideration and self-criticism, the very popular candidacy of Dora María Téllez never came to a vote due to the pre-selection of the slate; accordingly the nine-person Sandinista National Directorate remained an all-male club. Some of these men have encouraged British audiences to imagine a Nicaragua ruled by nine Margaret Thatchers; whilst the prospect is chilling, the argument is superficial and reflects an unwillingness or inability to seriously address this issue of the representation of women.

However, AMNLAE is a good example of how Sandinista popular movements, basically instruments of the party line, have either grown increasing independent or spawned new and more militant groups. For instance AMNLAE holds a basically orthodox left and FSLN view that women are not primarily oppressed by patriarchy but by the class system; this can be summed up in the attitude that says what is the point of talking to a woman about sexuality if she is starving? However, women within AMNLAE have become increasingly concerned, significantly in the so-called post-revolutionary period, that working within the FSLN's hierarchical, patriarchal structure has placed limits on them and has meant that sexism has been ineffectively challenged. After the Sandinista election defeat the National Feminist Committee (CNF) was set up to rival the aims of AMNLAE after its members decided they did not need a political father looking after them. Indeed, much of the popular movement has thrown off the top–down model and is no longer the party instrument it once was.[29]

It has been argued that US aggression, in the form of the contras and an economic blockade, may have helped the FSLN perpetuate the anti-imperialist nationalist myth, and thus prolonged Sandinista rule.[30] In my view, perhaps, but probably not! But if it is possible to see a positive side to the barbarity of the US sponsored assault it did stimulate a greater role for women in national life and pushed the Sandinistas into a more constructive partnership with the people of the Atlantic coast.

The positive and negative sides of Sandinista recognition of diversity is clearly evident in the Sandinistas' learning curve experience with regard to the Miskito Indians; initially misunderstood, largely thanks to historical separation, their differentness rather than otherness was ultimately accepted and incorporated more or less sensitively into the Sandinista nationalist project providing an excellent example of what Hazel Smith calls the Sandinistas 'remarkable flexibility and willingness to learn from the people'.[31]

Even so, despite all the errors of the Sandinista regime, admitted or denied, and notwithstanding certain counter arguments such as that of Dore and Weeks (above), it is difficult to see how a revolution which was patently anti-Yankee and was dressed by those same Yankees in the clothes of its public enemy number one, could possibly have survived in the sense of continued rule of the FSLN. The Sandinistas lost the election of February 1990 because the Contra war had left many dead, crippled and wounded. They lost because the economic and social infrastructure was in ruins and because even basic goods were in desperately short supply. As Vilas put it, a 'decade of harsh and insecure existence was not the creation of the Sandinistas, but the Sandinista government did administer it'.[32] That is what the people voted against.

Given the conditions of FSLN evolution, of clandestine struggle and the existence of various tendencies, it is not surprising that it became highly centralised, bureaucratic and vertical; this was needed to maintain discipline and contributed to the emphasis on nationalism rather than socialism as a unifying theme. Nor is it surprising that the revolution was not everything it could have been; not only did the US dictate the agenda of international debate about Nicaragua leading to a highly rhetorical pro- or anti-argument, but the US perception of Nicaragua as a low intensity conflict was certainly not valid from Managua where up to 50% of government expenditure was necessarily military. As Hazel Smith correctly notes 'there is no nation in history which has not placed wartime restrictions on its citizens' and this certainly goes a long way to accounting for some of the inadequacies noted here.[33]

Of course electoral defeat does not mean that it was all for nothing. Just as a decade of revolution does not erase half a century of brutal dictatorship or two of foreign control it can also be argued that when revolutions are authentic, as this was, they stamp an indelible seal on society's entire expanse.[34] Despite reverses, such as the election defeat, nothing will revert to what it was 'notwithstanding the nightmares of the vanquished or the fantasies of the victors'.[35]

With war, economic and natural disaster and policy error, the revolution cannot be considered either unimportant or over. As John Pilger has noted, under the Sandinistas the Nicaraguan population achieved a collective sense of worth. The word pobreterria or 'scum of the earth' disappeared.[36] If verticalism characterised the 1980s these years nonetheless set in motion a chain of events which by the 1990s saw the possibilities of fragmentation in the sense of the realisation of multi-faceted identities. After the 1990 elections the FSLN stated objective was to win the 1996 election and to defend the revolution. It is clear that 'losing the [1990] election doesn't mean losing the revolution'.[37]

The UNO coalition which won the 1990 elections was not a Somocista party, its allegiance to Nicaragua's constitution was not specifically questioned and in many ways it was 'just as much a product of the revolution as any other social structure and organisation which had emerged during the 11 years since the fall of the dictator'.[38] UNO chose not to destroy the FSLN state nor to do exactly what the US wants; it has had to live with an emancipated Nicaraguan people and the reality that Nicaragua's future is likely to be bedevilled by US animosity towards its independence. But it is clear that semi-colonial servility to the US is now unacceptable to almost all Nicaraguans.

If the Sandinistas sought to impose Nicaraguan national identity they would do as well to remember that nations are dual phenomena full of people with multiple loyalties and identities; essentially constructed from above, they cannot be understood unless analysed from below in terms of the assumptions, hopes, needs, longings and interests of ordinary people, which are not necessarily national and still less nationalistic.[39] In this sense, throwing off its stifling imperialist chains could be considered a first stage of something much more important. To slightly misquote Winston Churchill, the 1990 elections were not the end of the revolution, or even the beginning of the end, but perhaps the end of the beginning.

AFTERWORD

Despite the somewhat positive tone of this work, at the time of writing Nicaragua is, nonetheless, a forlorn nation, bedevilled by problems and descending ever further into political and economic crisis. Perhaps, after all, I fell into the trap mentioned in the foreword of wanting to make the revolution something more positive than it was?

In Nicaragua today, the politicians play populist games and swim in a sea of corruption, concerned more with their own position than the country's. Consequently, former Sandinistas have joined centre-right coalitions and 'the country seems like a bus in which the driver and his fare collector are embroiled in a fist fight'. While the citizenry, politically active until at least 1992, has not lost interest in politics, the politicians have lost interest in the people's concerns and needs. Politically and physically Nicaragua is truly impoverished today, and as the Nicaraguan magazine Envío notes 'social movements rarely manage to hold onto their unity and identity in conditions of extended extreme poverty'. Signs of the proud days of revolutionary defiance are disappearing; 'Nicaragua Libre' number plates are no more and Sandinista murals destroyed or defaced. But despite all this, Nicaragua has changed and so have Nicaraguans.[40]

Eleven years would never be sufficient, given the problems of such a small country in the shadow of a regional and global power in the form of the United States. However, whilst physical signs of the revolution may be removed the minds of the people have been changed. Nicaraguans experienced freedom from oppression. Nicaragua became a literate country and many people enriched its long poetic traditions. The underlying expectations of the people about their potential has changed. People found pride at last in national terms, yes, but also as individuals with other identities; the national revolution was but a first and vital step in realising these.

Carlos Vilas, supporter of the Sandinista revolution, notes sadly that 'the effort of the people is the most powerful weapon a poor nation has, but it is not enough'. In this case I can only hope that he is wrong; the changes which the revolution provoked within people provide Nicaragua's brightest, perhaps only, hope for the future. La lucha continua...!

152   *Identity and the Nicaraguan Revolution*

Notes

1. H. Smith, *Nicaragua: Self Determination and Survival* (London: Pluto Press, 1993, p. xv).
2. Pearce, quoted in Smith, *op. cit.*, p. xvi.
3. C. Calhoun, *Social Theory and the Politics of Identity* (Oxford: Blackwell, 1994, p. 9).
4. E.J. Hobsbawm, *Nations and Nationalism Since 1870: Programme, Myth, Reality* (Cambridge: Cambridge University Press, 1990, p. 13).
5. E. Dore and J.Weeks, *The Red and the Black: The Sandinistas and the Nicaraguan Revolution* (University of London Institute of Latin American Studies Research Papers, 1992).
6. G. Prevost and H.E.Vanden, *Democracy and Socialism in Sandinista Nicaragua* (Boulder, Col: Lynne Rienner Publishers, 1993).
7. Dore and Weeks, *op. cit.*, p. 22.
8. Smith, *op. cit.*, p. 3.
9. Dore and Weeks, *op. cit.*, p. 25.
10. Dore and Weeks, *op. cit.*, p. 11.
11. Calhoun, *op. cit.*, p. 10.
12. Smith, *op. cit.*, p. 4.
13. B. Nietschmann, *The Unknown War* (New York: Freedom House, 1989).
14. Smith, *op. cit.*, p. 225.
15. Hooker qouted in Smith, *op. cit.*, p. 239.
16. Smith, *op. cit.*, p. 224 ; p. 241.
17. P. Chuchryk, 'Women in the Revolution', in T. Walker, *Revolution and Counter-Revolution in Nicaragua* (Boulder, Col.: Westview Press, 1991).
18. Smith, *op. cit.*, p. 222.
19. P. Chuchryk, 'Women in the Revolution', in Walker, *op. cit.*, p. 158.
20. Smith, *op. cit.*, p. 217.
21. P. Chuchryk, 'Women in the Revolution', in Walker, *op. cit.*, p. 148.
22. *Ibid*, p. 147.
23. Belli quoted in Smith, *op. cit.*, p. 217.
24. Dore and Weeks, *op. cit.*, p. 37.
25. Hobsbawm, *op. cit.*, p. 13.
26. G. Vickers, 'A Spider's Web', *NACLA* Special Edition – 'Nicaragua', Vol XXIV, No. 1, June 1990, p. 19
27. R.Wilson (1995), 'Shifting Frontiers: Historical Transformations of Identities in Latin America', *Bulletin of Latin American Research*, Vol. 14, No. 1, January, pp. 1–7.
28. Vickers, *op. cit.*, p. 19.
29. M. Quandt, 'Unbinding the Ties: Popular Movements and the FSLN', *NACLA*, Vol. XXVI, No. 4, February, pp. 11–14, 1993, p. 11.
29. Dore and Weeks, *op. cit.*, p. 28.
30. Smith, *op. cit.*, p. 4.
31. Vilas, C., 'What Went Wrong', *NACLA* Special Edition – 'Nicaragua', Vol. XXIV, No. 1, June, 1990, p. 11.
32. Smith, *op. cit.*, p. 136.
33. T. O'Kane, 'The New Old Order', *NACLA* Special Edition – 'Nicaragua', Vol. XXIV, No. 1, June, 1990, p. 28.

34. Vilas, *op. cit.*, p. 18.
35. J. Pilger, *Distant Voices* (London: Vintage, 1992).
36. Bendaria quoted in Smith, *op. cit.*, p. 6.
37. Smith, *op. cit.*, p. 28.
38. Hobsbawm, *op. cit.*, p. 10.
39. Universidad Centroamericana, 'The Crisis is Bordering on the Intolerable', *Envío*, Vol. 14, No. 167, June 1995.

8 Re-reading Europe's Identities
Neil Renwick

The title of this essay is meant to surprise, disturb and hopefully intrigue the student of international relations. The title might be said to be trying to 'make strange' the familiar features of this field of study[1]. Strange or unusual approaches may produce strange or unusual responses; different ways of thinking about the complex European political environment in which we live. By focusing upon identities in Europe and by making the peculiar claim that these can be 'read' in some way, this essay tries to challenge our established way of thinking about European politics and to open up issues previously marginalised or disregarded. The essay begins by discussing what we mean by identity in international relations, turns to the idea that we can think about 'Europe' as a text and then considers the various textualities or ways that this political text can be 'read' and 're-read'.

ON IDENTITIES

The idea or concept of 'identity' has been largely dormant in the orthodox study of international relations. This is because it has not been regarded as a central problem or contested issue. International Relations has assumed that any questions we might want to ask about political identities are well-covered by our understanding of an individual's identification with the state (citizenship) or with the nation (national identity or nationalism) or with the synthesis of the two in the institutionalised form of the nation-state. Thus, the orthodox 'canon' is 'reductionist' in other words it reduces the complexities of identity to the state and the nation as the assumed building-blocks of inter-national relations.

Yet, as a growing body of writing testifies, identity and the activity of identification are much more complex than the orthodoxy permits. The orthodoxy's approach to identity as one governed by the presence of the national-state implies that identity is something that exists and can and should be uncovered and nurtured by the nation-state. This can be described as a type of essentialism; that there is a national essence that is waiting to be discovered, protected and promoted by the state. This view fails to account for the pliability of identities and their openness to manipulation. It is far more useful to conceive of identities as constructions. As one writer has described it, identities do not exist outside their making. Rather, they are socially created in specific social circumstances.[2] Consequently, the process of identification is of as much interest to us as identity itself. The sweeping changes in Europe in the closing decade of the twentieth century are wiping away established ideologies and ways of identifying differences between peoples. New computer, fibre-optic and satellite technologies producing different ways of working and new ways of communicating are underlining the existence of alternative ways of living in a social setting. This, in turn, highlights the contingent or unfixed nature of identification.

Identities, being socially constructed, involve choices between alternative and competing points of attachment. Moreover, given that there are many competing claims upon identities, from ideas, histories, geographic attachments to name only a few, identity cannot be said to be totally complete or absolute. As the societal context itself alters, so too are the mix of pressures constituting identity. If identities can be constructed, then they can also be de-constructed and re-constructed. This is a highly fluid image of identity. It also means that identity and the process of identification are fundamentally political in character and we can then try and explore the politics involved in the construction of identity. More of this later. Our starting point, however, is a question. How can we make sense of the political condition of Europe at the close of the twentieth century in which identities are being constructed and reconstructed?

STOP MAKING SENSE!

Does today's political Europe make any sense at all? Opinion is sharply divided between those who argue that Europe has fallen into a new Age of Barbarism and those who claim that there is every prospect of further advances in European civilisation and material progress.[3] Those who argue for an optimistic future for Europe point to the absence of general war in Europe for over fifty years, to a growth in overall economic prosperity, to improvements in health, education and housing, to the co-operation between governments in the European Union and to the end of the Cold War divide and collapse of communism. The challenge is to sustain and 'cherish our cultural achievement and at the same time continue civilisation's promise to extend its enlightenment to the whole of humanity not just a select few'. This belief in a project of rational progression is challenged by those who argue that Europe is beset by fragmentation, hatred and conflict. Ethnic war in Bosnia, rising racial violence, revivals of fascism, heightened nationalist sentiment and a mounting disillusionment with established political institutions and processes are said to provide ample evidence of the dangers of Modernity and of the barbarous character of today's Europe.

If we are talking about identity in international relations, this debate is being held within the accepted view that people identify primarily with the nation-state and that this is the main vehicle for advancing the emancipatory goals of Europe's three-hundred year-old 'Enlightenment Project'. This largely remains a state-centric approach. It explains contemporary European political developments in terms of the orthodox conceptual categories of sovereignty, the alignment of states and national identities, the interests of states and the distribution of power across the states' system. The extent to which this system of states is able to progress the Enlightenment's emancipatory mission, or descends into disorder and violence ultimately depends upon the virility of the members of the system and their commitment to domestic and inter-state emancipatory goals. This in turn is reliant upon the self-definition of state interest.

But is this enough? Are the concepts and categories of orthodox inter-state/inter-national relations sufficient to understand today's Europe? The orthodoxy emphasises states and their interactions as the principal way of explaining European political relations. This accepts unquestioningly the belief in a common evolution to a higher level of rational organisation. This is embedded in the historical tradition of Modernity and the Enlightenment's commitment to Reason as the engine of human progress. As suggested above, this story (often referred to as a 'discourse') tends to marginalise such considerations of identity as adjuncts to the state itself rather than as distinctive factors worthy of attention in their own right. This story largely excludes such considerations as culture in its attempts at explanation. In other words, this way of looking at international relations fails to take account of the diversity that helps us to understand the European condition.

This is particularly important as the debate over Europe outlined above prompts a deeper, more disturbing concern with the contemporary European political condition. This concern is best summed up as a perceptible shift in the sensitivity of Europe. By this is meant the feeling, hard to pin down, that the consciousness of Europe has changed. The growing references to living in 'post-history', 'post-culture', 'post-rational', 'post-ideological' or 'post-industrial' Europe has been noticeable in recent years. As Heller and Feher have noted, the use of the pre-fix 'post' indicates that this is a sense in which Europe is living 'after' some great experience; in this case the end of the dominance of 'Modernity'.[4] It is important to note, however, that this idea of being 'after' is not used in a chronological sense. Rather it is seeking to describe an altered condition in which the features of both Modernity and Post-Modernity are present; the latter acting as a kind of distorting presence, opening the way for new voices and histories to be heard and read.

The loss of the certainty and sense of direction that Modernity provides ties into the issue of how Europe is developing politically. Crucially, the issue is one of identity. Modernity provided a singular and tightly-bound idea of European identity centred upon the values of Reason, Emancipation and the State. The idea of identity as unfixed, as socially contingent, strikes at the very heart of this singular modernist identity. Laclau outlines the political implications clearly:

> Whether the proliferation of political identities in the contemporary world will lead to a deepening of the logic inherent in the democratic process, or whether it will lead, as some predict, to an implosion of the social and to a radically deregulated society that will create the terrain for authoritarian solutions remains to be seen. But, whatever the outcome, this is the question that sets the agenda for democratic politics in the decades to come.[5]

But, if this is the case, can we think about political Europe in a different, unorthodox, way that might shed more light on the complexities of this European condition?

EUROPE AS A 'TEXT'

One way in which we can try to think about European politics differently would be for us to make an imaginative leap and think about Europe as a 'text'. We are used to conceiving of texts as literary items that can be read and re-read over and over again. We also tend to accept an unspoken idea that the author has given the text a particular meaning and that this can be readily discovered by the reader and understood as the author intended. In this sense, we tend to describe the author as having some authority over the text and that there is a single 'authentic' meaning or reading of the text. We call this meaning (or reading or interpretation) the 'textuality' of the text. How do we use this metaphor to understand Europe?

As we have seen above, an orthodox 'reading' of the political 'text' that we call Europe can be seen to adopt this idea that there is a single story or 'textuality' to be found in the European text. This can be discovered by understanding the importance of human reason to the evolution of Europe. This evolution is explained as a progressive process of developing political spaces called states that provide sanctuaries of reason protecting people from the dangers of anarchy outside the state. The attachment of peoples to a particular state is reinforced by the promotion of the idea that the state and the nation are inextricably entwined. The idea of the nation-state thus reinforced the experience of separation arising from the inviolability of borders between states. The assertion of distinctiveness between peoples embodied in the national state has served to emphasise the vertical divisions between peoples in modern Europe over the horizontal divisions between 'Estates' that had existed across mediaeval Christendom. Modern Europe's development of the nation-state in stressing difference between peoples brought the idea of 'otherness' into the very heart of the practice and study of international relations.

At the same time as political and psychological borders were being drawn between peoples inside and outside the state, the internal development of government institutions and the accompanying political ethos were drawing borders between people within the state. The assertion of public and private spheres of activity, of civic and domestic 'service' and of familiar and 'foreign' gave practical form within the state to the experience of inclusion and exclusion at the centre of the modern state. This is the 'grand narrative' of the orthodox textuality found in the European political text. It is familiar. It is persuasive. Above all, it is misleading. Why?

The answer lies in two aspects of the story. First, we can borrow the idea of 'the death of the author'. In other words, the author of Modernist European politics – 'Sovereign Man' – no longer exists to write the European political script. On the face of it, this appears a fairly ridiculous idea: what do we mean by the 'death' of an author? The explanation rests with the way we view Reason's idea of the 'Sovereign Man'. This portrays the human being who exercises reason as the major agent of progress. This human agent is said to be a cohesive, purposive individual.

This view has been undermined by the psychological work of Freud who began to break down the individual into a number of conscious and sub-conscious dimensions with distinctive levels of awareness. Recent philosophical and psychoanalytical thinking has put forward the view that the individual has become 'de-centred'. By this is meant that the individual is being psychologically fragmented, eroded by the experience of living in an age that is wiping away the capacity of the individual to act with purpose. This is a portrayal of the individual as a psychologically displaced person, uncertain, directionless and without a belief in the future. If this purposive human agent is being erased then it follows that the 'authentic' meaning said to be conveyed by the author through the text must therefore disappear with the author.

Second, as Chris Brown's work on normative theory has noted, the death of both the author and authoritative meaning has three related consequences for the way the text is 'read':

(i) If there is no authoritative meaning or 'reading' of the text, then the way is open for each reader to read the meaning of the text in different ways. There is no definitive 'reading' of the text. Each 'reading' is thus as valid as any other. In the literary jargon mentioned above, a number of textualities arise from the 'authorless' text; political Europe, as a text, can be re-read in ways quite different from the reading offered by the Orthodoxy.

(ii) the death of the author breaks the direct relationship said to exist between the author and the author's text. Meaning no longer comes from the relationship between the author and the text but rather from the relationship between texts. This is the concept of inter-textuality. No text is pristine in its originality. All texts draw upon other texts such that a text merely consists of the weaving together of a whole range of many diverse texts; the fragments or traces of these other texts can still be read in the particular text being read. In the words of Umberto Eco, 'books always speak of other books, and every story tells a story that has already been told'.[6]

The European political text, therefore, is constituted by many different texts – literary, historical, geographic, cultural, philosophic, cinema graphic, artistic, economic, musical, racial or national. Our understanding of Europe results from our reading of the relationship between the various texts we see as constituting the European political text. Thus, we are concerned with the inter-textual rather than inter-national relations of Europe. This is a much more open-ended way of thinking about Europe. The 'world we inhabit loses its familiar pillars upon which we lean for some sense of certainty. Such freedom is an unsettling prospect for us for, as the Italian philosopher Gianni Vattimo suggests, we are entering a world of 'infinite interpretability'.[7]

(iii) the death of the author and 'inter-textuality' assumes that texts are constructed; that is, they are largely artificial ideas pieced together from many diverse texts. It follows that if they can be constructed then they can be de-constructed. Texts such as Europe can be de-constructed and re-constructed again and again and again. By doing this we can delve into the actual processes involved in how a text has been put together. We can ask questions and uncover the unwritten use of power in the construction of a text such as Political Europe and the promotion of its meaning. We can question the degree to which the information that is passed on to us (the 'received knowledge') as students of 'The Discipline of International Relations' is not neutral or 'objective' in character but full of other people's values, assumptions and judgements about what is worthy and what is not; what is to be included and what is to be excluded in the great story or Grand Narrative of International Relations. We are helped in this task by the work of French philosophers such as Jacques Derrida who have asked such questions of language. In particular, we can usefully borrow the idea of pairs of words being used together to suggest what is good and what is bad in international relations and elsewhere.

Such subliminal messages are carried in the language we use to describe and understand international relations. So we think about such pairs of words as order/chaos, state/anarchy, orderliness/justice, war/peace, power/ethics, realist/idealist, public/private, domestic/foreign as commonplace pairings of opposites ('binary oppositions') in our Discipline. But Derrida and others point out that these pairings of words stress the good nature of the first word in each pairing of oppositions and imply the bad nature of the second.

The first word in each pairing is thus privileged over the second and reflects a dominance of the former over the latter in actual life. Orthodox International Relations continues to stress the primacy of the state, the requirement of order, the ever-presence of war, the inescapability of power, the need for realism, the public sphere and responsibility to the Self. Together these constitute a dominant, even tyrannical, 'regime of truth' that represses and excludes the secondary and subordinate terms in the pairing. By breaking these 'binary oppositions' wide open, we can examine the patterns of power operating to repress and exclude in the way we think and practice International Relations.

This process of de-constructing is directly related to the textual fabric of Europe. What we are experiencing is a conjunction of simultaneous critical textualities. We can portray these critical textualities engaging us as challenges to (i) the precepts of the European Enlightenment, (ii) to the established body of European values, (iii) to the way we have understood and experienced political space, and (iv) to the way we have understood and experienced time.

Each of these related textualities raise fundamental questions about identity. The first confronts the Enlightenment's belief in a civilising mission based on universal Reason with the twentieth century's barbarism. Humanity's common journey collapses in the face of inhumanity and unreason. The second points to a break-down in 'uncivilised' values arising from the 'cult of origins' so evident in ethnic and nationalist conflict. The third questions the continued way we attach primary political identification with a space defined as and by the nation-state. Globalised patterns of trade and capital flows as well as communications from MTV and CNN to the Internet 'Superhighway' are re-defining our identification with particular political spaces. The fourth raises questions about the way in which our identities are tied up with our ideas of Time, History and Progress. Again, it is useful to recall that each of these challenges directly relates to the issues of power and exclusion discussed earlier.

ENLIGHTENMENT/BARBARISM

'The' Enlightenment textuality was really a collectivity of mutually reinforcing textualities from the 17th and 18th centuries. We can include the Reformation, the Scientific Revolution, the Renaissance, the Humanist and Rationalist philosophical movements. These movements included such famous figures as Martin Luther, Galileo Galilei, Copernicus, Erasmus, Rene Descartes and les Philosophes.

The common features of the Enlightenment are describes by Eric Hobsbawm as 'the establishment of a universal system of such rules and standards of moral behaviour, embodied in the institutions of states dedicated to the rational progress of humanity: to Life, Liberty and the pursuit of Happiness, to Equality, Liberty and Fraternity'.[8] This definition points out the key elements: institutionalism, humanism, universalism and the role of the state as the main agent for progress. We can see this in the pairings of ideas that have been used to describe the Enlightenment Project; the 'binary oppositions' that incorporate and reinforce patterns of inclusion and exclusion in our thinking about the world. These include: Reason/Intuition; Science/Myth-Romance; Object/Subject; Empirical-deductive/Interpretative-inductive; Universal/Particular. Each of the former terms is privileged over each of the latter; including the former and excluding the latter. Understanding the world and one's place in it following the demise of faith in the heliocentric or God-centred explanation of the world rested on the shoulders of humanity itself. It was to be the refinement and application of human reason to

Europe's problems that would advance human society. This was a project that would transcend time and place. It would provide universal meaning and universal ethical rules.

For Ernesto Laclau, the 'crisis' of the Enlightenment is 'a crisis of universalism'; a loss of faith or confidence in the possibility of universal meaning or morality. Reason, however, has not appeared to the world in a homogeneous form. For example, both liberal-capitalist and Marxist approaches to the world can be defined as rational explanations and prescriptions for human social relations. Both represent opposite sides of the same coin that is Reason. Yet, in the wake of the end of Cold War ideological confrontation, Europeans are living within a vacuum in which the universalist claims of Reason and its derivative cohorts lie discredited and de-valued. The 'gap' created by universalism's absence makes us all the more aware of its loss. There is 'a consciousness of the contingent, precarious, limited character of what remains.'[9]

The Marxist historian Eric Hobsbawm argues that there has been a rise in barbarism during the twentieth century. Barbarism is defined here as a 'reversal' of the Enlightenment project and as 'the disruption and breakdown of the systems of rules and moral behaviour by which all societies regulate the relations among their members and, to a lesser extent, between their members and those of other societies'.[10] Two world wars, the advent of 'total war', millions of combatant and civilian deaths, the systematic genocide of the holocaust, the atomic bomb, Hiroshima and Nagasaki, the wars of decolonisation, the crushing of the 1956 Hungarian uprising and 1968 'Prague Spring' and the 'ethnic cleansing' of the Bosnian conflict are held to stand testament to the failure of the civilising mission of universal Reason.

Enlightenment Reason is also held to be suspect because of the way it has evolved into an oppressive technocratic form. The philosophical influence of Rene Descartes' empirical method and Auguste Compte's 'Positivism' helped evolve a form of reason privileging facts over values, objective over subjective. The universalism of such reason was increasingly believed to have fallen into the abstract search for 'essences' and to reduce the complexities and nuances of the world to the rigid strictures of rational thought. Such Reason has been thought to suppress legitimate differences of identity. Just as there are multiple identities, it is argued, Enlightenment-derived thought has produced 'multiple oppressions.'[11]

Whilst the principles of the Enlightenment have held sway over the development of political ideas and institutions in Europe, its dominance has never been total. The emotional, spiritual and irrational have remained powerful, although subordinated, features of the political text.

Movements such as nineteenth century Romanticism emerged as a reaction to the so-called 'cage of reason'. Ironically, Reason and Romanticism feed off each other; sometimes with horrific consequences. For example, in Hitler's Germany the romantic-mythical idealism of the German 'nation' was fused with the construction of a powerful rationally-organised state. The Holocaust's systematic mass murder drew upon the powerful ideological and state forces that differentiated and oppressed those who were 'different'. This combined with the ruthless, rational technical efficiency of the Nazi's system of murder: genocide.

Whilst for Hobsbawm, such barbarity partly results from the breakdown of the Enlightenment's progressive, civilising values, for writers such as Stjepan Mestrovic the 'barbarian temperament' is ever-present and is merely 'repackaged' by Modernity. We simply delude ourselves that our barbarism is expelled by our Reason.[12] Such barbarism is evident not only on the 'killing fields' of Bosnia but in our contemporary experiences of sharpened antipathy towards 'foreigners', the homeless, jobless and dispossessed of Europe; in the resort to fortress-like defence of homes and work-places from Moscow to Manchester; the resort to spiritual or, more interestingly, mystical sources of solace and meaning. This is intertextually woven into the changing character of dominant European political values.

VALUES/DE-VALUES

Hobsbawm's articulation of barbarism as 'the actual adaptation of people to living in a society without the rules of civilisation' is attributed to an 'obsolescence of traditional social mores'.[13] For Julia Kristeva, this was directly related to today's European 'cult of origins'.[14] To Kristeva, the end of ideological certainty has resulted in a 'fragmentation of individuals'. This has led to a dangerous decline into common bonding found in the 'imaginary identity' of national origins. This cult of imagined identity is evident in many ways in today's Europe. The most obvious example is the 'barbarism' of the conflict in Bosnia-Herzegovena in the 1990s. The stress upon ethnicity and claims to common heritage embodied in shared histories differentiate and demarcate in this conflict. The instances of mass rape, torture and a return to the use of concentration camps merely underline the scepticism raised against the claims of universal Reason.

Other signs of the cult are evident in the xenophobia displayed in calls of 'Germany for the Germans' or 'France for the French'. The exploitation of such sentiments by neo-Fascist groups has been obvious enough across Europe, not only in Germany and France. Russia, Italy, Belgium have also experienced the consequences of the power of originatory identification. Political parties with openly xenophobic anti-immigration policies have made significant gains in political representation. The success of the Freedom Party in Austria is but one example.

Directly related to this cult of origins is the description of the Enlightenment crisis as one 'marked by the incommensurability of different articulations of identity'.[15] This is the politics of diaspora. Diaspora refers to the idea of communal spaces that are experienced as simultaneous identities. This is the experience of living in a particular political space (such as a state) with its physical and imagined sources of identification whilst simultaneously identifying with other, external, sources of cultural identity.

This diasporic experience is particularly acute in the post-colonial textuality of Europe. The complexities of identity faced by those who have come to Europe from other countries and former colonies as well as Europe's gypsies is clear in their experience of simultaneously living inside and outside the dominant cultural identity of a nation-state; living in the 'real' and 'the imagined' at the same time. The binary oppositions used to 'locate' such peoples highlights the assumptions of inclusion and exclusion at work: native/immigrant, white/black-coloured, national/ethnic.[16] This psychological dimension of the socially-directed process of identification[17] gives rise to accusations of the new Europe as one for 'pan-European whiteness'[18] and to an active counter-assertion of non- white identities; thus making differences absolute.[19]

The work of Homi Bhabha helps put the diasporic into focus. As we noted above, the use of 'post-' is not meant in a chronological sense but is used to suggest a changed, more pluralistic idea of Europe. Bhabha describes the 'post-' pre-fixed concepts (for example post-colonial) as 'enunciative boundaries'. By this he means that these are new boundaries at which previously suppressed 'voices' can be heard and hidden stories be read at last: minorities, women, migrants, exiles, refugees, AIDS sufferers and 'the bearers of policed sexualities'. Bhabha argues that we need to recognise the ambivalence of cultures and the partial identities that result from living in a space between cultures; such is the post-colonial experience for many people and societies.[20]

The historical narrative of European Modernity has largely rested upon a belief in the northern European roots of European civilisation. Yet, this has been challenged by writers such as Martin Bernal, who has claimed 'afroasiatic' origins. Bernal's location of 'western civilisation' in Near Eastern (Egyptian-Phoenician) roots leads him to conclude that, if he is correct, it will be necessary not only to rethink the fundamental bases of 'Western Civilisation' but also to recognise the penetration of racism and continental chauvinism into all our historiography; our philosophy of writing history.[21] The claim to an African presence throughout European history, yet unacknowledged by the history constructed by white Europe, is advanced by writers such as David Forbes and Simon Hinds.[22]

But the question of values carries many different textual nuances. The question of a de-valuation of values takes us deeper into the cultural textuality of Europe. The debate about European values and culture has frequently turned on the question of whether the distinction between 'high' and 'low' culture has broken down and, if so, has this led to a loss of our capacity to remain a 'civilised' community. Does a loss of 'high' culture undermine the drive towards continual improvement; to acquire higher plains of achievement?

The value of culture and the culture of values have been contested ideas for centuries. The concept of 'culture' means different things to different people. In some definitions, culture means those forms of representation that carry Humanity beyond the drudgery of the de-humanising existence of every-day life. Great paintings, poetry, sculpture, literature, music or architecture thus represent the best of human existence. This, in turn, fuels claims that Art and the Artist carry a special responsibility to society to both depict the 'essence' of that Humanity whilst simultaneously transcending it. Modernist art sought to achieve both; expressing the essence of industrial society's mechanistic, rapidly changing character whilst seeking the abstract essence of Humanity that allowed it to transcend the industrial epoch's de-humanising impact. Aestheticism, the theoretical discourse of Art, thus portrayed the role of Artists, the avante-guarde, as social guides.

Writing in 1936, the German essayist Walter Benjamin argued that this claim to aesthetic 'Truth' and distinctiveness was being challenged by 'The Age of Mechanical Reproduction'.[23] The ability to re-produce by mechanical means, Benjamin argued, erased the originating genius of the producer and a cultural artefact's 'aura'. Art thus became just another commodity. This point was taken up by other German writers, Theodor Adorno and Max Horkheimer of the so-called 'Frankfurt School' in the 1940s. Culture in capitalist society was simply another industry with its products bought and sold like any other item in the marketplace.[24] More recent writings have suggested that the arrival of 'decibel culture' ('The

Beatles'. . . . or 'Primal Scream'?), the indistinctiveness of Art and advertising – the use of the Classics to sell dog food, chocolate or automobiles
– and the street cultures, performance art and Muzak-infested shopping
malls have de-valued societal appreciation of quality leaving little in the
way of benchmarks against which to make judgements as to what is worthy and what is not.[25]

This point is related to the challenges being mounted against the
accepted canons of wisdom in music, theology and literature amongst
others. The accepted 'discourse' of music is being savaged by the gender-
focused critique of Marcia Citron. The supposed unity of the early Christian Church and the rationale for its male domination are undermined
by the works of Elaine Pagels. The literary form, the novelistic tradition,
is challenged by works such as Umberto Eco's 'The Name of the Rose'.[26]
What these critical de-constructions are doing is undermining the
accepted, dominant and exclusionary 'stories' or texts that have provided
the legitimating benchmarks for so long. The certitude of the Grand Narratives is being washed away.

SPACE/NON-SPACE

'Space' is political. It is moulded, constructed and distrusted. It is
contested by alternative, competing interests. Reason has sought to reconstruct and control Nature. Little of the contemporary European
topography can be said still to be 'natural'. The urban cityscapes are the
battlegrounds of different identities; the differentiation of each district/
suburban 'persona'.

The modern nation-state has formed the principal focus for political
identification in Europe. Yet this politicised space is said to be subject to
contemporary pressures of 'balkanisation'.[27] In addition, the corrosion
of the state's practical sovereignty by the globalising processes of trade
and capital flows, the erosive effects of the global Internet, a global culture epitomised by MTV or CNN are believed to be tearing apart the traditional compact idea of the state. Political space is being dissolved and
re-constituted.

Here a textual relationship with the changing character of capitalist
society comes into play. The shift to more knowledge-intensive forms of
production involving the utilisation of new technologies carries significant implications for identification. Such technologies move people
into 'cyberspace' thereby removing them from the traditional locators of
Time and Space. This process is a further movement of inclusion and

exclusion. Access to cyberspace raises questions of relative wealth and poverty. The influence upon language is also significant. Language has remained a key element in the process of identification. The strict requirements of Internet communication language promote a distinctive, globalised lexicon. It poses an additional question as to exclusion and identity. Does the experience of cyberspace promote closer attachments between globally dispersed participants than between physical neighbours? This affects political identity in different ways.

The globalising influence has an obviously broadening affect on the identificatory perspective. Yet, such globalising forces have the effect of fragmenting the established political space and associated identity and throwing people back onto the cult of origins discussed above. Arthur Schlessinger has commented that: 'The more people feel themselves adrift in a cold, impersonal, anonymous world, the more desperately they embrace some warm, familiar, intelligible, protective human unit – the more they crave the politics of identity. Integration and disintegration are the opposites that feed on each other. The more the world integrates, the more people cling to their own in groups increasingly defined in these post-ideological days by ethnic and religious emotions'.[28]

TIME/PERPETUAL PRESENT

One of the most important textualities of Modernist political Europe is the Sense of History. The notion that we gain a sense of individual and collective meaning, of identity, from our relation to a past and to a future. Our feeling of our place in history is tied into a deeper sense of time. Modernity's text has given us a sense of time that we rarely question. This is a feeling that we are travelling through time that has a beginning and an end. 'Time', therefore, acts as a provider of location for identity in History. This is what we call a teleological understanding of time and human history; a progressive, linear and ascendant idea that can be traced all the way back to the Greek philosopher Aristotle. The establishment of the state is portrayed as the creation of a reasoned space as an answer to the problem of avoiding anarchy. Europe's historical textuality has stressed the progressive perfectibility of the political space that is the state. Space has been privileged over Time.

Yet, the stretching and tearing of political space in contemporary Europe is due in part to a qualitative change in the way we experience time. This has been well expressed in the imagined history in reverse of

Martin Amis' novel *Time's Arrow*. At one layer of experience 'real time' communication has dissolved time differentials spurring a timeless existence. At another, perhaps more profound layer of our experience, there is a sense that we have lost faith in the idea of the future. The implications of a de-centred 'sovereign being' are clear here. Lacking purpose, the sense of future disappears. The past and the present must therefore take on added importance for our sense of identity. Where we have come from helps to answer the question of where we are now. The central and eastern European experience of time has been significantly affected by the events since 1989. The loss of the state-socialist parameters of Time embodied in socialist history and the uncertainty of an unknown future leads to a greater emphasis upon the past and present as important locators of identity. This reflection on the past is evident in the cult of origins. Turning to an imagined shared beginning, differentiating you from 'Others' and marking your present existence was regarded as central to the conflict of the Balkans during the late 1990s.

However, at a further level of experience, History itself can be said to be disappearing. 'History', like identity, is constructed. It is not an unchallengable, absolute truth. History as a story is selective; it has actively included and excluded. History is characterised by amnesia or an 'active forgetting'. In this sense it is more useful to think about History as a history of silences. This forgetfulness has excluded or marginalised issues of morality and justice. It has relegated women to the 'private'. It has subordinated non-European stories to mere sub-plots of the main European text. The construction of national cultural histories is insistent that 'a veil of forgetfulness should discreetly cover obscure internal differences... oblivion must cover the internal differentiations and nuances within any one politically sanctified culture'.[29] A good example of such active forgetting is that of post-reunification Berlin. With reunification Berlin experienced frenetic change. Eastern Berlin became a virtual construction site. This represents an active obliteration of the communist past – an active forgetting moulding eastern Berlin into the history of the post-Second World War liberal-capitalist western Berlin. This process was reinforced by the re-naming of streets in eastern Berlin. This experience of History is inter-textually linked to the changing political space of Berlin. An awareness of European political History as artificial and as artifice (a device deliberately designed to exclude) pervades contemporary disillusionment with established institutions. With the future and the past both rejected, identification is subject to the experience of living continually in the present – the perpetual present. Live-for-the-moment not for a tomorrow that can never come.

This altered sensitivity to Time is seen in disparate ways from 'joy-riding' to the proliferation of 'historical' theme parks complete with 'authentic' smells of the period!

READING EUROPE'S IDENTITIES

The very nature of European political inter-textuality does not allow us the luxury of 'conclusion'. No 'quick fix'! This response is, at the very least, frustrating for those who need conclusions. But, if there are no answers what does any of this offer the student of European Intertextual Relations? Inter- textuality offers us a way to experience the European text in complex diversity, unrestricted by the imposition of a Modernist International Relation's prison of categories and exclusions.

Hopefully it spurs us to think about the constructed nature of meaning and the free play of competing constitutive influences woven together to provide the multiple dimensions of experience that form the contemporary European political condition. It spurs us to understand critically the Russian doll-like character of the different textualities of European identities: to look inside one and find another and another... each related to the other yet with a distinctive personality. We are jettisoning the notion of categories in favour of unseparated 're-readings' of the European political text.

This allows us to think more easily about the textualities we encounter: the distortion of 'Space', the erosion of 'Time/History', the erasure of the 'sovereign being'. Ask the question of the received, conventional wisdom: where did this 'knowledge' come from? What are the privileged ideas it contains? Who or what does it include and exclude? Who and what constructs our political identities in Europe, how are they constructed and... why?

Much of the criticism directed at this approach centres upon the possibility of 'relativism'; that there is no way of judging between alternative interpretations. The claims that Europe has an underlying unity or that it is a fragmented entity play to the either/or assumption. As Moretti as suggested, 'complex Europe' carries meaning as a welter of contradictory, yet co-existent, forces.[30] This is 'a productive enmity'. It is a dynamic and necessary creative tension between elements of orderliness and chaos, unity and disparity. The textualities of Europe are not mutually exclusive categories but each helps constitute the other. None of these textualities is ever complete and each is contingent upon the play of the other. Inter-textuality is, therefore, both a productive irreducible condition of contemporary Europe and a fruitful approach to better understanding the complex character of this condition.

Notes

1. J. Der Derian and M.J. Shapiro (eds), *International/Intertextual Relations: Postmodern Readings of World Politics* (Lexington: Lexington Books, 1989, pp.xiv–xv.
2. S. Macdonald, 'Identity Complexes in Western Europe: Social Anthropological Perspectives' in S. Macdonald (ed.), *Inside European Identities* (Oxford/Providence: Berg, 1993, p. 6).
3. E. Hobsbawm, 'Barbarism: A User's Guide', *New Left Review*, No. 206, July–August 1994, pp.44–54; L. Jardine, Beware Prophets of Doom, *The Sunday Times*, May 1, 1994, p.12.
4. A. Heller and F. Feher, *The Postmodern Political Condition* (Cambridge: Polity, 1988, Repr. 1991, Ch. 11).
5. E. Laclau (ed) *The Making of Political Identities* (London: Verso, 1994, p.5).
6. U. Eco, *Reflections on the Name of the Rose* (London: Secker & Warburg, 1983 Rpr. 1985 p. 20).
7. G.Vattimo, *The End of Modernity* (Baltimore: Johns Hopkins Press, 1988).
8. Hobsbawm, *op.cit.*, p. 45.
9. Laclau, *op.cit.*, p. 1.
10. Hobsbawm, *loc.cit.*
11. D. Harvey,'Class Relations, Social Justice and the Politics of Difference' in M. Keith and S. Pile (eds), *Place and the Politics of Identity* (London: Routledge, 1993, p. 56).
12. S.G. Mestrovic, *The Barbarian Temperament* (London: Routledge, 1993).
13. Hobsbawm, *loc.cit.*
14. J. Kristeva, *Nations without Nationalism* (New York: Columbia University Press, 1993, pp. 3–4).
15. M. Keith and S. Pile, 'The Politics of Place', in Keith and Pile (eds), *Place and the Politics of Identity* (London: Routledge, 1993, pp. 18–19).
16. S. Patterson, *Dark Strangers: A Study of West Indians in London* (London: Penguin, 1965).
17. Homi Bhabha, Foreword to F. Fanon, *Black Skin, White Masks*, (1952) (London: Pluto, 1986 edn pp. vii–xxv).
18. L. Back and A. Nayak (eds), *Invisible Europeans? Black People in the 'New' Europe* (Birmingham: AFFOR, England, 1993, p. 4).
19. W. Jones and C. Harris (eds), *Inside Babylon: The Caribbean Diaspora in Britain* (London: Verso, 1993).
20. H. Bhabha, *The Location of Culture* (London: Routledge, 1994).
21. M. Bernal, *Black Athena: The Afroasiatic Roots of Classical Civilisation* (London: Vintage, 1991 edn, p. 2).

22. D. Forbes, 'In and Out of Europe: A Black European Perspective' and S. Hinds, 'Roots in Europe: The African Presence and European History' in Back and Nayak, *op.cit.*

23. W. Benjamin, 'The Work of Art in the Age of Mechanical Reproduction', in W. Benjamin (trans. H. Zohn), *Illuminations* (London: Jonathan Cape, 1970, pp. 219–253).

24. M. Horkheimer and T. Adorno, 'The Dialectic of the Enlightenment' (Excerpts) in S. During (ed.), *The Cultural Studies Reader* (London: Routledge, 1993).

25 G. Steiner, *In Bluebeard's Castle: Towards a Re-definition of Culture* (London: Faber & Faber, 1971, repr. 1989, Ch. 3).

26. M.J. Citron, *Gender and the Musical Canon* (Cambridge University Press, 1993); E. Pagels, *The Gnostic Gospels* (New York: Vintage, 1981 edn); Umberto Eco, *Reflections on The Name of The Rose* (London: Secker & Warburg, 1985).

27. S. Mestrovic, *The Balkanisation of the West: The Confluence of Postmodernism and Postcommunism* (London: Routledge, 1994).

28. A. Schlessinger, 'Three Steps to Tame Tribalism and Unify Europe', *International Herald Tribune*, June 17, 1994, p.6.

29. R. Ashley, 'Living on Border Lines: Man, Poststructuralism, and War' in Der Derian and Shapiro, *op.cit.*, p. 262; E. Gellner, *Culture, Identity and Politics* (Cambridge University Press, 1987, p. 10).

30. F. Moretti, 'Modern European Literature: A Geographical Sketch', *New Left Review*, No. 206, July/August 1994, pp. 86–109.

9 Colonialism and Sub-Saharan Identities
Nana Poku

INTRODUCTION

Unlike Europe, where nation-builders aimed to replace the older empires with nations that represented some combination of cultural, linguistic, and patriotic unity, African states are building nations based on new identities defined by the boundaries of their colonial past. Recent studies suggest that this might not be as different from other historical experiences as commonly presumed. Benedict Anderson, for example, provides a convincing account of how most nations of Latin America were built on the administrative divisions left by the Spanish empire. Africa's colonial past, however, has left a legacy of multiple identities and a crisis of legitimacy for post-colonial governments. Almost everywhere on the continent the remnants of colonialism remain deeply rooted in contemporary events. For the relics of colonialism lie deep in African societies.

This chapter will emphasise the complexities of the group identities that the African state faces and, relatedly, the impact of these identities for the politics of interaction on the continent. The chapter assumes a complex and constant engagement of rival interest in the contemporary political arena and a complex interaction among various groups mobilised to secure public resources from those in political authority. Thus, the accent upon organised group action in the political arena and upon expressed collective claims to resources, participation and security accounts for the many political identities on the African continent. I will begin by providing a brief introduction of European colonialism in its African context, then turn to the implications of this for the formation of contemporary African states and examine the concept of identity in this context. The chapter will conclude by considering the implications of these identities for what is argued here to be a current drive towards democratisation on the continent.[1]

Before proceeding, however, it is important to clarify the point that in referring to Africa I am primarily concerned with Black Africa. That is, although Africa is geographically a single entity, it is politically and culturally heterogeneous. The normal division of the continent is provided by the Sahara desert, bringing the Maghreb states of the predominantly Islamic north, and combining the rest to the south – including South Africa – as sub-Saharan or Black Africa. It must be stated that, historically, this distinction has served more as a bridge than a barrier between north and south. Goods, people and ideas have freely moved across it, and these contacts continue today in such forms as Pan-Africanism, the Organisation of African Unity, and the collaboration in addressing Third World concerns in the United Nations. For the purpose of this essay, however, although references will be made to the Maghreb states, it is within the context of Black Africa that the essay will be largely constructed.

THE COLONIAL LEGACY

As a geographical entity, Africa has a rich cultural inheritance: the Zulu nation, the Pharaohs of Egypt; the Ethiopian civilisation; Great Zimbabwe; the sophisticated education and cultural metropolis of Timbuctu and the brave Ashanti warriors of Ghana; all point to an impressive past.[2] Yet the manner in which Africans were drawn into world politics, as objects of external rivalries and interests rather than as protagonists in their own right, has undoubtedly had the most profound impact on contemporary African identities. Admittedly, here is not the place to analyse the full history of Black Africa. Yet, one cannot construct a meaningful understanding of what constitutes contemporary African identities without first considering Africa's recent history. As will become clear, the modern identities of Black Africa cannot be separated from the continent's colonial legacy.

Among the peoples of Africa and Asia, imperialism and colonialism are generally viewed as monopolies of people of European origin – 'the white man'. The terms denote a power relationship of one political entity over another. Imperialism describes the process of establishing that power relationship, and colonialism has to do with the pattern of domination and rule once the relationship has been consolidated. Motivated by a mix of economic and geo-political considerations, at the conference of Berlin in 1884, European leaders finally decided the rules for the partitioning of what James Mayall described as the 'last great land mass': Africa. This in turn produced what historian often refer to as the 'great scramble for Africa'.

To the colonisers the strategy was simple, whenever they occupied a piece of land they could legitimately integrate that territory into their empire. This extension of the European notion of sovereignty brought with it a total compartmentalisation of political space in which there were no empty areas. Only 10 per cent of the continent was under direct European control in 1870, but by the end of the century only 10 per cent remained outside it.[3] From the ownership of a landholding through a hierarchy of political administrative areas such as the community, county, state, and nation, all pieces fit together with neither overlap nor extension. The resulting pattern contains comparable administrative units and clearly defined boundaries.

Within their colonial boundaries, the colonisers constructed African economies to serve European rather than African interests and integrated African markets into the global division of labour. The rapid construction of commodity export economies (cash crops and minerals) was undertaken, as exemplified by groundnut, cocoa and palm oil from Nigeria, cocoa and gold from the Gold Coast (now Ghana), cotton from Benin and Burkina Faso; coffee from Kenya, Uganda and Tanzania; and ores from Liberia, Guinea, and Sierra Leone. (As will become apparent, this construction of Africa economies and the manner in which they were integrated into the global economy has had a significant impact on post-colonial development.)[4] As large-scale plantations developed and expanded on the continent in order to service the demands for these products, so too was an influx of a significant number of European settlers. These settlers were concentrated heavily on the Eastern and Southern parts of the continent as well as in Algeria, altering the socio-economic and political structures of these regions considerably.[5]

African's involvement in the First World War gave a great boost to their opposition to external rule. It was, however, the Second World War which led directly to 'mass' nationalism, the call for self-determination and eventually independence.[6] Political strategies varied, but nationalist movements in most colonies challenged their colonial leaders by demanding better representations on all the apparatus of the state. The period from the end of the Second World War to the 1960s, saw the domination of African politics by a cascade of constitutional formulae and bargaining processes which eventually led to the emergence of native rule states on the continent.

As one might expect, the pattern of decolonialisation differed considerably from empire to empire. In a characteristic style, the French attempted to slow or even freeze decolonialisation in the late 1950s and early 1960s. The strategy was to create a sort of community of Francophone states which would offer the colonies equal status in their dealings with France. Guinea opted out of this scheme and took full independence in 1958; this initiated a process which led to over a dozen Francophone countries becoming independent by 1960. In an equally typical manner, the British adopted a pragmatic style of decolonialisation, granting independence whenever a colony was viewed as 'ready' – such as Ghana in 1957, Nigeria in 1960 and Sierra Leone in 1961. The British empire in Africa continued to be disbanded in a piecemeal but careful fashion, each territory being treated individually according to its preparedness for independence as judged by the British: not always as objectively as claimed.

In contrast to the Belgians and the Portuguese, the decolonialisation process went relatively smoothly for the British and the French despite the occasional problems (Algeria for the French, Rhodesia (now Zimbabwe) for the British). Within days of the Belgians leaving Congo in 1960, a civil war broke out that exacerbated superpower rivalries and drew in the large United Nations military forces in ONUC (UN Operation in the Congo). Equally chaotic was the Portuguese withdrawal from Mozambique and Angola (and also Guinea-Bissau) in 1975, following a long war of attrition and the subsequent intervention of South African, Cuban, Soviet, and American interests. Even today, the legacy of this conflict is still with us and the wars have still not been fully resolved.[7]

One of the most important observations to be made about this transition from colonial rule to independent states (at least for our purpose), is the fact that the boundaries of the latter changed remarkably little. That is, post-colonial African states are, with very few exceptions, territorially identical to the European colonies they replaced. That this must be so, was stipulated at the 1964 meeting of the Organisation for African Unity (OAU). The implications of this for the politics of identification will be examined in greater detailed later, for now however, it suffices to say that every boundary on the continent cuts through at least one cultural area. The Nigeria-Cameroon boundary divides fourteen, while the boundaries of Burkina Faso cross twenty-one cultural areas. At the micro level such boundaries sometimes divided town from their hinterlands, villages from their traditional fields and even families from their communities.

During the colonial period, this artificially created them/us (or to use the jargon, inside/outside) had little significance primarily because the state could and did maintain a more or less impartial supervision over the disparate elements over which it ruled. Territorial identification was never a colonial priority, hence, the colonial powers did not expect their subjects to develop any emotional attachment to the territory as a whole:

instead, they emphasised a common loyalty to the metropolis. The colonial state thus resembles a Hobbesian state of nature where security and equality becomes the primary national concern. The role of the state in this context was one of providing a security umbrella for national subjects to live and move freely within a colonial boundary. The post-colonial significance of this will be examined in greater detail later. For now, however, we are at the point where we need to bring our historical narrative up to date. The intention here is not to cover every aspect of post-colonial life; rather we will concentrate on those aspects that will later inform on our discussions about contemporary African identities, and relatedly, the current advancement of democratic principles on the continent.

FROM COLONIALISM TO NEO-COLONIALISM

At independence, the former colonies looked firmly towards an opportunistic and optimistic future. To a large extent they regarded their colonial past as at least best forgotten; a history of exploitation and humiliation which had left their people poor and under-developed. Yet, over four decades of independence has not fulfilled any of their optimistic dreams or expectations. Indeed, the most obvious observation to be made about the history of post-colonial Black Africa is that the populations of these countries have on the whole witnessed an absolute decline in their living standards since becoming independent. According to a recent World Bank report, the rate of Gross Domestic Product (GDP) for the whole of Sub-Saharan Africa showed a decline from 3.9 per cent in the 1970s to 1.9 per cent in the 1980s (excluding Nigeria, from 4.1 per cent to 1.6 per cent), while per Capita income growth over all showed a decline of 1.3 per cent to 0.8 per cent in the same period. If Nigeria is excluded, the low and middle income countries – Benin, Burundi, Chad, Djibouti, Ethiopia, Gambia, Gunea-Bissau, Mali, Niger, Rwanda, Sierra Leone, Somalia, Togo, Uganda, and Upper Volta, to mention but a few, actually had a negative per capita growth rate between 1980 and 1991. Indeed, the total Gross National Product (GNP) of all fifty-two African states in 1991 was only about 7 per cent of that of the United States.[8]

Over the past two or so decades, academic interest in the causes of African poverty have been strong. Approaches and theories to an understanding and explanation of the problem abound – almost as many theories as theorists. By far the most dominant theoretical explanation for Black Africa's contemporary ills (at least for policy-makers and financial institutions) has come from what we shall call the 'over-extension school'.

Suffering from a chronic shortage of capabilities, African governments, this school argues, after independence took on too many tasks and, as a result, their social and other (i.e defence) commitments exceeded their economic capabilities. Far too often these governments extended the activities of the state through embarking on over-ambitious social and economic policies designed to achieve rapid economic growth. In Ghana, for instance, within two years of independence, Nkrumah had run the Ghanaian reserves from £200 million down to just £4 million and the country's external debt up to nearly £300 million in order to finance his rapid industrialisation programme.[9] In reality however, these policies were, more often than not, accompanied by inefficiencies, inadequate funding and corruption.

The persuasive nature of this over-extension thesis has found ready support not only from contemporary western academics, but (and as mentioned earlier), western financial institutions. In 1985, for example, a World Bank report on Africa's development crisis concluded that, 'African governments should change their policies of government intervention... if they are to improve their disappointing growth record... The role of the government... should be one of safe-guarding the mechanisms of growth in the market place, rather then being the artificial generator of short lived economic booms'[10]

How valid are these criticisms? While it is true that post-colonial governments over-extended themselves, it is far from axiomatic that their inability to develop economically was solely related to this over-extension. A more productive way of analysing why post-colonial governments have been so unsuccessful at developing their countries might be to place it within the context of both colonialism and decolonialisation. At the time of decolonialisation, the optimism was based more on hypothesis than on fact or historical experience. In many cases colonial leaders and academic commentators took the favourable conditions of the post-war (and in retrospect artificial) economic boom as their model for post-colonial development. Killick makes that point that most of their basic assumptions were as false as the very pessimistic projections being made ten years earlier, which were themselves based on an equally untypical 1930s.[11] The reality was that young African states were quite incapable of carrying through the highly sophisticated development schemes that western experts drew up for them. For example, industry could not, given the size and character of most of these states, take the rest of the un-modernised economy along with it. Import-substituting industries could not generate an efficient intermediate or capital goods industry in the short term.

Equally, far from being at their strongest at the time of independence, most of the colonial economies were weak and fragmented; reflecting centuries of colonial subjugation and exploitation. In Black Africa, industries and most of the basic economic infrastructures (i.e transport and communications systems) needed to stimulate economic growth after independence were virtually non-existent. In addition to this, virtually all the ex-colonies had suffered from years of Colonial or metropolitan policies that deliberately inhibited industrial and economic development, and instead promoted a heavy reliance on export of primary products.[12] Here, the British rule in India provides a classic example. Britain, it is argued, systematically destroyed the Indian handicraft textile industry in order to provide market for Lancashire's cotton industry.[13] Klein relates how until independence, Senegal had to export peanuts in their shells to France because the latter levied high tariffs on imports in order to protect its own vegetable oil industry.

The problem with this form of dependency is that it has carried on since independence. Through their domination of the global political economy (especially world trading markets, capital and technical knowledge), the ex-colonial powers still control the revenues to ex-colonies through their ability to fix raw-material prices and determine the volume of raw material sales on the international market. This position is usually referred to in the literature as 'neo-colonialism' or new-colonialism. This term denotes a many-sided attempt by the former metropolitan powers to tie the new 'nation' closely to the interest and need of their own economic growth. At times this is overt; for example, when France imposed military agreements on its former colonies, so that many of them, when becoming independent, had still to accept the presence of French troops on their soil.

It is rather the structural (or covert), economic relationship between former colonial powers and their colonies that has given content to neo-colonialism. The argument holds that colonialism fostered economic dependency through turning colonial economies into cash-crop economies. The post colonial impact of this are twofold: firstly, this has rendered post-colonial regimes highly vulnerable to fluctuations in world market conditions that affects primary products. Secondly, the weakness of their economies has placed them at a disadvantage in their dealings with former colonial leaders at the global level.

In 1974 an assortment of states identifying themselves as under-developed countries, complained at the United Nations Assembly that they were treated unequally and were becoming increasingly dependent on their former metropolitan rulers through neo-colonial exploitation and the unjust nature of the international economic order. It was argued that the underdevelopment of these territories was functionally related to the development of the core. The structural nature of the emergent Global Political Economy has permitted the advanced core to drain the periphery of its economic surplus, transferring wealth from the former colonies to the former metropolitan rulers through the mechanisms of trade and investment. Consequently, dependency does not merely hold back the full development of the former colonies; it actually immiserizes the less developed economies and make them even less successful than they might otherwise have been.

In this context, dependency cannot be ignored. Yet, by its very nature modern international relations is conducted in an arena of inter-dependency. This is further strengthened by the shape of modern inter-dependent economic markets. While there is a merit in the argument that inter-dependency of the world's economy based on free trade, specialisation and international division of labour, facilitates domestic development,[14] there is no merit in having a system that structurally undermines the developmental efforts of certain regions.

Developing countries efforts to improve their economies are constantly being undermined by the present world economic order and the growth in power of their neo-colonial instruments; such as multinational corporations. Whereas liberal economic thinking stresses the dual but flexible nature of domestic and international economies (that is, the contrast between the modern sectors integrated into the national and international economies and the backward, isolated, and inefficient sectors), it could be argued that there is only one functional integrated whole. Within this system, the underdeveloped periphery is necessarily backward and underdeveloped because the periphery is systematically exploited and prevented from developing by international capitalism and its reactionary domestic allies in the Third World economies themselves.

This functional or organic relationship between the developed and underdeveloped countries was arguably created by colonialism. In the colonial period, international companies, the agents of world capitalism, invested in the primary producing sectors of less-developed countries. Productive export sectors linked by capital to the international economy existed as enclaves in otherwise under-developed economies unable to take advantage of such external economies as were potentially available. In the decade before 'mass' decolonisation and for a time afterwards, transnational companies, seeking to integrate production worldwide, invested in industrial and manufacturing as well as the traditional primary producing sectors. For the recipient nations, the benefits, often described as 'trickle-down', were limited. Local markets have been systematically under-developed because even after independence, profits are repatriated to the host state and the better known, better organised transnational companies attract local savings away from indigenous firms. As the work of Theotonio Dos Santos has demonstrated with reference to Latin America, this process of dependency could not have been sustained after independence without the support of local elites who, as he quite rightly concluded, 'are integrated into a class alliance with the transnational bourgeoisie, adopting their life-style and consumption patterns.'

For different reasons, this transnational class alliance has also played a critical role in the history of contemporary Black Africa. It was precisely this curious identity of interests between the new African elite (almost all educated in Europe) and the colonial oligarchy that facilitated the peaceful transfer of power in Black Africa. Once it had become apparent that the trade and economic policies of the colonial power could be conducted without the apparatus of direct political control, then the logic of maintaining expensive overseas colonies became less attractive. 'Gabon is independent', President M'ba is reputed to have said, 'but between Gabon and France nothing has changed; everything goes on as before.' Indeed, in the study of African societies after independence, one can be forgiven for thinking that de-colonialisation left them as states without independence or sovereignty.

As will become clear, what constitutes contemporary African identities are directly related to this relationship between pre and post-colonial developments. This said, we have arrived at the point where we need to bring our discussions back to the theme of this chapter: namely, the issue of contemporary African identities. We begin by clarifying several key concepts.

NATION, ETHNICITY, NATIONALISM

As used in the context of this essay, ethnicity denotes a subjective perception of common origin, historical memories, close ties, and shared aspirations. Ethnic group pertains to organised activity by persons, linked by a consciousness of a special identity, who jointly seek to maximise their corporate political, economic, and social interests. The orthodox definition of a nation usually refers to a social collectivity which share some or all of the following characteristics: a sense of common identity, a history, a language, perceived ethnic or racial origins, religion, a common economic life, a geographical location and a political base. The common element in modern nations are (i) a state which sets the parameters of social advances, particularly in terms of language and education, and (ii) historical myths which project into the past the legitimacy of the nations associated with the state. Nationalism implies either an attachment to an existing state recognised as sovereign by the international community, or the aspiration to establish such a state. In myth each nation corresponds to one culture. In reality, the cultural variety within a recognised nation may be enormous. The nineteenth and twentieth century myth of the nation-state, in which cultural boundaries and state boundaries coincide, is the exception rather than the rule in historical reality. Eric Hobsbawm, for example, notes that in 1789 only half the population of France spoke French.

In a similar vein, Smith notes that, of the 132 independent states existing in 1971, 'only 12 were ethnically homogeneous, representing 9.1 per cent of the total, while another 25 (or 18 per cent) had a single ethnic community comprising over 90 per cent of the state's population'.[15] In this context, the concept of nationalism appears to be a super-ethnic collectivity – that which binds people together who would otherwise find their greatest sense of belonging in ethnic group, religious groups, productive units, and so on. However, while the nation-state gives territoriality to a community of people that usually includes many ethnic groups, it does not exclude political competition between ethnic groups over territory or political independence. This gives rise to what is usually referred to as 'political nationalism' (an idea to which we shall return).

As will become apparent, national loyalties may coexist with loyalties to subnational groups, which may be labelled in ethnic, tribal, linguistic, religious or regional terms. These subgroups too, however powerful the sentiments attached to them, change over time. Their boundaries and their meanings shift, and their significance for political rivalry or war cannot be simply derived from the magnitude of the cultural distinctions. The term tribe is particularly misleading. It conveys an unrealistic image of similar small-scale primitive communities rather than groups as varied in their histories and internal dynamics as the 'nations' and 'ethnic groups' of other continents.

Certainly, when most commentators use the concept 'tribes' to distinguish between African societies and to explain contemporary political uncertainties, it generally has pejorative connotations. In this context, it suggests primordial attachments to primitive and savage ways of life, sharply distinguished from the 'civilised' ways of Europeans. Certainly, neither Serbs nor Croatians are ever referred to as tribes. Neither is the

Quebecois in Canada. The term 'tribe' however, offers very little scope for critical academic analysis. Even less so when it functions as an explanatory tool for large-scale killing and destruction on the African continent. Narratives in this sense are no trivial matter. Whether they are 'true' is not immediately at issue. What matters is that they are accepted as adequate to make sense of contemporary events and political behaviour.

Elsewhere, John Berger remarks that, 'if every event which occurred could be given a name, there would be no need for [such narratives]. As things are here, life outstrips our vocabulary. A word is missing so the story has to be told.'[16] In telling the story about contemporary African identities, perhaps there are two words missing: History and Progress. The former refers to Black Africa's colonial past and the latter, its impact on contemporary African events. As I have sought to demonstrate, contemporary African economic development (or lack of) is functionally related to (i) the construction of African economies during colonialism and (ii) their integration into the global capitalist economic system. The story of African identities are not too dissimilar from this in the sense that they too are the legacies of colonialism. What colonial leaders grouped together as 'tribal' units for administrative purposes, function today as the basis of ethnic and political identities on the continent; these occasionally explode into secessionism and warfare, as in Nigeria, Chad, Sudan, and Ethiopia.

THE CONSTRUCTION OF AFRICAN IDENTITIES

The dominant narrative of international relations is one of an arena characterised by three features: (i) it is anarchic, without any higher authority, (ii) states all perform the same functions and are equivalent units, and (iii) there is an uneven distribution of resources and capacities among states. Every state comprises of a mixture of ethnic, cultural and linguistic identities, commonly referred to as nations. Each nation gives primacy of belonging to some sub-state group, however defined and measured. Thus, for instance, some people within the province of Biafra in Nigeria recognise their sub-State regional identity as having primacy, that is, as Biafrian identity. A population subset not having any allegiance to what is otherwise a national identity is problematic in any State. This is even more so when identities function as the only avenue for securing limited public resources from the various institutions of the state.

Far more than in any other parts of the former colonial world, the identities of African state as we know it today are a direct product of European colonialism. Its boundaries are the lines drawn on maps by colonial governments, generally with startling unconcern for the people whom they casually allocated to one territory or another. Note for example, all the straight line boundaries on an African map. These usually were drawn from divides between the coastal nodes of competing powers and extended inland until they conflicted with another colonial power.

Although it is naive to suppose that the realities of any environment can, or should, dictate the configuration of a state, it is equally foolish to overlook the impact of predetermined shapes on future defence, communications, and governance: in other words, on the shaping of political identities. Whereas the reality of a straight line drawn across the Sahara or the Kalahari may be of little consequence, the impact of similar delimitations across populated areas, such as between Kenya and Tanzania, Angola and Zambia, and Ethiopia and Somali Republic, obviously has socio-political implications. What resulted from this was a compartmentalisation of each country into so-called tribal areas that were supposedly different from one another. In some cases, one or at most two or three very large groups were dominant, such as in Dahomey, Upper Volta, and Swaziland. In others, several large groups were interspersed among more numerous smaller ones – Kenya, Nigeria, the Conger (Zaire).[17]

This was particularly true in British-governed areas under the policy of indirect rule, where locating indigenous leaders and specifying the prevailing social-political traditions were essential. What resulted was the creation of many new self-conscious identities.[18] A typical example of this would be the Sandawe of Tanzania who, despite their unique language and many customs that set them off from surrounding ethnic groups, never seem to have possessed a sense of solidarity and separate identities until they were organised into an administrative subchiefdom and virtually told who they were.[19]

The Manyika people of Zimbabwe provides further example of how colonialism created ethnic identities and the manner in which these identities have been manipulated to serve political and economic interests. Before 1890 the Manyika shared a common Shona language and cultural traits with the other Shona groups. They 'were not conscious of a cultural identity, still less a political one'. Colonial manipulation of territory and, more importantly, the language work of mission stations that privileged a written language based on the Manyika dialect, led to the creation of an ethnic identity around this sub-unit of Shona-speakers.

The Manyika migrants, further, benefited from literacy skills that gave them access to much desired jobs in domestic services – they came to be seen as 'natural' domestic servants in towns or southern Rhodesia and South Africa. Even migrants from areas where Manyika ethnicity was resisted had to capitulate in the urban areas and claim to belong to this ethnic identity in order to gain employment.

This colonial legacy has been inherited, and indeed accepted, by the present independent African governments. Politicians in Kenya play off Kikuyu against Luo and against Kambo and against the various minority groups. Sierra Leone must contend with a Creole/indigenous split, with the indigenous peoples being fragmented by a Temne-Mende conflict. Nigeria worked to bring the Ibo back into national life, and Zaire, despite several proclamations declaring all its citizens as equal, regularly has to play politics with over 250 recognised ethnic groups.

Indeed, throughout the continent states preside over divided societies containing widely divergent ethnic groups. This has made it particularly difficult for post-colonial states to generate a moral basis for government which endows rulers with legitimacy or authority, rather than with the mere control of the state machinery. Though the notion of government is accepted on the continent, the political institutions through which its powers are exercised are generally treated with remarkable indifference. The history of contemporary Africa is littered with examples; here we find that multi-party systems have been replaced by a single-party state, and in turn by military regimes.

This position arises because the ruling elite, deeply engaged in carrying out the duties of running the state machinery set and left behind by the former colonial elite, have done little, if anything, to establish a meaningful relationship with the large number of peasant dwellers and workers in the remote countryside. Given the diverse interests of these groups (due to the differences in their ways of life), each live 'beside' the other without any meaningful contact or awareness of the other, though they are of common origin. The elite are an active social group for they are aware of their common belonging, ingrained further by the constant competitive conflict between them. The peasants, on the other hand, form a passive social group. They are unaware of their being a distinctive class in the society. Nor are they aware that those others who portray elements of difference from them – like possession of cars, big houses and so forth – have anything to do with them.

This has given rise to a situation where nations have greater attachment to their localities (or local communities) than to the overarching state.[20] In reality, the boundaries of this community rarely corresponds to an 'ethnic group' as defined in its classical or 'western' sense. Here, we find that ethnicity and ethnic group identities are basically a political and not a cultural phenomenon, and the concepts operate within contemporary political contexts and are not an archaic survival arrangement carried over into the present by conservative people.[21] Though these identities may derive in part from pre-colonial states or cultural commonalities, in general they are relics of Black Africa's colonial past.

Such artificiality has created a condition in Africa where ethnic groups generally lack homogeneity and cohesiveness. This in turn has allowed for the emergence of multiple identities and interests among group members. For instance, the individual member, variously involved in economic roles such as worker, professional, businessperson, or administrator, develops crosscutting ties of economic class, religion, and so forth, that modify the exclusivity of primary group obligations.[22] It is primarily within their dealings with the territorial entity or the apparatus of the state, that members assume the mantle of the group identity. As such, ethnic group identity becomes an instrument for mobilising and aggregating interests in competition with other ethnic groups, for state-controlled political and economic resources.

This situation arises because governments are in the business of allocating resources. Public officials must decide where to locate clinics, wells, schools, roads, market places and so on. These same people distribute crucial appointments, government contracts, public-funded loans and licenses. National groups or sub-groups manoeuvre to influence these important decisions. In this context, ethnic group identity provides a ready-made vehicle through which to work.[23] The membership usually negotiates a common position within the group and continually acts so as to maintain the unity and strength of the heterogeneous units before they engage in meaningful encounters at the state level. The importance of the state in this context cannot be under-stated. The state's capacity to allocate resources and to mediate societal conflicts makes it a central link in any political process. Here, cultural elites mobilise identities to secure political and economic resources from the state. As they mobilise these identities for their political purposes, they help to shape which particular identity, or mix of identities, come to the fore.

THE POLITICISATION OF ETHNICITY

By manipulating identity in this manner, ethnicity is moved into the arena of competition for political power, privilege and wealth against other groups. Elsewhere an astute observer remarked that, 'ethnic identities are frequently manipulated and mobilised in the service of class and political interests'. Most students of international relations will find this observation not particularly surprising given the fact that ethnic groups are such strong representations of common identities and carry such powerful mobilising sentiments within them. As we have discussed, this strength arises from the multiple reinforcement (cultural, emotional, historical) that they enjoy and the multiple needs that they service (social support, historical motivation, ideological clarification, and economic well being). The politicisation of ethnicity directs these strong bonds towards a goal that has no essential link to ethnicity.

In the case of South Africa, for example, leader–follower relations (or patron/clientelism) among the majority of Zulu supporters of Inkatha are hardly based on ideological identification but on reciprocal instrumental advantage and ethnic symbolic gratifications. Inkatha's poor and illiterate constituency depends on patronage handed out by strong leaders and local power-brokers in return for loyalty regardless of the leaders' ideological outlook or ethical behaviour. Past political powerlessness reinforced the importance of African auxiliaries to whom the impoverished could turn for protection and favour. This leads to the emergence of a classical system of clientelism and patrimony.

'Unlike "class" and "ethnicity", both of which are group phenomena', René Lemarchand and Keith Legg note that, 'clientelism refers to a personalised and reciprocal relationship between an inferior [client] and a superior [patron] commanding unequal resources'.[24] This relationship is brought about by several developments unique to the African setting. Critical, here, is the already discussed relationship between African states and their citizens. The weakness of the African state institutions and the fragile nature of its public acceptance provide a unique sociopolitical environment which encourages informal networks of personal relationships between powerful and well-placed individuals (patrons) and the rest of their ethnic communities (clients).

Thus, for example in the early 1960s, various groups among the Yoruba contested power in the then Western region of Nigeria. Each faction (in particular, the Oyo Yoruba around Chief Samuel Ladoke Akintola and the Ijebu Yoruba who looked to Chief Obafemi Awolowo) vied for political power in the region. It was to build linkages between these competing interests within the larger Yoruba community that Chief Awolowo played an instrumental role in organising a pan-Yoruba cultural organisation, the Society of the Descendant of Oduduwa, which subsequently led to the founding of a Yoruba-led political party.

However, the, 'divisive rivalry between traditional Yoruba groups'[25] continued into the 1960s and combined in the 1962 proclamation of a state of emergency in the Western Region and the subsequent trial and imprisonment of Chief Awolowo for possessing arms and ammunition illegally. Some fifteen years later, commenting on Chief Obafemi Awolowo's consolidation of various Yoruba ethnic subgroups for electoral purposes in 1979, Richard Joseph asserts that, 'By sweeping Yorubaland so convincingly, Chief Awolowo became leader of the Yoruba with a completeness whose significance can be fully comprehended only when placed in the context of the historical rivalries among the Yoruba subgroups.'[26]

Thus, politicised ethnicity (ethnic nationalism) moves social identity to political agencies, providing the means for political mobilisation and organisation, and submits the ethnic identity and groups to another set of rules – those of competition for political power and economic privilege. Here, ethnic consciousness is neither irrational nor ephemeral. From the perspective of the ordinary African, ethnicity appears no less sensible a basis for political mobilisation than socio-economic class. It is, however, far from axiomatic that politicised ethnicity is identical to nationalism. Nationalism can be, and most often is, multi-ethnic – the nation-state, the territorial form most nations exist in or strive for, usually involves a 'plural society' in which distinct ethnic groups 'share the same political and economic order'.[27] The Afrikaner settler community of South Africa provides a noticeable exception to this generalisation.

We have noted how Africa was pre-eminently the continent of European conquest. Throughout the continent, but particularly in the southern third, the right to rule was defined in racial terms. In an intriguing analysis of ethnic mobilisation, Dan O'Meara set out the way in which the ideological 'call' to Afrikaners to adopt a particular ethnic nationalism (or identity) developed in competition with other interpretations of Afrikaner nationalism. Limited word space does not allow for detailed discussions of this important work here, however it suffices to say that the process showed many of the characteristics already discussed: the nation had to be established as 'the primary social unit from which all individuals draw their identity'.[28] Class divisions had to be overcome in order to promote a socio-cultural unity. In the words of Nico Diederichs (a former finance and state president of South Africa); '[I]f the worker is drawn away from the nation, we may as well write Ichabod on the door of our temples ... He must be drawn into his nation in order to be a genuine man. There must be no division or schism between class and class.'[29]

In order to politicise ethnicity in this context, the national identity of the Afrikaners – the *Volk* – was used as a justification for strengthening the boundaries of the group.

Such general considerations serve as a caution to pay attention not just to cultural diversity but to the particular historical factors making some subnational identities more prominent than others. Only a few of the possible separate identities come to channel political competition; even fewer serve as rationales for claiming dominance within a state or establishing a separate state. Indeed, and in contrast to the European experience, few of Africa's ethnic groups spawned 'nationalist' ideologies. Among the few exceptions were Somali nationalism, aiming to unite Somalis dispersed under different colonial administrations, and Baganda separatism in Uganda. Following African independence, there were only a handful of secessionist civil wars. They were generally based on colonial administrative divisions rather than ethnic boundaries (east Nigeria, southern Sudan, Katanga). The Eritrean and Western Saharan nationalist movements were based on colonial territories incorporated forcibly by larger neighbours.

IDENTITY AND DEMOCRATIC PROSPECTS

This discussion has suggested some ways in which to conceptualise the construction of political identities and their multiple roles in contemporary African societies. From it, we can deduce that Africa's political inheritance from its colonial past was a tradition of bureaucratic autocracy, scarcely yet affected by democracy and bolstered by a multiplicity of cultural, linguistic and political identities. These were political structures in transition which could either move forwards to true democracy or backwards to centralised authoritarianism. The prospects were in fact bleak, despite the immense euphoria of the moment of inheritance. At the international level, we have noted how post-colonial states have been co-opted into an international political economy which has structurally worked to impede their developmental efforts. Their domestic efforts have also been hampered by multiplicity of identities which have produced layers of claimants to state power and wealth. The common result has been a fundamental political instability usually concealed under monopolistic or oligopolistic authoritarian regimes.

The collapse of communism in the Soviet Union and the ending of the cold war has created an opportunity for democratic transition, not only in Europe and the former Soviet Union, but also in Africa. Giddens notes that 'over the period from 1989 to mid-1993, more than twenty countries in Africa alone sought to introduce constitutionalism and democratic parliamentary institutions.'[30] This apparent shift towards democracy and democratic principles poses a fundamental question about the survival of democracy – at least in its western format – on a continent with little democratic tradition.

Robert Dahl and others have identified many procedures and institutions that seem to be necessary to fulfil a true democracy. Dahl posits a procedural minimum for democracy that includes secret balloting, universal adult suffrage, regular elections, partisan competition, associational freedom, and executive accountability.[31] In institutional terms, this requires multiple political parties, representative institutions (such as legislatures) with policy-making powers and an executive who is accountable either to the population (such as the popularly elected U.S president) or to the legislature (such as the prime minister in the United Kingdom). For all this to work, there must be a rule of law which limits the power of the government and legally guaranteed civil liberties which protects individuals from government power and provides the legal space necessary for political activity.[32]

In Africa, most of these institutions (if they were ever strong) are weaker today than they were in the immediate post-independent period. Throughout West, Central and Eastern Africa, political leaders have treated their respective countries as personal patrimonies. As a result, the common people in whose name these leaders contested political power before and after independence, have become frustrated with false economic and development promises. Disenchantment has grown, first with the rulers, then with the institutions through which they were chosen, and then with the institutions with which they wielded their power – the legislator and their assemblies, the judiciary and their courts, the security services and their police, the civil service and their bureaucracy. In this context, the first challenge for democracy is how to generate a moral basis for government.

The task, of course, does not end here. Political leaders must also find ways of dealing with the diversity among various ethnic groups by managing and recognising the rights of individuals to promote their ethnic identities. Such a strategy need not entail the denial of cultural variety, ethnic consciousness or the desirability of a range of social identities. It should, however, shift these into a democratic practise within society (an encompassing social structure, capable of acknowledging and welcoming variety) as a whole. Such an approach will demand enormous change, not simply a glib commitment to democratic principles. The problem of ethnicity, which involves the manner in which it has been mobilised for conflictual politics in Africa (as elsewhere), is not going to be solved through an overnight disposition towards democratic principles.·

Notes

1. Within the short space of this chapter, it will not be possible to engage in the type of in-depth analysis of African societies and relatedly, all the prominent identities within. Thus, the chapter serves only to introduce the student of international relations to some of the basics of what constitutes contemporary African identities.
2. In fact, one thousand years of Islamic influence prior to European intervention had left a significant legacy, one that is most obviously seen today with half of Africa's population being Muslim.
3. P. Gifford and W.R. Louis, *France and Britain in Africa: Imperial Rivalry and Colonial Rule* (New Haven: Yale University Press, 1971).
4. The reader here, is referred to amongst others, the work of A.G. Hopkins, *An Economic History of West Africa*. This work deals with the manner in which West Africa was integrated in the World economy.
5. With serious implications witnessed up to the present day. Unfortunately, word space does not allow for any serious analyses of this particular group within the context of this chapter. A useful introduction to the subject, however, is provided by G. Mare, in *Ethnicity and Politics in South Africa* (London: Zed Books, 1993).
6. A useful introduction is B. Davidson, *Modern Africa: A Social and Political History* (London: Longman Group, 1990).
7. A good introduction to this conflict is W. Minter, *Apartheid's Contras: An Inquiry into the Roots of War in Angola and Mozambique* (London: Zed Books, 1994).
8. A useful introduction to contemporary African problems is provided by I.L.L. Griffiths, in *The Atlas of African Affairs* (London: Routledge, 1994).
9. Peter Calvocoressi, *Independent Africa and the World* (London: Longman, 1981, pp. 65–100).
10. This is well in line with the liberalist tendencies of the World Bank in relation to separating politics from economics.
11. The reader here, is referred to T. Killick, 'Trends in Development Economics and their Relevance to Africa', *JMAS*, vol. 18, no. 3, 1980.
12. In general, the metropolitan rulers, encouraged the development of single commodities, such as peanuts, coffee and cotton, and to a large extent discouraged founding local industries. According to D.K. Fieldhouse, the main reason way this occurred, was because, it was in the metropolitan powers interest to make the colonies peripheral extensions of their own economies. Since the metropolitan powers were to a large extent industrialised, it was important to make the colonies non- industrialised, in order

for them to provide the raw-materials necessary for the former to maintain their economic dominance.
13. See V. G. *European Empires from Conquest to Collapse: 1855–1960* (London: Fontana, 1931).
14. If this was the case, then why are the American and the British economy in absolute decline. Added to this, why also, has countries in Latin America, who have enjoyed more then 200 hundred years of independence, not amongst the most industrially vibrant economies in the world.
15. A. Smith, *The Ethnic Revival in the Modern World* (Cambridge University Press, 1981, pp. 9–10).
16. J. Berger, *Once in Europe* (London: Granta Books 1991, p. 77).
17. A good introduction to this subject is A.I. Asiwaju (ed.), *Partitioned Africans: Ethnic Relations across Africa's International Boundaries* (London: Hurst, and Lagos: University of Lagos Press, 1985).
18. The Ewe in Ghana and Togo, the Ibo in Nigeria, the Kikuyu in Kenya, and the Soga in Uganda are typical of such altered societies.
19. An interesting and informative study of this particular group is provided by J.L. Newman, *The Ecological Basis for Subsistence Change Among the Sandawe of Tanzania* (Washington, DC: National Academy of Science, 1970).
20. This is a characteristic of rural population everywhere, not only in Contemporary Africa.
21. A. Cohen, *Customs and Politics in Urban Africa* (Berkeley: University of California Press, 1969, p.190).
22. The possible exception to this generalisation is the white settler communities of Africa – the so called 'while tribes of Africa'. In South Africa, for example, the exclusivity of primary group obligations forms the basis of their socio-economic position.
23. R. Sandbrook, *The Politics of Africa's Economic Stagnation* (Cambridge University Press: 1993, p. 77).
24. René Lemarchand and Keith Legg, 'Political Clientelism and Development: A Preliminary Analysis', *Comparative Politics*, 4, no. 2, January 1972, p. 151.
25. See R.L. Sklar, 'Nigerian Politics: The Ordeal of Chief Awolowo, 1960–65' in G.M. Carter (ed.) *Politics in Africa: 7 Cases* (New York: Harcourt Brace & World, 1966, p.18).
26. Richard A. Joseph, 'Democratisation under Military Tutelage', *Comparative Politics* 14, no. 1, 1981, p. 92.
27. Giddens, A. *Sociology* (Cambridge: Polity Press, 1989), p. 244.
28. D. Harrison, *The White Tribes of Africa* (London: BBC Publications, 1981). This Book provides an interesting insight into the settler communities of South Africa.
29. Quoted in D. O'Meara, *Volkskapitalisme; Class, Capital and Ideology in the Development of Afrikaaner Nationalism 1934–1948* (Johannesburg: Ravan, 1983, p. 71).
30. A. Giddens, *Beyond Left and Right: the Future of Radical Politics* (Cambridge: Polity, p. 104).
31. Robert A. Dahl, 'Procedural Democracy', in P. Laslett and J. Fishkin (eds.) *Philosophy, Politics and Society* (Oxford: Basil Blackwell, 1979, p. 97–113).

32.   Some scholars posit even more extensive requirements for a liberal democracy.Valerie Bunce, for example, mentions five characteristics: rule of law, extensive civil liberties guaranteed by law, representative government, Weberian bureaucracy, and some dispersion of economic resources. She sees the fourth as necessary to make the bureaucracy accountable to the public and the fifth to avoid excessive concentration of resources in the hands of the government.Valerie Bunce, 'The Struggle for Liberal Democracy in Eastern Europe', *World Policy Journal*, 7, no. 3, Summer 1990, p. 399.

10 Citizenship: Identification and the Global
Roy Smith

Few would deny that a broad array of processes have contributed to a growing awareness of 'global' issues. These processes range from increasing environmental degradation to the promotion of satellite broadcasting. However, it is far from clear how the recognition of such issues impacts on senses of identity and the concept of citizenship as dealt with in the traditional terms of the politics of the nation-state system. This chapter will consider how various global issues present a challenge to national governments. It will also look at the ways in which national identities relate to these issues and the possibility of developing a sense of global citizenship.

A GLOBAL POLITICAL AGENDA?

There remains a great diversity of experiences within and between various cultures and societies. Despite this diversity there are undeniable processes that have emerged which have an increasing global impact. Foremost among these is the trend towards following the Western model of industrialisation and economic growth. This is significant in terms of a developing *global* political agenda, for two main reasons. First, it reflects the adoption of particular values and practices across a growing number of societies.[1] Second, one of the consequences of the adoption of this model of development is environmental decay. The degree of this decay has varying local impacts. However, the overall trend is one of non-sustainable development practices at the local level which have environmental impacts at both the local and global levels.

Rapid industrialisation and resulting environmental decay highlight the issue of the overlap between national policies and global consequences. One of the fundamental aspects of the processes of globalisation is the way in which national governments have declining control over key issue areas. Trans-boundary pollution is a notable example of this. Similarly the free flow of capital, foreign direct investment and the ability of transnational corporations to transfer operations around the world can also undermine the decisions of national governments. As such this lack of control can be argued to have led to a form of 'identity crisis' for *national* decision-making.[2]

The hierarchical nature of the nation-state system allows power relationships to develop between states in various issue areas. This leads to different peoples and governments feeling either more or less secure in relation to particular issues at particular times. The processes described above can be incorporated into an analysis of international relations that fits this hierarchical model. For example, it is possible to argue that some states, or regions, are more at risk from environmental decay than others.[3] An example of this would be the low-lying areas of the world threatened by a potential rise in sea level. Similarly there is a gradation of vulnerability to the vagaries of the global economic system. However, it remains the case that even the most powerful states are increasingly subject to forces out of the control of their governments.

Given that governments face growing restrictions on their autonomy it is understandable that many individuals are reassessing the benefits of national citizenship, and to what extent this concept relates to their personal sense of identity. This is evident in the growth of new social movements such as gay and lesbian groups, religious orders and issue-based pressure groups. The promotion of a sense of national identity and national interests is a fundamental element of the role of governments. These concepts in themselves are open to much debate with many governments facing separatist movements and the existence of varied, even conflicting, interest groups within states. Examples of these range from groups seeking their own statehood, such as the Basques, Kurds and Timorese, through to multinational corporations with company rather than national allegiances. However, despite an apparent resurgence in nationalist movements within particular states, notably in Eastern Europe, it remains the case that national governments face an increasingly difficult task in establishing their legitimacy.

In both liberal democracies and authoritarian regimes there appears to be a growing awareness of the difficulties national governments face in preserving their autonomy within the decision-making process. A degree of autonomy can be maintained in the domestic political arena through the legislative process and, to a lesser extent, the control of government spending. Similarly the control of legitimate agencies of organised coercive force remain under the remit of national governments. Yet even in these areas there can be external pressures. One of the most enduring features of the concept of sovereign rule has been the acknowledgement of the international community that each state has ultimate jurisdiction over its own domestic affairs, especially in relation to defining criminality and its subsequent policing and control. Elements of censure, for example regarding perceived human rights abuses, may occur towards particular states. Such criticism is likely to come from groups such as Amnesty International or Human Rights Watch but might also be voiced at the governmental level. However, such criticism is rarely followed through with significant penalties. A case in point would be the United States' renewal of China's Most Favoured Nation status in 1994 despite strong criticism from the Clinton Administration of China's human rights abuses. Clearly, in this instance, trade concerns were given priority over the moral stance.

Far more pertinent is the issue of the control of government spending. The actual allocation of funds to particular government departments may appear to be a matter wholly under domestic jurisdiction. Certainly the division of the central budget can be seen as a matter for national governments. Yet external factors, such as a balance of payments deficit, have implications for the total amount of money to be allocated. Similarly, other factors may be relevant. For example, border disputes and the potential threat of invasion is likely to lead to an emphasis on military spending over other sectors of the economy. Within a global political economy the operations of transnational corporations and world market commodity prices can seriously undermine the fiscal policies of many governments, particularly in developing states.

Two main points arise from the above argument that national governments are experiencing a growing lack of autonomy in achieving their policy objectives. First, it begs the question regarding the extent to which governments can retain their legitimacy given that they are losing control of key areas of governance. Why should citizens maintain an allegiance to a dysfunctional institution? Second, assuming that governments can continue to maintain at least a vestige of political control is it possible for national governments to co-ordinate their efforts to address the emerging global political agenda?

With regard to the first point, citizen dissatisfaction with national government can manifest itself in a broad array of ways. These might range from a campaign to replace a government on Party political grounds through to either a desire for greater autonomy at a more localised level or a grander vision of regional, or even global, governance. For the vast majority of people the most likely prompt for dissatisfaction with government policies will be the extent to which they perceive the immediate impact on their own lives to be enhanced or degraded by such policies. By this criteria one might expect the majority of anti-government movements to reflect the aspirations of a territorial unit within an existing state. Most separatist movements campaigning for self-determination would fit this model.[4] However, a similar dissatisfaction may also be felt by those without such a localised agenda but with an acknowledgement that global issues are not being adequately addressed by national governments. Again, several new social movements would be relevant to this point with the promotion of universal human rights, including expression of sexual preference, the promotion of sustainable development policies and the desire to meet the basic needs of the world's population regardless of their nationality.

There is not necessarily a direct contradiction between recognising the current failings of national governments in dealing with global issues and a continuing affinity to a particular national identity. Moreover, it could be argued that, without a viable alternative, national governments remain the only appropriate actors to manage the processes of globalisation. Furthermore, unlike citizenship, which is conferred by national governments, a sense of identity is far more self-generated. Clearly this development of self-identification with cultural values and norms is deeply rooted in the whole process of socialisation. However, it is important to recognise that a *national* identity is but one of a range of identities individuals possess.

NATIONAL AND GLOBAL IDENTITIES

Each individual simultaneously experiences a range of identities. A sense of national identity can range from xenophobia to a vague indifference toward an identity imposed by an accident of birth at a given location. Other identities may revolve around relations with family members; political allegiances; religion; gender; sexual preference; race; age; wealth or position within a societal class structure. Depending on circumstances a particular identity, or combination of identities, will become of significance to individuals and those they interact with. In much the same way a sense of global identity has more to do with an individual's self-consciousness than being imposed by any higher authority. Ultimately, of course, we are all global citizens in the sense that we all inhabit one world. However, as an element of self-awareness many people would not think in these terms. Even the recognition of a global political economy or an understanding that the Western model of economic growth is non-sustainable may not be sufficient in themselves to alter self-perception. A key element here is the extent to which individuals can be 'other regarding'. This relates to the ability to define one's own identity within the context of a greater community. Significantly this community could include future generations.

Having acknowledged that we are all amalgams of multi-layered identities the question is raised concerning how this relates to the processes of globalisation. Taking the common denominator as being our participation in the organic whole of the natural world there are a range of sub-sections within this scenario. These can be crudely divided into three basic categories that reflect various levels of awareness. First, there is an extremely low, or non-existent awareness of global processes.[5] Second, there is an awareness of these processes but responsibility for dealing with them is deferred to national governments. Third, there is an active dissatisfaction with national government policies which are perceived as failing to deal with the global political agenda.

The above divisions each include a vast spectrum of degrees of awareness, with resulting implications for identity formation. Even the first category can be sub-divided further taking into account the varying impact on global processes, such as environmental decay, that the actors in this category can unwittingly inflict. These categories are further complicated by a fluidity of identification and subsequent actions by actors within each category. For example, an individual in the third category may be an active campaigner on a global issue such as environmental protection. His or her world-view may be strongly at odds with the whole conception of the nation-state system. Yet despite a desire to reject this system there remains an acknowledgement that he or she does have an imposed national identity. Moreover, it is through the lobbying of the national government that the most significant impact on the global political agenda is likely to take place.

NATIONAL AND GLOBAL INTERESTS

There is a strong correlation between a sense of identity and interests. The emotive power of nationalist propaganda linked to a dominant cultural experience of socialisation into a particular group is likely to generate an association with a related set of perceived interests.[6] Depending on the level of analysis the appropriateness of a range of perceived interests can vary considerably. In particular this can vary when a temporal element is taken into consideration. For example, the reliance on fossil fuels for energy generation may appear beneficial in the short term. Yet if other factors, such as their non-renewability and polluting effects are taken into account, it becomes apparent that other means of energy generation are more beneficial in the longer term. Similarly the promotion of a national interest in competition with those of other states must also be viewed in terms of how such an interest has been defined. In many instances the longer term consequences of policies designed to further a particular state's interests can eventually prove counter-productive.

Disputes over access to decreasing fish stocks such as those between Iceland and Britain, Canada and Spain or Russia and Japan are examples of various governments giving priority to their short-term interests of promoting their respective fishing industries. However, without coordinated management of fisheries the depletion of these resources will continue. The longer-term effect of this will be detrimental to all national fishing industries. This reflects what has been called the 'tragedy of the commons'. Without effective management the logic of individuals or governments with access to commonly held resources is to make optimum use of these resources, but without considering the impact this has on the resource or other users. This example encapsulates the whole range of issues related to the linkages between communities, resources, identities and citizenship. In particular it reflects the trend to retreat within short-term self-protection measures at times of shortage or other crises. This trend does not negate the possibility of global governance or global citizenry. However, it does highlight the difficulties faced in achieving these goals.

How to manage the global commons is an issue that has become a key element of the emerging global political agenda. It also serves to highlight the need to address the ways in which processes of globalisation are relevant to discussions surrounding identity formation and the concept of citizenship. In order to overcome the abuse and over-exploitation of common resources there needs to be a re-evaluation of self-identity, at both an individual and governmental level. This, in turn, has implications for the concept of citizenship. Certain aspects of citizenship bestowed by national governments could remain unaltered. These could include the right of abode, access to education, health and welfare provisions. However, the successful management of common resources and various additional aspects of the global political agenda require a significant shift away from traditional conceptions of national identity and interests.

A central element in altering conceptions of identity in terms of a global political agenda relates to conceptions of time. The temporal element has largely been under-estimated in the majority of approaches to the study of international relations. This is particularly relevant in relation to environmental pollution and resource depletion.[7] Structuralist approaches to the study of international relations do take into account the significance of the historical development of the contemporary international political and economic systems. The work of both Wallerstein and Gunder Frank is explicit in acknowledging the ongoing relevance of the age of empire-building by the European powers and the role of the United States in dominating the major institutions of the post-1945 period. However, they are generally remiss in projecting forward to forecast the longer-term consequences of current policies.

Previous attempts at promoting elements of embryonic world governance, such as the League of Nations and the United Nations, have been subject to criticisms of being naively idealistic. This is largely unjustified given the restricted remit of both organisations. Any popular perception of either as supranational bodies far exceeds the intent of the founders of both bodies. Whist attempting to manage conflict between states there has remained an acknowledgement that domestic sovereignty retains an almost sacrosanct status. Certainly there is abundant evidence of the failures of previous tentative regimes of governance. The dissolution of the League and examples of defiance of UN Security Council resolutions support this view. However, the processes of modernisation and globalisation are strengthening the argument that a system of global governance is required. Admittedly it does not necessarily follow that an increased need for such a regime will make the achievement of this objective any easier. Yet national governments and individuals are faced with mounting evidence that their own interests can only be fulfilled within the context of a regime of some form of global governance.

The dominant actors within the nation-state system remain national governments. It is clear that the most powerful of these states are already adopting policies which acknowledge the advantages of co-operation with each other. There is a long-standing history of both conflict and co-operation between national governments. The key motivation remains the promotion of perceived national interests. Yet as the evolution of a shared global political agenda has been recognised it is becoming apparent that national interests are best served by way of co-operation. The growth in membership of inter-governmental organisations demonstrates this trend.[8] In addition to the broad range of agencies within the framework of the United Nations, governments are cooperating through numerous multi-lateral agreements. The formation of trading blocs such as the European Union, the North American Free Trade

Area and Asia Pacific Economic Cooperation are examples of regional groupings. The creation of the World Trade Organisation suggests a willingness to coordinate a global trading regime. Although a great many conflicts, even to the point of armed aggression, can be cited the predominant trend is one of co-operation.

The majority of conflicts tend to take place within rather than between states. Military expenditure is increasingly geared towards fighting civil wars and controlling a state's own population.[9] A partial explanation for this may be the perceived inability, or unwillingness, of national governments to address the issues of importance to their populations. Although many of these grievances will relate to localised agendas and issues of self-determination many will also relate to issues relevant to the global political agenda. It is within the context of the latter set of issues that global governance pertains directly to domestic policy-making.

There is an undeniable ideological element to the issue of how best to achieve the goal of citizens' welfare. For some regimes free market forces are the driving force behind policies. Others choose a more interventionist stance with state subsidies and public ownership of key utilities. The nature of the global political economy is such that state intervention is necessarily restricted by international pressures. However, despite these restrictions there remain a range of policy options that governments can implement to meet basic needs. Few regimes will openly admit that they pursue policies which operate counter to the interests of sectors of their population. Yet clearly it remains the case that several states, particularly in the developing world, are failing to fulfil the basic needs of a significant proportion of their populations. How can this be justified and to what extent should this issue be seen as part of the global political agenda?

PROVISION OF BASIC NEEDS

The meeting of one's basic needs, in terms of access to food, water and shelter, is a fundamental aspect of identity formation. The failure to meet these needs negates one's very existence. It is debatable, and a matter of political orientation, the extent to which the meeting of these needs is the responsibility of national governments. Social contract theory and similar approaches argue that welfare provision is an integral part of the role of government. Even 'hard-line' Realists, such as Morgenthau, would generally adhere to the belief that the welfare of the majority of a state's citizens should be promoted as a broad national interest.[10]

The legitimacy and ability of citizens to claim certain rights from governments are moot points. Although there may seem to be a form of moral imperative to prevent life-threatening hardships there remains no *unquestionable* position regarding which, if any, authority holds responsibility for alleviating such hardships. Because of the mainstream acceptance that national governments have the legitimate authority over given areas of territory, any such responsibility is deemed to devolve to them. In more recent years there has been greater public recognition that certain issues, such as famine relief or the prevention of genocide, fall within the realms of a concern beyond that of a national interest.

If one acknowledges that issues such as the welfare of citizens of another state are to be considered this immediately transforms the traditional conception of the primacy of pursuing domestic interests. In certain circumstances it may be possible to argue that there are self-interests in operation if, for example, one feared the consequences of the potential collapse of a neighbouring state's government.[11] Zaire's concern regarding the situation in Rwanda in 1994 was doubtless heightened by the sharing of a national border. Yet many recent examples of concern for the plight of citizens of other states, from Ethiopia to Bosnia, do not have obvious connections to the national interests of the states and citizens voicing this concern. This appears to be a further example of an emerging political agenda focusing on issues in addition to those of traditional domestic concern.

Taking citizen welfare and the meeting of basic needs as a relevant part of a global political agenda begs the question of who is responsible for meeting these needs and by what mechanisms. In both Somalia and Rwanda in the 1990s it has been apparent that the national governments were incapable of alleviating the suffering of significant numbers of their populations. If their own governments could not provide assistance could the people of Somalia and Rwanda reasonably expect to appeal to the international community for aid? If human life is to be valued as part of a global political agenda this would seem a fair expectation. This assumes that there is a degree of international *identification* with the suffering experienced by people in other communities. Although it is impossible to quantify this sentiment throughout the world's population the success of humanitarian appeals such as the Band Aid and Live Aid phenomena illustrate its existence.

The United Nations system has been viewed as either an ineffective talking shop or an alternative forum for the dominant states to continue a slightly modified form of power politics. Yet for all this criticism it remains the closest approximation to world governance. Specialised agencies such as the World Health Organisation and the UN Development Programme have remits to contribute towards meeting basic needs on a global scale.[12] In a sense the United Nations, through the contributions and political will of its member states, has accepted a degree of responsibility for maintaining the welfare of 'global citizens' – regardless of their nationality.

There are a number of implications that arise from developing a concept of global citizenship and identification. Citizenship is a *loaded* term implying that certain rights and duties arise from this status. There is also the assumption that one is the citizen of a particular and defined political unit. In the case of global citizenry there is currently a mismatch between the level of identification with the situation and experiences of other people around the world and the codification of this into a legitimised regime of global goverance. Senses of identity and identification are largely self-defined and reinforced. In contrast the creation of some form of global government at the institutional level will have to be the subject of much negotiation, compromise and debate. As such this latter element is far more problematic. Not least because it brings into question fundamental aspects of the existing international political system.

To talk in terms of a global citizenry would appear to challenge accepted norms regarding what citizenship involves. Certainly although there are numerous issues that justify reference to a global political agenda it is a more extreme claim to point to the emergence of a global citizenry with all that this implies. If it is accepted that citizens can reasonably claim that their basic needs should be provided for this raises questions regarding the relationship between their national government and any higher global authority. In particular the question of intervention becomes a potential problem, especially if the host government either objects or is deemed by the wider international community to be failing to meet its obligations towards its own population.

SOVEREIGNTY AND INTERVENTION

The international community's response to the crises in Somalia and Rwanda in the 1990s are both examples of the complications surrounding the issue of outside intervention into the domestic affairs of sovereign states. The concept of sovereignty remains central to contemporary international politics. The growth in both numbers and significance of non-state actors linked to the declining autonomy of policymakers has undoubtedly raised challenges to the operation of the nation-state system. However, despite these challenges, of all the rules and norms associated with the nation-state system it is the issue of sovereignty that retains the greatest significance. This relates to both the practical operation of the international political system and also the more amorphous elements of emotive attachment to particular national identities.

Even in the most extreme examples of famine relief or intervention to prevent civil war there is likely to be an element of resentment that foreign forces are being deployed in one's own state. This is largely an issue of attitude and perception. To accept such intervention requires an alteration of one's basic mind-set away from traditional conceptions of international politics. This remains the most difficult barrier to developing a sense of global citizenship. For most people, including citizens of the most developed industrialised states, what are regarded as local issues with immediate impact on daily are likely to be seen as priority concerns. In the context of life threatening situations this is to be expected. However, to identify oneself as a global citizen there needs to be an awareness of both global issues and how they relate to all individuals' lives.

The contentious nature of the issue of intervention highlights the ongoing difficulty in dealing with individuals as global rather than national citizens. As mentioned previously there does not necessarily have to be direct confrontation between global and national identities. Yet it remains the case that where any potential conflict takes place it is the appeal to nationalism that has the advantage of both familiarity and more obvious short-term advantages. This position is reinforced even within parts of the United Nations system. In particular many peacekeeping operations, although often carried out by multinational forces, are still perceived as reflecting the interests of certain states.[13] Part of the problem here is that the United Nations has developed few mechanisms that are seen as independent from the interests of individual members.

In relation to peacekeeping, or any similar form of UN sponsored military intervention, each operation is dealt with individually on an almost ad hoc basis. There is no standing military force under a defined UN command structure. As such the national contributions towards each operation becomes an issue of relevance. Given the military capabilities of some states compared to others it follows that there is a likelihood particular states will play a disproportionate role in such operations. The Gulf War is a case in point with a massive military contribution from the United States. Regardless of the degree to which US interests coincided with the aims and objectives of this UN operation popular perception, especially in several Arab states, was that this was an operation led not only militarily but also politically by the United States.

One of the main reasons for the view that the international response to Iraq's invasion of Kuwait was determined by US interests relates to a failure to respond in equal measure to similar situations elsewhere. The example of Indonesia's invasion and occupation of East Timor has been cited in this context. There are a myriad of legitimate reasons why the United Nations, or individual states, appear inconsistent in their responses to international events. One fundamental aspect is that of resources and capabilities to respond. Even with a standing military and humanitarian relief force it would be logistically impossible for the United Nations to respond to all international crises. Assuming that the resources were available there would still need to be political decisions taken to prioritise crises. It is with regard to this point that the issue of ethnocentrism is likely to be problematic. Whilst acknowledging many aspects of globalisation the identification with 'global values' remains a hotly debated topic. Disagreement over the formulation of universal human rights is one example of this.

At the political level it could be argued that the United Nations system is fundamentally flawed in relation to achieving global governance. With very few exceptions the UN remains little more than the collective will of its member states. It has not yet evolved to the stage whereby it is perceived as achieving fully independent autonomy of action. Any disciplinary measures taken against a member state has to be accepted voluntarily or imposed by force. The decision-making process by which such censure would take place remains integrally linked to the views of the representatives of the member states. Moreover, the key role of the Security Council can be seen as an ongoing reflection of the dominance of particular states.[14]

The earlier argument that there need not be a conflict between national and global interests and identities would appear to be countered by the above point. Certainly it is unlikely that complete consensus agreement will take place over what policies should be adopted on a global scale. There will always be regional or more local variables to be taken into consideration. Under such circumstances negotiation and compromise would be required. Such a regime of global negotiation is not unimaginable. The United Nations could be said to go a long way towards providing a forum for such negotiations.[15] However, the very make up of the UN's membership and its language and culture remain to a large extent state, as opposed to globally, oriented.

Many would advocate the need for a revolutionary change in the contemporary international political system. The argument being that whilst the United Nations continues to be so dominated by the culture of interactions between the representatives of national governments it cannot adequately deal with the global political agenda. Even if the logic of the overlap between national and global interests and identities is accepted it appears to be impossible for national governments to pursue policies which seem to run counter to their own short-term interests. This reflect *particularist* rather than *global* cultures and identities. Under such circumstances it is worthwhile to consider what evidence there is that greater global governance can be achieved within the contemporary international political system. This will go some way towards assessing the likelihood of such a regime being developed further.

EMERGING GLOBAL GOVERNANCE

To some extent the very existence of the United Nations demonstrates the evolution of a form of global governance. It is often overlooked that despite ongoing interstate and intrastate conflict there is also significant co-operation under the auspices of the United Nations. The origins of much of this co-operative action considerably pre-dates the formation of the UN. Organisations such as the International Postal Union and the International Labour Organisation were established well before 1945. These and similar organisations have functional origins and emerged as a natural consequence of greater interactions between states. A myriad of international activities from aviation control to the protection of intellectual property rights now have a place within the framework of the UN.[16]

Much of the co-operative work currently operating by way of the UN is clearly an extension of the pursuit of individual national interests. However, it is also possible to identify processes and policies that, although collaborative, favour certain states over others. An example would be the establishment of the World Trade Organisation. This is a refinement of the General Agreement on Tariffs and Trade regime. Despite the attempt this makes to coordinate international trade it does not necessarily follow that there will be an equitable distribution of benefits. Given that the structure of the global political economy is already hierarchical it is not surprising that the gains and losses within this structure reflect this hierarchy. Such examples seem only to reinforce the view that the dominant states will continue to maintain the status quo with all the short-term advantages that follow from this.

There appears to be a basic incompatibility between allowing market forces free reign and managing development policies in a sustainable manner. This is largely due to the inability, or unwillingness, to include environmental and other social costs in the development equation. Without such inclusion the adoption of the Western model of industrialisation will continue to have devastating long-term environmental effects. Although there is increased political rhetoric relating to the need to adopt sustainable development policies the number of cases where such policies have been adopted remain a small minority. Therefore it is clear from the examples of both GATT and the WTO that the establishment of global regimes for issue areas such as international trade are not in themselves representative of effective global governance.

To pursue the issue of environmental protection further it is useful to look at the ways in which governments have attempted to debate this at the global level. Again the United Nations has provided the context for these discussions. The 1972 Stockholm Conference is widely regarded as the first attempt to address this issue in a global context. Virtually all of the UN member states participated. For the first time the connection between poverty and environmental degradation was made explicit. The establishment of the UN Development Programme and the UN Environment Programme seemed to demonstrate a commitment by the member states to pursue co-ordinated policies with regard to environmental protection. Despite the undoubted benefit of promoting discussion on environmental issues the Stockholm Conference largely failed in reversing the trend of global environmental decay.

Twenty years later the 1992 Earth Summit in Rio provided an opportunity to review progress and establish a more comprehensive regime for environmental protection.[17] Again the coming together of the majority of the world's heads of government can be seen as fulfilling an element of the criteria for global governance. Yet to be truly successful such governance needed to demonstrate far more than being able to organise a summit meeting. There needed to be outcomes that seriously addressed the issue of environmental decay beyond the established rhetoric of appealing to the 'Green' vote. To some extent this was achieved with the establishment of the Commission on Sustainable Development, the Global Environment Facility, and the signing of Conventions on Biodiversity and Climate Change. However, it has already become apparent that such measures continue to clash with the pursuit of national policies.

Although several significant measures for environmental protection arose from the Earth Summit there is little evidence to suggest that these measures have had their desired effect. The most comprehensive of these measures was the establishment of a regime to monitor climate change, with particular reference to curtailing greenhouse gas emissions. In comparison with other similar international agreements the Climate Change Convention has been unusually precise in setting targets for the reduction in greenhouse gas emissions.[18] Yet despite this apparent success there are many flaws within the climate change regime. First, the targets fall well short of actively countering pollution. At best they lessen the rate of continuing environmental decay. Second, as with other international agreements each member state agrees voluntarily to abide by its commitments. Not all states are party to this Convention, and those that are face minimal censure if they fail to meet their targets.

Given that the above Convention can be cited as one of the more successful outcomes of Rio this is an indication of why some commentators viewed the Earth Summit as a relative failure. Despite a recognition of the harmful effects of the pollution associated with industrialisation there was little governmental enthusiasm to reduce the impetus for greater economic growth and resource consumption. Where this did occur it was generally aimed at curtailing the consumerist aspirations of the populations of the developing states. Again this can be seen as a reflection of the way in which the more developed states tend to dominate. Their patterns of consumption are well established and it would appear that their populations will strongly resist attempts to modify these patterns.[19] This has a direct link to the issue of identity formation in that these consumerist patterns do not appear to include the 'other regarding' element of acknowledging the needs of both future generations and those adversely affected by these patterns.

NGOs AND GLOBAL GOVERNANCE

The role of non-governmental organisations (NGOs) is a major feature of the global political agenda. Many of the processes of this new agenda are more appropriately considered in relation to NGOs than to national governments. Whilst not denying the continuing political legitimacy and relevance of national governments it is often NGOs that are the key players associated with some of the more significant issues on the contemporary agenda. Much of the spread of industrialisation and the adoption of more consumerist oriented lifestyles is the result of the operations of privately owned transnational corporations. Although not as readily associated with the concept of global governance as national governments such corporations have played a significant part in both the development and, in part, the management of the global political agenda.

In addition to these transnational corporations other types of NGOs play important roles on the world stage. The major religious faiths are becoming increasingly recognised for their part in both identity formation and the impact they can have in both international and domestic politics. A great many single issue pressure groups are relevant to the whole debate surrounding the global political agenda and the ability of national governments to maintain their legitimacy in the eyes of their populations. By associating with one, or several, of these pressure groups citizens are not necessarily denying their allegiance to a particular national identity. However, many of these groups, demands relate to issues that reflect the global rather than national agenda.

Again environmental and conservation issues are prime examples of the types of issues raised where citizens have an identification with a concept of world order that can be at odds with that of national governments. In many instances this may not be the case. For example a supporter of Greenpeace or Friends of the Earth might have a personal interest in very localised environmental issues. He or she might not question in the slightest the legitimacy of their national government. Indeed the whole focus of their campaigning could be the lobbying of their government with a view to influencing policies.[20] Yet other campaigners, whilst recognising the value of lobbying governments, are better represented by their identification with more fundamental global interests.

Individuals falling into the latter group are likely to be those more readily accepting of the concept of global citizenship. NGO pressure groups can give expression to this element of self-identification. However, there remains a huge divide between an awareness and acceptance of the concept of global citizenship and the actual implementation of such a concept into the practicalities of the political sphere. Various NGOs can be argued to represent forums perhaps more appropriate to debate and the tackling of issues of increasing relevance to the global political agenda. This might be in conjunction with national governments or in a more independent manner. Yet at the same time national governments retain a large degree of control over the world's resources, including the legitimate use of force.[21] Under these circumstances there are serious doubts surrounding the ability of this nascent global citizenry to evolve into a political entity comparable with established forms of citizenship.

A GLOBAL CITIZENRY?

The assessment regarding the degree to which a global citizenry has evolved is significantly related to what expectations there are of what the characteristics of such a citizenry will be. If the expectation is that it should reflect established conventions of state citizenship it is clear that this criteria has not been met. There is no legitimacy of authority for a world government in the same way as exists for most national governments. The right to appeal for the fulfilment of meeting one's basic needs has not been established.[22] Despite being subject to the consequences of increasingly globalised structures and processes the world's population has yet to match this transformation of its social environment with an appropriate response in terms of political organisation.

The most fundamental element surrounding the conception of a global citizenry relates to the holistic approach of 'One World'. This acknowledges the existence of the nation-state system. However, the emphasis of this analysis focuses far more on the collective human experience of life on Earth, rather than the atomised view of competing nationalities. This holistic view recognises that there is a great diversity of human experience. Yet this can be subsumed into separate categories within the greater collective experience. From this perspective there is some justification for discussing a global citizenry in terms of the broader longer-term aspects of ensuring the promotion of sustainable development policies.

There seems to be ample evidence to support the case that, with the growth of global issues and interests, it is no longer sufficient to analyse international relations solely within the context of competing national interests. Similarly this has implications for both self-defined and imposed identities. Even the most unreconstructed state-centric analysts cannot deny the emergence of a global political agenda.[23] Citizen participation within this agenda, however, remains an issue that has yet to establish clearly defined norms within this agenda. Certainly there is a lack of control and autonomy felt amongst a great many individuals, even more extreme than that experienced by national governments. Almost by definition when one talks in terms of global issues, without a well-established system of global governance, individuals will feel disempowered to influence events significantly.

The examples of emerging global governance mentioned above, the World Trade Organisation and the United Nations system, have very limited opportunities for the active participation of individuals. Both organisations are effectively intergovernmental.[24] As such, despite the huge influence both organisations have on the world's population, the greatest influence the majority of individuals have over these organisations is by way of lobbying their national governments, with widely varying degrees of success. Participation and/or representation in decision-making can be seen as a major characteristic for defining citizenhood. For the majority of the world's population there are very limited opportunities to play an active role in this process.

ONE WORLD – MANY IDENTITIES

In terms of identity it has been possible to highlight a great range of identities that individuals can experience simultaneously. Several of these may be in conflict with each other. The most significant of these would seem to be national and global identities. Earlier I have argued that there does not have to be a conflict between these two areas of identity. The nation-state system may yet be able to incorporate co-operative national policies to address the global political agenda. Evidence so far would suggest that there is a long way to go towards achieving this aim. Despite this rather pessimistic outlook there remains some hope that the increasingly obvious existence of shared national interests will advance the development of a greater sense of a global citizenry.

Current trends do suggest that although there seems to be a growing awareness of global issues the dominant culture remains the pursuit of short-term national interests.[25] Eventually it will become apparent that even these interests can no longer be met. Crucial to this process is the point at which longer-term interests are recognised. If individuals and national governments continue to pursue short-term interests, even in the face of recognising the implications of this, then there is little hope for sustainable global governance. Objectively there is only one world. To maintain this world requires a subjective assessment of one's own identity, and lifestyle, and how that relates to both national and global governance.

Notes

1. Cultural differences may still be marked, but the promotion of economic growth, increasing industrialisation and the shift in emphasis from urban dwelling are the norm in most societies.

Concluding Thoughts
Jill Krause and Neil Renwick

In these concluding thoughts, we are going to consider two questions. Firstly, what are the key themes that have been exposed by the various essays in this book. Secondly, how does the subject of *identity* actually relate to being a student of international relations?

KEY THEMES

The chapters of this book have all sought to address the increasingly complex political world in which we live by following a different and hopefully more interesting avenue of understanding than that associated with conventional approaches to the subject. By looking beyond the boundaries that we erect by thinking about the world through the privileged concepts of state, citizen and nation it is hoped to provide alternative concepts and greater understanding of the problems facing peoples across the world.

As the Introduction indicated, although each contribution offers a distinctive perspective, all the contributions focus upon the questions of how individuals and social groups develop a self-awareness; an understanding of who they are, how they relate to others. By examining these questions, the assumed conventional wisdom locating identity at the level of the state with an attachment to the *imagined community* of a homogenised nation, is subjected to a critical re-evaluation. These critical re-assessments focus upon the theoretical and practical processes of inclusion and exclusion in the way that international relations has sought to understand individual and collective attachments and feelings of *belonging*. In particular, these studies have illuminated the way in which established ways of understanding identity in international relations are inherently distorted in their suppression or exclusion of the complexities of ethnicity, gender, race, religion and ethno-centricism. The patterns of *constructed* and *re-constructed* identities clearly are intimately related to processes of social formation, cultural difference and the impact upon the way we experience space and time as a result of a globalised political economy. Fundamentally, these are questions and issues of power. By exploring these processes of attachment, of identification, these studies have exposed an inherently hierarchical ordering of dominance and subordination that transcends our established notions of political membership, participation and symbolic representation.

At the heart of this pattern of power is Modernity. Modernity has many faces: political, economic, historical, cultural, economic, artistic, musical or architectual. Modernity is about an accelerated sense of time. From the increased beat of the European and North American industrial revolutions to the contemporary world of global telecommunications and Internet *superhighways*, the sensitivity to change in human society has been profoundly influenced by the end of traditional patterns of life governed by seasonal time. Modernity is also about space; in particular, *ordered space*. As the chapters by Farrands, Youngs and Scholte illustrate, Modernity is inextricably linked to the notion of organised space and the creation of boundaries. This is most notable in the process of state-building.

Politically, Modernity is embodied in the modern state and popular representation through single or multi-party systems. Popular collective identification with the state is reinforced by the linkage of nation to state and the construction of national identity. *State* and *Nation* are mutually reinforcing. Each offers a *holy grail* of an *ordered* and *orderly* social system. The creation of centralised political institutions supported by a homogeneous national identity established a reasoned, stable space for human improvement. Beyond the secure boundaries of this reasoned space, however, lay the dangerous sea of irrational, unpredictable anarchy: the space of *international* relations. In economic terms, Modernity's logic has been evident in the canonical and inexorable law of supply and demand within capitalist societies and in the structured control imposed by central-planned systems of production, distribution and exchange.

In historical terms European Modernity offers a potent story of human development. Starting with the collapse of Christendom and the guiding hand of God's *Divine Providence*, Humanity's search for social rules to regulate its behaviour and improve its condition turned to Reason. The Enlightenment, the Protestant Reformation, the Scientific Revolution and the nineteenth century industrial revolution together formed a powerful narrative of advancement grounded in an unshakable faith in Progress: the Unbound Prometheus.

To these political, economic and historical aspects of Modernity have been added aesthetic and cultural features. Modernity has sought to cut through the flux and turbulance of human activity to delve deep for abstract principles to illustrate the essence of life. Modern painters, musical composers and architects have tried to portray the essence of human existence through abstraction; simple lines, cold materials and mechanistic images.

Yet, the dominance of Modernity and Reason is being questioned and challenged. Theories of *postmodernity* are critical of Modernity's ideas and practices. Reason, they argue, has become a tyrant seeking to impose order upon all. The story of Modernity, they say, is a story of exclusion and repression. To paraphrase from a certain popular science fiction series, *the needs of the One* (in this case Modernity) *have suppressed the needs of the Many.* Non-Europeans, non-whites, women; all have been excluded from the story; at best sub-plots to the main narrative. At the same time, the emphasis upon Reason has reduced people to mere objects in social scientific study. It has excluded values and subjectivity, categorising and ordering human activities such a war and genocide. As such, then, it has failed to offer a satisfactory means of understanding the world in which we live.

A recognition of the practical failings of Modernity is one of the more obvious of today's societies; the obvious loss of faith in inevitable progress, in the inevitable benefits of technology and in the ability of states to lead their peoples to higher levels of material and spiritual existence, has combined with the explosion of voices at the close of this century. The raising of the lost voices of the womens' movements, Gays, Blacks, Asians, immigrants, gypsies or muslims is fracturing the myth of homogeneous national identities. Each caries a distinct culture, history, value-system and resultant identity. Each, in fact, offers a distinct subjectivity threatening to pull down the Inside/Outside division; the systems of inclusion and exclusion operating within states and between them. Language, culture, aesthetics, economics and politics are threatened with *de*construction – the exposure of the underlying relationships of unequal power and their radical overthrow.

Having recognised these raised voices and the importance of subjectivity and identity, it is evident that there are significant consequences for established international relations: the sovereignty of state-centricism, the integrity of nationally-defined identity, the belief in universal political principles such as a universal ethical order transcending all community distinctions.

For some authors this change of aspect or angle of criticism is profoundly disturbing. This is not only because it is a radical approach challenging the orthodoxy, but more importantly, because they believe it strips away the established principles and rules that provide a *necessary* restraint upon human behaviour and thereby allow individual and collective freedoms. In effect, they believe that this approach threatens to leave us with nothing to hold onto. If all behaviour is governed by particular circumstances, in other words, if good behaviour is *contingent* upon specific circumstances, then there can be little or even no common or commonly-accepted rules of right and wrong. A free-for-all can ensue and no authoritative arbitor can exist, leaving the way open for the exercise of *Might is Right* approaches to societal order.

Responses to this perspective have been firstly, that *Might* already operates in a subliminal way and that it is necessary to expose this to prevent or limit it. Secondly, the recognition and acceptance of a *plurality* of legitimate cultures or voices does not necessarily exclude commonality or shared assumptions about how to conduct community affairs without conflict, indeed it may promote it through mutual recognition of cultural worth and identities and through tolerance. Thirdly, this approach does not exclude Reason or reject its worth, what it rejects is its hegemonic and exclusionary nature and role. The plea is to restore the human element to the heart of the study of international relations.

WHERE DOES THIS TAKE INTERNATIONAL RELATIONS STUDENTS?

The answer to this question lies in a range of related points. The first point to make is that to approach international affairs from the angle of identity is deliberately disconcerting. It moves the observer away from the comfortable sanctuary of orthodox theory and understanding by focusing upon new types of boundaries and divisions located at previously *hidden* sites of repression among societies. Second, this emphasis upon identity forces us to reconsider the usefulness of our chosen tools of the trade. We are familiar with the fairly settled concepts of State, Nation, Power, Sovereignty. *Identity* is conceptually unsettling. It leads us into avenues of language, signs, culture, socialisation and psychology that redefine our sense of differentiation; where do we as political beings draw boundaries of Self and Other – at the territorial and legal boundaries of the State or in specific, contextually-defined political spaces that owe no allegiance to traditional definitions of inclusion and exclusion? To ask these questions is to make these traditional tools less definite, less omnipotent as means of explaining the political world around us and as means by which we can seek answers to the problems of this world.

Fourth, it reinstates the subjective to our way of thinking about international affairs. By this we mean that we are seeking to better understand the maelstrom of social, economic and political forces that are surrounding people in their day-to-day lives rather than seeking to understand these relations as primarily *objective* social categories. In other words, we are concerned with the way that influences associated with the play of identity *closely* impinge upon humanity's daily life. This attempt to restore the human factor through identity is as much about *meaning* or *self-worth* as it is about factors of ethnicity, nationality, race, history or culture that together contribute to our sense of identity. In seeking a closer proximity to the world we seek to understand, human needs, rights, fears and hopes become much more than mere categories and acquire a colour and vibrancy lost from the more stand-offish orthodox approaches. Fifth, the inclusion of identity into the lexicon of international relations drives us to greater sophistication in the prescriptive advice on improving the lives of people. It requires us to be sensitive to the detail and nuances of daily life. This facilitates the mutual recognition and respect necessary for a more tolerant, more equitable, more democratic and more peaceful world in the twenty-first century.

Index